GRAFTON ELLIOT SMITH
The Man and His Work

Sir Grafton Elliot Smith, MA (Cambridge), DLitt (Manchester),
DSc (Liverpool), FRCP (London), MD, ChM (Sydney), FRS, Croix
de Chevalier de la Legion d'Honneur

GRAFTON ELLIOT SMITH
THE MAN AND HIS WORK

Edited by
A. P. ELKIN and N. W. G. MACINTOSH

SYDNEY UNIVERSITY PRESS

SYDNEY UNIVERSITY PRESS
Press Building, University of Sydney

UNITED KINGDOM, EUROPE, MIDDLE EAST, AFRICA, CARIBBEAN
Prentice/Hall International, International Book Distributors Ltd
Hemel Hempstead, England

NORTH AND SOUTH AMERICA
International Scholarly Book Services, Inc., Portland, Oregon

First published 1974
© Sydney University Press 1974

Library of Congress Catalog Card Number 73-84903

National Library of Australia registry card number and
ISBN 0 424 06790 0

This book is supported by money from
THE ELEANOR SOPHIA WOOD BEQUEST

Printed in Australia at The Griffin Press, Adelaide

CONTENTS

CONTENTS

LIST OF ILLUSTRATIONS

PLATES

FIGURES

CONTRIBUTORS

P. O. BISHOP, MB, BS, DSc (Sydney), FAA
Head of the Department of Physiology, John Curtin School of Medical Research, Institute of Advanced Studies, Australian National University

H. D. BLACK, MEc, HonDLitt (Sydney)
Chancellor, University of Sydney

RAYMOND A. DART, MSc (Brisbane), MB, ChM, MD (Sydney), HonDSc (Natal), HonDSc (Witwatersrand)
Professor Emeritus (Anatomy), University of Witwatersrand

A. P. ELKIN, CMG, MA, HonDLitt (Sydney), PhD (London)
Emeritus Professor (Anthropology) and Editor Oceania Publications, University of Sydney

WANG GUNGWU, MA (Malaya), PHD (London), FAHA
Professor of Far Eastern History, The Research School of Pacific Studies, The Institute of Advanced Studies, Australian National University

S. L. LARNACH, MSc (Sydney)
Research Fellow, Shellshear Museum, University of Sydney

JOHN LOEWENTHAL, ED, MS (Melbourne), MB, BS (Sydney), FRCS, FRACS, HonFACS
Head of Department of Surgery, University of Sydney, and President, Royal Australasian College of Surgeons

H. G. OETTLE, MB, ChB (Witwatersrand)
Division of Forensic Medicine, Department of Health, New South Wales

F. D. McCARTHY, DipAnthrop (Sydney)
Principal, Australian Institute of Aboriginal Studies 1963-72, formerly Ethnologist, Australian Museum

N. W. G. MACINTOSH, MB, BS, DipAnthrop (Sydney), FRACS (Hon), FRACDS (Hon)
Challis Professor of Anatomy, University of Sydney, and Chairman, Australian Institute of Aboriginal Studies

E. C. B. MACLAURIN, BA, BD (Sydney), MA (Cambridge)
Head of the Department of Semitic Studies, University of Sydney

G. SELBY, MB, BS, MD (Sydney), MRCP (London), FRCP (Edinburgh), FRACP
President of the Australian Association of Neurologists and Consulting Neurologist at Royal North Shore Hospital

J. R. SIMONS, MSc (Sydney), PhD (London)
School of Biological Sciences, University of Sydney

T. D. STEWART, AB (George Washington), MD (John Hopkins)
Anthropologist Emeritus, Smithsonian Institute

J. PETER WHITE, BA (Melbourne), MA (Cambridge), PhD (ANU)
Lecturer in Prehistory, Department of Anthropology, University of Sydney

PREFACE

This book is a record of the commemoration by The University of Sydney, of the centenary of the birth of one of its most distinguished graduates, a man of genius, Grafton Elliot Smith (1871-1937). His was a 'big name' in the fields of anatomy, human evolution and ethnology. He added to knowledge, inspired research, challenged accepted ideas and caused controversy.

Although he lived and worked abroad for nearly all his post-graduate life, he never failed to serve his and our University when occasions arose, and these were many.

Very few people, commemorating the centenary of a great man's birth have had personal contact with him or are aware of the significance of his contributions to the building of the temple of knowledge. And so it was with Grafton Elliot Smith. However, there were a few scientists abroad and in Australia who through study of the relevant literature or through personal association had a deep appreciation of his work and, in the latter case, also a vivid recollection of the man himself.

We hoped that three who, as post graduates, had worked with him would take part in the commemoration, each a specialist in one of the three fields in which he made his principal contributions. These were retired though active, Professors, A. J. E. Cave (Anatomy, London), R. A. Dart (Anatomy, Witwatersrand) and A. P. Elkin (Anthropology, Sydney).

The Vice-Chancellor, Professor B. R. Williams, who had come to Sydney from The University of Manchester where Elliot Smith had been Professor of Anatomy (1909-19) and had left a great name, authorized a small committee to plan the commemoration. He (and later the Senate) agreed that there should be a special function in the Great Hall, presided over by the Chancellor, at which Professors Cave, Dart and Elkin would speak, from personal knowledge, about Elliot Smith and his work. This was to be followed by a symposium lasting three days, each day to be introduced by one of the same three scholars and to be devoted to the Elliot Smith field in which he had specialized.

After correspondence with Professors Cave and Dart, who were enthusiastic, and with the help of Mr J. H. Elliott of the Registrar's Department, dates were fixed, and other arrangements made. Unfortunately, a short time before the event, Professor Cave became suddenly ill, and was unable, as well as forbidden, to come to Australia, much to his great disappointment, as well as ours. Dr D. T. Stewart, Anthropologist Emeritus of the Smithsonian Institute, at very short notice, accepted the University's invitation to take part in the symposium.

The University Commemoration in the Great Hall, held on 30 October 1972 and attended by over 200, was addressed by H. D. Black Esq., Chancellor, by Professors Dart and Elkin on Elliot Smith, and by Professor N. W. G. Macintosh, Professor of Anatomy in the University, and Professor John Loewenthal, Professor of Surgery and also President of the Australasian College of Surgeons. The symposium (31 October to 2 November 1972) was attended each day by about 80 persons. Questioning and discussions were good. The title of the first session was *In the Beginning*. Dr Stewart opened it with a paper on 'The Relationship of the Neanderthal Group to Modern Man'; papers followed on aspects of human evolution. Professor Dart gave the opening paper on the second day for which the theme was *Early Man*, and Professor Elkin introduced the theme of the third day, *Diffusion of Culture*.

The papers as published in this volume vary a little from the order in which they were given, as some overlapping of themes was unavoidable in arranging the programmes. Moreover, some of them, being partly or wholly talks to slides, have been written or rewritten since the symposium. No text is available of Professor Dart's very personal talk in the Great Hall but essential points he made are included in his first symposium paper.

We thank those who took part with us in the symposium and who took great pains to make their printed papers worthy of the occasion. We also thank the Trustees of the University of Sydney Anatomy Research Fund for the substantial subsidy which made this publication possible.

University of Sydney
July 1973

A. P. ELKIN
N. W. G. MACINTOSH

OPENING ADDRESSES

OPENING ADDRESS

WELCOME TO THE CENTENARY COMMEMORATION

H. D. Black

I bid you welcome to this, the Centenary Commemoration of Sir Grafton Elliot Smith, by The University of Sydney in association with the Royal Australasian College of Surgeons.

If ever it could be justly said, then Nature could stand up and say of Grafton Elliot Smith: 'This was a man.'

Proper it is to commemorate and to honour a mind which ranged expertly over many fields; which gave stimulus along many lines of inquiry; and which made contributions of lasting significance to human knowledge: proper it is to recall and commemorate a man in whose personality many people found qualities of integrity and charm, whose utterance was ever in noble voice, the bass resonance of it being much remarked in his time, and whose style was gracious, flowing English prose, whose presence elevated every gathering. I saw and heard him only once as a young man and indelibly one recalls the handsome, noble head, and the whole generous measure of the man.

We should not—we should never—forget those whose contribution has flowed into the general fund of knowledge. We are where we scientifically are, and we have the insights which we have because countless others have cleared the scientific path for advances to the present state of knowledge; and the 'here and now' of that present knowledge will also prove no final resting place, for the quest is always for truth, for the further truth.

But, unless we actively seek to inform ourselves of our intellectual debt to the forerunners of science, we will unjustly forget the work of earlier scientists, and bury their memory in an anonymous past: from which they can be rescued only by such centenary commemorations as this one. Happily this evening we have two former students of Grafton Elliot Smith to evoke the man for us, namely Emeritus Professors A. P. Elkin and R. A. Dart.

Perforce, in the passage of time, not only will a man's scientific contribution pass into the body of accepted knowledge, and be absorbed often without personal reference to his particular discoveries; but perforce also in the passage of inquiry the great hypotheses with which a man is associated in his day will come under further and subsequent scientific scrutiny. New facts will demand new formulations. Upon a

3

Newtonian universe falls an Einsteinian re-formulation. It is interesting that in Grafton Elliot Smith's case, one of his intellectual mentors was the great T. H. Huxley; and it was that same Huxley who said what all scientists come to know—Grafton Elliot Smith included no less—that the most beautiful theory can be slain by one ugly fact. I say this because if it be that the diffusionist theory of culture which was one of his great hypotheses has met a powerful stream of critical evaluation and modification—as, for example, a result of the writings of such men as A. L. Kroeber with his concept of stimulus diffusion—it is still true that rich, imaginative, powerful minds make contributions by the very way they attempt to grapple with what the philosopher, Alfred North Whitehead, once called 'the welter of fact'; and their hypotheses bring into sharp focus and point the issues, even if they be wrong in the theory advanced. As Huxley once said, so could it be said of Grafton Elliot Smith: 'he burns that others may have light'.

I make next another general point. There was a catholicity of scientific interests which Grafton Elliot Smith displayed which distinguishes—and even distances him somewhat—from scientific practitioners today. It could be said of him, as it cannot be said now of some individual scientists, that he exhibited a general scientific culture, a habit of mind which illuminated whatever it turned to. He was not a limited specialist, but a mind which brought its intellectual calculus into play always on all the material evidence before him. It is immensely important to restore to the scientific community the image of one man who displayed this general, pervasive scientific culture—so much the richer in influence in so being a general culture—rather than a single-line expertise. Aspects of his wide-ranging contributions will be covered by subsequent speakers.

He was born on 14 August 1871, in Grafton in northern New South Wales, and died in London on 1 January 1937. He was so named Grafton as the first of the family to be born in that attractive town. His remarkable Father had employment first as a child in a London shop; yet so well did he study at a Workingman's College that he secured a post as teacher with the Department of Education in New South Wales after migration to these shores; subsequently becoming Headmaster at Grafton, and a Lecturer at the Sydney Teacher's College.

When young Grafton was but ten years of age, this Father put into his hands an elementary text on physiology. A seed was sown. And in Sydney, some years later, the boy attended the evening class in physiology given by the Dean of Medicine at the University of Sydney, Professor T. Anderson Stuart; and in due course he entered this University in the Faculty of Medicine, graduating, and distinguishing himself en route in anatomy and neurophysiology. He became a Demonstrator under Professor J. T. Wilson, affectionately known to all students and his friends as 'Jummy', who greatly esteemed the young man. By 1895, he became Doctor of Medicine, with a gold medal for his thesis; and in 1896 a travelling scholarship took him to Cambridge University.

In the University of Sydney he had, in those days of a smaller and more intimate University, been surrounded by an intellectual atmosphere created by the mutual co-operative enthusiasm of men with revered names . . . Haswell, biology, and J. P. Hill; Wilson, anatomy; C. J. Martin in physiology; and Edgeworth David, geology and polar explorer, and Anderson Stuart. He had experienced an interactive cross-fertilization of minds in different disciplines.

Small wonder that this fine mind, with this background and its potential, should carry enthusiasm and skill into all its subsequent life-work, and the great story of his work thereafter had these happy and fortunate antecedents and beginnings in both a stimulating family and University background, in Australia. For, if much of his life was lived subsequently abroad, this remained his homeland; he loved it, came frequently back to it, and is a son of it. But much of the work of his life was to be performed elsewhere.

The full flavour of his performance, and of the man himself, is beautifully expressed or suggested by a poem written by S. Sassoon of another archaeologist, but agreed by the poet to be included as appropriate in the memorial volume on Grafton Elliot Smith, assembled and edited by Warren R. Dawson. This extract in particular—

> Five thousand years
> He guided us through scientific spaces
> of excavated History; till his lone
> Roads of research grew blurred; and in our ears
> Time was the rumoured tongues of vanished races,
> And Thought a chartless Age of Ice and Stone.
>
> The story ended; and in the darkened air
> Flowered while he lit his pipe; an aureole glowed
> Enwreathed with smoke: the moment's match-light showed
> His rosy face, broad brow, and smooth grey hair,
> Backed by the crowded book-shelves.

Something in these lines, you may agree, evokes the ranging quality of an inquiring scientific mind; and evokes also the agent, the quiet man, for Grafton Elliot Smith was thought by many, at least in his earlier years, to be reserved in manner. The easy sociability flowered later.

Work at London and Cambridge filled his days; and at the British Museum he began the cataloguing of its enormous collection of brains, which took till 1902 to complete. Then, marriage, a happy one, to Kathleen Macredie; and off to accept the Professorship of Anatomy in Cairo, in the Government School of Medicine. By this act, he had taken the first step into the study of what Macredie called 'the magnificent material for anatomical work'. He liked Cairo, and set about organizing the Medical School.

His researches were now early Egyptaic, on prehistoric and 12th Dynasty people; with a break in 1902 to visit Australia, and 'Jummy' Wilson again.

Back in Egypt, he put the first mummified Pharaoh under X-ray photography, and described the physical character of Tuthmosis IV.

In 1909, the Chair of Anatomy in Manchester beckoned; and he left for it, but not before being decorated by the Khedive, Abbas Hilmy. In 1911 his book, *The Ancient Egyptians* appeared; and there soon broke upon the world the so-called 'diffusion-heresy'. A most furious controversy was aroused; but I leave judgment on it all to others.

He worked, and travelled much also; and during World War I he carried on his duties at the university, attending also at military hospitals, and serving on the General Medical Council.

Ten years after Manchester, University College, London, called him to the Chair of Anatomy, which he occupied until retirement. He lived variously at Hampstead, Gower Street, Regent's Park, and in the final period in a nursing-home.

His work in London was, as ever, a full-blooded response to the opportunity afforded. His writings attest the range of his interests and his capacity . . . dealing with man, his evolution, fossil remains, neanderthal man, classification of races, and the beginnings and diffusion of culture and civilization. The earlier formative influences in his life caused him to favour closer relations between various disciplines, such as anatomy, cultural and physical anthropology, and psychology. He travelled widely . . . to Java, the United States, Spain, Australia in 1929, and to China. In 1934 he was Knighted. As early as 1912 he had received the Royal Medal of the Royal Society; yet in the midst of his long and unwavering researches he never failed to find time to encourage the young budding scientist. In 1924, for example, he had welcomed to England from the University of Sydney none other than John Irvine Hunter, of brief and tragic fame, as an anatomist of promise.

But in 1936 he suffered two blows . . . his son lost his life in an accident; and his wife, too, suffered an accident which confined her to hospital. He retired from the Chair in 1936, the Professorial Board recording a generous and just appreciation of his services. Late though it was in day of his research activities, he was awarded the Huxley Medal; whereas much earlier he had been awarded and honoured with the Honorary Gold Medal of the Royal College of Surgeons in 1930.

His health, for long robust, weakened; the journey made just before Christmas in this year so crowded with its triumphs and tragedies, to see his wife, taxed and tired him; but he was happily re-united with his family, and he passed away on New Year's Day, 1937.

In Dawson's memorial volume there are 34 pages of his listed writings of all kinds, from his letters to *The Times*, to his striking anthropological works, like *The Diffusion of Culture*, and his numerous works as an anatomist. He left a fragment only of an autobiography; and one reads how early-on this Australian began presciently to collect and study live bandicoots. His friend, Professor J. T. (Jummy) Wilson, in a biographical sketch of his earlier career, foreshadowed the scholar to come: 'from the

6

first' he said, 'it was easy to recognise Elliot Smith as a student of outstanding quality and of eager interest'.

Some others have remarked a certain pungency of comment belying a warm and friendly nature; some even said 'pontifical'. His artistic and musical interests were wide; and he was a sociable man. His colleagues spoke of his devoted care and loyalty; and he readily acknowledged assistance rendered to him by others in a scientific field. His mind, said one, 'had that luminous quality which enabled him to reduce a seeming chaos of ideas to an harmonious unity'. It was structural, architectural, in bent.

It is especially our honour to recall that he was an alumnus of the University of Sydney, taking his first degree here in medicine with first-class honours. And it is proper that we pay tribute here, and in this Centenary Commemoration, to a great and remarkable man.

It is our good fortune that to give body to this, my introductory sketchy outline of the man, we have, speaking in the order set out two former students who will recall him, *l'homme même*, namely, Emeritus Professors Dart and Elkin; and that then by good fortune also we hear from the Challis Professor of Anatomy, Professor N. W. G. Macintosh; to be followed by the Head of the Department of Surgery, Professor John Loewenthal, who is also by happy coincidence on this occasion, President of the Royal Australasian College of Surgeons, all of whom will take us in some depth into the man and his achievements.

SIR GRAFTON ELLIOT SMITH: THE MAN AND HIS WORK

A personal testimony

A. P. Elkin

In Australia, 1914

In July 1914, in this same Great Hall where we are tonight, Grafton Elliot Smith gave a series of four University Extension Board lectures on 'Ancient Egypt and the Dawn of Civilization'. As was his custom, he spoke to slides. One of these still remains clear and vivid in my mind. It was of a mastaba: I see the drawing of the rock-hewn tomb deep-down and the shaft up from it to the surface, to the temple or mortuary chapel which contained the portrait-statue of the deceased and in its forecourt a place for offerings brought by the mourners. The lecture was on the development of burial customs from the simple grave to the pyramid and dolmen.

Elliot Smith, then 43, was on the high plateau of achievement and fame where he had been for a decade and would be for another two decades. A Fellow of the Royal Society of London and Professor of Anatomy in Manchester, he was renowned in the fields of anatomy, physical anthropology and ethnology.

But why did such a distinguished person visit Australia in 1914? Because in August of that year an event took place which marked the coming of age of Science in Australia. After much thought and preparation, the British Association for the Advancement of Science held its eighty-fourth meeting in Australia, the sessions being in the several capital cities. A large contingent of British and European scientists generously gave of their time to make the sea journey. Not the least among them was Grafton Elliot Smith. Indeed, he seldom missed a meeting of the association wherever it was held. He always had a newly discovered fact to talk about, an idea to put forward, a theory to propound.

This Australian meeting was a very exciting one for him. In the Sydney Session Professor Edgeworth David of Geology, whose fascinating lectures I attended in 1912, and Professor J. T. Wilson of Anatomy with whom Elliot Smith had been both a student and an assistant, exhibited a cranium from Talgai, near Warwick, southeastern Queensland. This specimen of early man in Australia was 'news', and that very night,

21 August 1914, Elliot Smith referred to it in a brilliant public lecture in Sydney Town Hall. In the years which followed, his brother, S. A. Smith, for some time Acting Professor of Anatomy in the University of Sydney, worked on the cranium and prepared a report which Elliot Smith presented to the Royal Society of London for publication. And for years now, up to this present, Professor N. W. G. Macintosh of Anatomy (1955-73) has studied in the laboratory and in the field, the various aspects of Talgai, that youth who with his people lived in the Warwick district about 11,000 years ago.

More exciting for Elliot Smith, however, was the opportunity to see three Torres Strait Islander mummies, for he recognized in them several procedures which were used in mummification during the XXIst Dynasty of Egypt. Moreover, his reading showed that features of the associated ritual were similar in both places. He had published a book in 1911 to show the influence of Ancient Egyptian culture in Europe and in the near East, but he also thought that certain elements had spread east to India and beyond. Now, here in these Torres Straits Islander mummies he saw sound evidence for that hypothesis.

He expounded his views with enthusiasm at the Melbourne session a few days later. But there his joy was turned into sorrow by the doubts and criticism he met, especially when a distinguished scholar said the procedure in the Torres Strait was 'natural'. This implied that the complexities of the procedure and the associated rituals which took millenia to develop in Ancient Egypt, were reinvented by these Islanders —in most unfavourable conditions. This was too much of a shock to Elliot Smith, and so the intellectual battle was joined: an appropriate time for World War I had just been declared.

Returning to England he prepared and published his basic monograph: 'On the significance of the Geographical Distribution of Mummification—A study of the Migrations of Peoples and the Spread of Certain Customs and Beliefs'. This was followed by papers and books substantiating the eastward diffusion of certain cultural elements, which modified and added to in India, Southeast Asia and Indonesia, eventually influenced and contributed to the rise of the high civilizations in the region extending from Peru to Mexico. But loud and hard and clear was the reaction of ethnologists, especially in the United States of America, in a country then being constrained by the World War I situation to depart from the Monroe doctrine of isolationism—a doctrine unconsciously pushed back into the pre-Columbian period. Here was this British-Australian scientist suggesting that the native Indians of Mesoamerica, of Peru and Mexico, did not invent of themselves striking features of their civilizations, such as pyramids, mummification, calendars, art motifs and symbolism, but received the ideas and stimulus through diffusion from the Old World! A shocking concept to be vigorously opposed! This, however, is another story, not for our commemoration night. In the meantime, Elliot Smith served in war-time shell shock hospitals, and lectured and wrote.

Post World War I

The early 1920s were years of increasing public interest in the evolution of man and in the development of his culture. This was kindled by several discoveries. In particular, the remains of a very primitive human type, with some features suggesting Neanderthal man, were found in 1921 in a cave at Broken Hill, Northern Rhodesia; Elliot Smith contributed to the report on this find. In 1924, thanks to the perceptiveness of Professor Raymond Dart, a man-like ape skull was discovered at Taungs, Bechuanaland. Elliot Smith was thrilled by this and by Professor Dart's interpretation. He wrote about it in *Nature*, in *The Illustrated London News* and in *The Times*. In addition, arguments about the reconstruction and significance of the cranium and jaw of the Piltdown 'find' (later to be proved a hoax), were current in these years, with Elliot Smith in the thick of the arguments. While Pithecanthropus of Java, which was only just being received into the Human Family, Talgai in Australia, and Neanderthal in Europe continued to be of news value. These various, early types were discussed by Elliot Smith in his *Essays on the Evolution of Man*, 1924, which was reprinted in the same year. (A second edition appeared in 1927.)

In the meantime, the remarkable tomb of Tutankhamen had been opened in 1922. This event inspired Elliot Smith to write a series of articles for the *Daily Telegraph* (London) on the wider significance of the discoveries in the tomb. A redrafted version of the articles was published in 1923 in a delightful, small book, *Tutankhamen and the Discovery of his Tomb*.

The relevance of these finds and discussions to this commemoration address on 'Grafton Elliot Smith, the man and his work' is that during 1923-5 I gave series of lectures in Newcastle to University of Sydney Adult Education Classes on the evolution of man, early man and present-day primitive man, and on the rise and spread of culture. The members were solid citizens, whose reading included the *Illustrated London News*, *The Times* and various magazines. They, by their questions, kept me up to date on anthropological and ethnological issues. To them Elliot Smith was a *big name*, a widely-known name, for he was a compulsive spreader of knowledge and ideas—in newspaper articles and journals, and through publication of abstracts of his addresses which seemed innumerable. I have referred to a series of four lectures on 'Ancient Egypt and the Dawn of Civilization' which he gave in our Great Hall in July 1914, just before the meeting of the British Association. Similarly, when he came to Australia in September, 1924 to inquire into the proposed foundation of a Chair of Anthropology, he took the opportunity to give a series of four popular science lectures in the old King's Hall, Hunter Street, Sydney, on 'The Origin of Civilization' and related topics.

Pacific Science Congress—1923

The Second Pacific Science Congress was held in Melbourne and Sydney from 13 August to 3 September. Elliot Smith did not attend, but he was represented by W. J. Perry, his collaborator, and at the Sydney Session also by his brother, Dr S. A. Smith. The former, the author of the recently published *The Children of the Sun*, was Reader in Cultural Anthropology in University College, London, in the Department of Anatomy to which Elliot Smith had come from Manchester in August 1919. After conversations with Mr Perry, I decided to go to London for post-graduate study in anthropology. At that time, there were no University courses in Australia in the subject. So with my wife and young son, I spent two years, 1925-7 in England. Attached to Elliot Smith's Department, I did library research on the Australian Aborigines, and also attended classes in physical anthropology, including lectures on early man and on the brain, its evolution and the localization of areas in the cortex.

As others found, Elliot Smith did not seem to notice his post-graduate students, and certainly neither he nor Perry *directed* my research. But after a while, articles, reprints and references appeared on my table, with the suggestion that this or that might bear on my work. In other words, help and guidance were indirect.[1]

And when the student had finished his research and thesis, what made all the work worthwhile was not just the degree, but the use Elliot Smith made of one's results. If he referred to these in a book, he didn't just put one's name in a footnote in small type. No! he put it boldly in the text, and sometimes wrote 'as my friend, Mr. or Dr. so-and-so, has shown'. That indeed, was honour of a Companionate of high order!

So much for work. My time at University College was brightened by lunch times in Perry's room. Elliot Smith usually came in, and so did S. H. Hooke a Semitic Scholar, and for each a roll and butter, a banana and cheese, and a pot of good tea. And the conversation? Anatomy, evolution, diffusion of culture? Definitely not. What then? Just gossip. Like any normal Australian, Elliot Smith gossipped and yarned, sometimes about fellow scientists. Thus, I realized that distinguished men, Fellows of the Royal Society, authors of important books, were still ordinary mortals, possessing human frailties and foibles. This was revealing and reassuring to me whose background was mainly the Australian country-side. My home immediately before going to England was in the small village of Wollombi, where Elliot Smith's father was schoolmaster in the 1860s, and where his elder brother, S. H. Smith, a future Director of Education in New South Wales, was born.

During one lunch, the conversation turned to the subject of genius. Elliot Smith said that six persons, including himself, each of whom was regarded as a genius, had agreed to bequeathe his brain for anatomical study. The purpose was to search for features in the brain structure

---

[1] One book, the beautifully produced *Egyptian Mummies*, by himself and Warren R. Dawson, marked on the dust cover 'For Elkin' had added value to me: inside was the inscription, 'A. P. Elkin with Elliot Smith's kind regards'.

which could explain, or be correlated with, whatever genius is. He already had one such bequest duly preserved, but he dared not touch it lest he destroy the relevant feature in the structure. He had no solution for the old, old problem of the relation of brain and mind, of body and soul.

On another occasion he told us how non-plussed he was on the occasion of his first radio broadcast. He was a gifted public lecturer, needing no notes, so when the radio medium became available he agreed to use it. So into the studio he went, as on to the platform, but seeing no one to talk to, only a metal gadget, he was momentarily struck dumb. However, he managed to get started and then was all right. But after that, he always took some notes so that he could get going.

Books

I have already referred to four of Elliot Smith's books, and will mention only two more. *The Evolution of the Dragon* appeared in 1919. It is a very erudite study of symbolism. He looks for the meaning of symbols and symbolic actions in their history, e.g., of incense, libations, shells and the dragon. Even quite ordinary mundane things or practical actions of one period, may become in certain situations cherished symbols of a later period. He was fond of the line, 'he who runs may read', but *The Evolution of the Dragon* cannot be read as you run. It requires steady, thoughtful study. In some of his books he dispenses almost altogether with footnotes and references, but this one is fully documented, and the notes require reading.

The second book, published in 1930, is *Human History*. It is long, but it is easy to read. He had, as it were, talked his way through it, that is, had given a course of lectures, or rather talks, at Bedford College, University of London, and then wrote them out without footnotes in such a way that indeed 'he who runs may read'. In doing so he aimed at resolving the conflicting allegiances of natural history and the humanities by merging them in 'a Greater Humanity, which might be called Human History'. So here we have an anatomist and physical anthropologist writing a book on the whole course of our history, physical and cultural, from pre-human phases, throughout the stone and later ages and in all regions, with the underlying theme of continuity in space and time. And following that theme he is never lost in the abounding labyrinth of materials. He never lost sight of the wood in the entanglement of the trees, in itself a mark of genius.

In this book Elliot Smith showed his readiness to tackle new subjects. One of these, suggested mainly by Perry's research, was the innate peacefulness of primitive man. If left to his own hunting and food-gathering way of life, with no worries about material possessions, which indeed were encumbrances to mobility, with nothing to take and nothing to lose, primitive man had nothing to fight about. He just had occasional rows about women. To Elliot Smith and Perry, it was the invention of gardens, villages, property and especially civilization which resulted in violent behaviour. This became a 'pet' topic of his later years.[2]

The Foundation of the Department of Anthropology, University of Sydney

Finally, I must emphasize Elliot Smith's role in the firm establishment of the Department of Anthropology in this university. The Pacific Science Congress of 1923 in its Sydney Session resolved that such a department should be established for training New Guinea Administrative Officers in Anthropology, for conducting field research in the subject and for teaching undergraduates and producing research workers. The Australian National Research Council was asked to implement the resolution. It gained the co-operation of the University of Sydney and of the Commonwealth and State governments (for finance), and then asked the Rockefeller Foundation for research funds.

In 1924 Elliot Smith was lecturing at universities in the United States of America. The executive officers of the foundation knew him through his co-operation with them in setting up the Institute of Anatomy at University College, London; therefore they asked him to go on to Australia to find out from the Commonwealth government, the Australian National Research Council and the University of Sydney, whether a Department of Anthropology would definitely be established. He did this and reported favourably, whereupon the foundation agreed to make liberal grants to the Australian National Research Council for research in Human Biology. He had worked out with the secretary of the foundation that this objective would come within the terms of the foundation's charter and also would cover all aspects of anthropological research.

Thus, the Chair of Anthropology in this University was founded in 1925, and A. R. Brown (later Radcliffe-Brown) backed by Elliot Smith, took up the position in 1926. Five years later, however, the future of the department was in jeopardy. The Commonwealth government indicated that the grant towards its cost would be either drastically reduced or else discontinued. Radcliffe-Brown resigned in mid-1931, and his acting successor (R. W. Firth) did likewise at the end of 1932. I was then invited to take charge of the department for 1933, probably its last year.

But Elliot Smith had been busy. He appealed directly to the Australian Prime Minister, Mr J. Lyons, to reverse the government's decision, mainly because if the department were closed down, the Rockefeller Foundation would most likely cease to make grants for anthropological research. Elliot Smith also asked Mr S. M. Bruce to use his influence with Mr Lyons. Mr Bruce was Prime Minister when Elliot Smith

[2] He devotes two long chapters (V and VI) in *Human History* to the subject. Compare W. J. Perry, *The Primordial Ocean*, Chapter X, 'Violence'.

interviewed him in 1924 with regard to government support for the proposed Chair. As the result, mainly of these approaches, an annual grant for five years was made. I was appointed to the Chair, 1 January 1934. Before long, the Vice-Chancellor (Robert Wallace) agreed with me to ask the Prime Minister to double the duration of the grant and to increase the yearly amount so that a 'permanent', full-time lecturer could be appointed, and thus I would be able to plan a forward-looking programme of teaching and research. I also wrote, asking Professor Elliot Smith to put my case personally to Mr Lyons who was about to visit England. In spite of being seriously ill, he did so, arguing that when he recommended me for the Chair, he took for granted that the Commonwealth government would give me the means to develop the department. In February 1936 I received a letter of eight words from Sir Grafton (as he was by then): 'The Prime Minister will do what you want.' He did.[3]

Of course, my department was not the only one around the world on which Elliot Smith kept a watchful eye. Other departments included those whose professors had, as it were, gone out from him, e.g., Witwatersrand, Hong Kong and Peking.

And all the time, he ran his own department in London, and was involved in very many activities until his health failed throughout 1936. He died on New Years Day, 1937.

Sir Grafton Elliot Smith

There be those whose memorials appear everlasting; such are structures of stone, like those of the rulers and the wealthy in ancient Egypt with which Elliot Smith was familiar: pyramids, the apex of which, pointing to the sky, was the symbol of the sun: or solid rock-hewn tombs with hieroglyphics and designs on the walls of their associated mortuary chapels, ensuring that the names of the deceased would not be blotted out.

But there be others whose memorials are the building stones of human well-being, of learning, of science, which they have shaped and put in place. Tablets here and there mark where some of them have laboured. It is our privilege to remember them, by following in their train, by adding to the temple of learning and to the pyramid of aspiration, and by clearing away some of the unstable sands of ignorance and illusion from the sphinx—the riddle of the universe: a riddle which we shall ever strive to solve, but which like the sphinx itself, will ever stand in defiant challenge.

Outstanding among these builders of the temple of learning and the

---

3 For a full account of the establishment and early years of the Department of Anthropology see, A. P. Elkin, *The Journal Oceania*, 1930-70, especially pp. 10-24. (The Oceania Monographs, No. 16, being a reprint from *Oceania*, Vol. XL, No. 4, pp. 243-79, 1970.)

pyramid of aspiration was Grafton Elliot Smith. And the purpose of our celebration of the centenary of his birth is to remember him—this Australian; this graduate of our University; this friend, scientist and good companion.

AN APPRECIATION

N. W. G. Macintosh

It is my duty to express thanks. First to the Chancellor, Vice-Chancellor, Senators and members of Convocation for their approval and support for this Commemorative function and for their presence here tonight. Also to the Royal Australasian College of Surgeons and particularly to the President of the College, Professor John Loewenthal. Collaboration by the College is particularly appropriate because Sir Grafton Elliot Smith originally intended to embrace a surgical career, but Professor Loewenthal will speak to you in relation to surgery.

I now thank the two orators Professors Dart and Elkin.

Emeritus Professor Raymond Dart of the University of the Witwatersrand first revisited Australia in 1949 and delivered the Hunter Memorial Oration. The subject was the Australopithecines—little creatures from one million to two and a half million years ago, small in stature but with relatively large brains. Raymond Dart was the first to recognize their existence and that the first skull representing them—the Taungs skull—was human-like rather than ape-like. That was in 1925. A very few of the great minds agreed with his opinion but he had to wait twenty years for further discoveries of similar fossil representatives of the Australopithecines before he was vindicated. And this has been his role throughout his life. He has many times made the first discovery but always some years elapse before he is proven right. So far he has emerged triumphant and long may that continue. An example which is pertinent to recent work in Australia follows. Dart believed that man took to the sea in water craft some 60,000 years ago. This opinion flew in the face of all classical belief. Man, it was said, had not acquired the technical skill necessary to cope with the sea earlier than 6,000 years ago, subsequently extended to 9,000 years ago. Our work in Australia has helped to vindicate Dart because we have shown that Aboriginal man must have come by sea earlier than 32,000 years ago which makes the Aboriginal the world's first known mariner, on present evidence.

When Professor Dart visited here in 1949 the late Professor Joseph Lexden Shellshear was Research Professor of Anatomy in this University. Dart and Shellshear had worked together under Grafton Elliot Smith in London and were sent by him to America soon after World War I (in which incidentally Shellshear, a colonel of artillery, was awarded a DSO). Elliot Smith then sent Dart to the Witwatersrand and Shellshear to Hongkong as Professors of Anatomy. Their re-meeting in

Sydney in 1949, and their discussions together constituted a tremendous stimulus to those of us privileged to listen then to their erudition. Now tonight we have been privileged to have Raymond Dart with us again with his inimitable and exhilarating stimulation in no way diminished.

I ask your indulgence to allow me to speak further about the late Professor Shellshear whose intense affection, admiration and regard for Elliot Smith was probably only equalled by that of Dart. The continuing influence of Elliot Smith on the writings of Shellshear and Dart has been profound. Shellshear's publications were not numerous, but those that were published were formidable. His monograph on 'The brain of the Australian Aboriginal: a study in cerebral morphology', published in 1937 in the Philosophical Transactions of the Royal Society of London would in the hands of other authors probably have been expressed as a series of maybe twenty progress papers. I must refer to another, 'A comparative study of the endocranial cast of Sinanthropus' by J. L. Shellshear and G. Elliot Smith, published in 1934 in the same Transactions. Davidson Black whose work on Sinanthropus will remain a permanent classic, had asked them to make the study; they did so independently and then having combined their work, it is significant that Elliot Smith elected Shellshear, his former pupil, to be the senior author.

I also mention an occasion in 1929 when Shellshear and many anatomists and prehistorians from Australia and the Far East assembled in Java. There under the guidance of that colourful prehistorian Dr van Stein Callenfels, the most stimulating and exciting discussions took place in the temple of Borobudur. These were based on the influence of the Buddha, in which the stupendous knowledge of Elliot Smith so impressed the exceptionally knowledgeable Callenfels, who was not easy to impress, that he was provoked to say to Shellshear: 'Joseph, you did not warn me, I have been today in the presence of a truly great man.' If time permitted I would like to recount all the anecdotes Shellshear told me of this genius Elliot Smith, but that one anecdote will have to suffice.

For nearly thirty years I have never known whether any utterance I made was in any degree original to me, or stemmed totally from Shellshear, and therefore stemmed from Elliot Smith. We are all so much a part of our predecessors.

Emeritus Professor A. P. Elkin of our own University is well known to you all, as the doyen of Australian anthropologists whose influence and prestige in anthropological ranges has been of extraordinary breadth, flowing into social and political as well as academic spheres. His impress on a multitude of facets of Australian life has been and still is profound.

Elkin's association with Elliot Smith began in 1925 when he enrolled as a PhD student in University College, London, reading for the full physical anthropology and prehistory course, although myth and ritual earned him his PhD in 1927. He was at once invited to field work and research in the Kimberleys as a Rockefeller Fellow, which with a transfer of funds under Elliot Smith's influence, became converted to make him the first Australian National Research Fellow.

Appointed to the Sydney Chair in November 1933 he faced the task of securing its viability. He appealed to Elliot Smith to enlist financial sympathy from the Right Honorable J. A. Lyons when he visited London. Elliot Smith succinctly wrote Elkin in February 1936, 'the P.M. will do what you want'. For the first half of his twenty-four years tenure, his was the only department in Australia teaching anthropology and any requests he made in those early years to Elliot Smith were similarly supported.

This influence wielded by Elliot Smith in Australia was very evident as early as August 1914 when the British Association for the Advancement of Science met in Sydney. The Talgai Skull was announced and demonstrated by Professor Sir Edgeworth David and Professor J. T. Wilson at that Meeting and it was Elliot Smith's persuasiveness which enabled the skull to become the property of the University of Sydney.

Elkin's retirement in May 1956 merely opened up numerous other fields of activity, including Membership of Senate, and his multiple activities remain undiminished as you have been able to perceive.

My own association with Professor Elkin stems from when he accepted me as his student for a Diploma in Anthropology, and our close association and collaboration has continued for twenty-eight years.

We are honoured indeed to have on the platform with us Dr Dale Stewart from the Smithsonian Institution in Washington. He is probably the world's most renowned physical anthropologist and expert on the forensic interpretation of the modern human skeleton and on fossil man, particularly the Neanderthal race and he is the interpreter of the most recent find, Shanidar man from Iraq.

Dale Stewart and I have the curious distinction of being honorary citizens of the town of Humpolec in Czechoslovakia together with about a dozen other physical anthropologists or anatomists from around the world. Humpolec was the birthplace of Ales Hrdlicka whose 100th Anniversary was celebrated in 1969. Dr Stewart and his charming wife generously agreed to interrupt their very heavy schedule in North and South America to be present at this function, and he will be leading the first day of the three days Symposium beginning tomorrow. Also he has kindly brought with him copies of correspondence between Dr Ales Hrdlicka and Grafton Elliot Smith, which I had not known existed. In this, Hrdlicka recommended to Grafton Elliot Smith that he should influence appointment of a Professor of Physical Anthropology. Unfortunately or otherwise, Grafton Elliot Smith had already intervened and obtained appointment of a Social Anthropologist, A. R. Radcliffe-Brown. How different many things might have been if Hrdlicka had written earlier. To me it is a very great personal pleasure to be again in the company of Dr Stewart.

I must now mention the English anatomist Emeritus Professor Alec Cave, who had agreed and was enormously enthusiastic to make a trip to Australia and be one of the speakers tonight, singing the praises of Sir Grafton Elliot Smith. It was a blow to receive word six weeks ago that he had suffered a severe heart attack, and while he is now reasonably fit and well, he has been forbidden to indulge in any travelling for a further six months. It was he who wrote the eulogistic chapter in Dawson's symposial biography of Sir Grafton Elliot Smith, that chapter being entitled the Master Anatomist. I have spoken to him by telephone to London and he sends his most ardent good wishes for the success of this commemoration.

Finally I thank you all ladies and gentlemen for your attendance and for your appreciation of Professor Dart's and Professor Elkin's remarkable expositions about their former mentor.

ON BEHALF OF THE ROYAL AUSTRALASIAN COLLEGE OF SURGEONS

John Loewenthal

It is a great honour for my college to be allowed to be associated with the university in these commemorative proceedings. On behalf of my fellowship, I do thank you, Mr Chancellor, for allowing us this happy conjunction. We of the college are represented on this dais by the actual extremities of our fellowship; I as president am at least titular head of the organization. Professor Macintosh is our most junior fellow as he was awarded, only a few weeks ago, our jealously guarded distinction of Honorary Fellowship of the College. This award, only the 56th ever to be made in the nearly 50 years of existence of the College, puts 'Black Mac' in the same company as a highly selected group of most distinguished surgeons, peers, professors and politicians. Let me say on this occasion that it gives me the deepest pleasure to be able to state that none of the other 55 have earned the award more than Professor Macintosh. He has made outstanding contributions to the training of the young surgeon in this country, has blazed many trails and if ever a man has worked in the Elliot Smith tradition of being a truly major contributor to surgery through anatomy he is that man.

Macintosh and Elliott Smith shared many enthusiasms but perhaps not the least of these was their enjoyment, separated by no less than half a century of time, of the old pastime of giving the surgeons hell. In *The Lancet* of 25 October 1913 there is a letter to the editor from Grafton Elliot Smith at The University of Manchester of which the first paragraph reads:

> I think that all who take a real interest in the welfare of the teaching of anatomy and the maintenance of a right standard of knowledge of that subject will view with regret the action of the Council of the Royal College of Surgeons of England in selecting only one of the four examiners in Anatomy for the Fellowship from the ranks of the professed anatomists.

Elliot Smith goes on to indicate how this fellowship provides the one great incentive existing in the country to induce graduates to continue their study of anatomy and feels 'that such a policy will exercise a disastrous influence and react upon the whole methods of teaching'. He states that the college is the custodian of the greatest anatomical museum in existence which refers, of course, to the Hunterian Collection and after belabouring the college for its inadequacies in that regard finishes by saying,

> By appointing as examiners surgeons whose energies are necessarily devoted to work other than mere anatomy the College is driving students to the crammer and the text-book-monger and paralysing the work of those teachers who are endeavouring to instruct their advanced students in the knowledge of the whole structure of the human body and its real significance.

Let me tell you, however, that from 1919 to 1923 Elliot Smith set the springs for the revival in anatomy and laid the foundations of his broad conception of human biology. A great many of the consulting surgeons in the medical schools of Great Britain and the colonies, as they were then called, attended the Primary FRCS classes at that time and Elliot Smith was persuaded to lecture to the Primary Fellowship class. The statement is made by his biographer that this persuasion was effective on the grounds that, to quote verbatim, 'there were several young ex-army officers from the Botany Bay who were anxious to kiss the Pope's foot'. I must admit that the notion of the Professor of Anatomy in the University of Sydney ever being regarded as having either a Papal distinction or any element of Papal infallibility is an attractive but, alas, an unacceptable one. It is, however, true that Elliot Smith had the great concept of the anatomy of the future being something entirely different from the dry as dust topographical anatomy classically taught in the past. It was to his mind no longer simply the handmaiden of surgery but it was indeed the foundation of a broad conception of biology. He himself invented the student demonstrator system, whereby both students and recent graduates were able to teach and tutor others and in this way implant and consolidate their own knowledge. Professor Shellshear took this up in this school and Macintosh has used it over the last 17 years in the surgical training of 170 candidates who were successful in their Primary FRACS examination. Of those I believe that on 12 occasions the coveted Gordon Taylor prize for first place at this examination was awarded to one of the Sydney University demonstrators.

And so you will understand why it should be that at a time when men of deep learning and knowledge are offering their scholarship to the memory of one of the greatest scholars in their field we, the artisans and craftsmen, should be included in the group. The origins of our association lie deep in pre-history as it is in fact true that a skull exists which was excavated in Peru and which has a nice rounded hole in it, the edges of it being quite smooth to establish the fact that it was carried out during life and a long time ante mortem. It is assumed that it was done by primitive man as an elective operation 'to let the devils out'. There are fewer operations of this type being carried out in the second half of the 20th century although there are a few procedures both in surgery and psychiatry which bear more than a passing resemblance to it.

Mr Chancellor, my colleagues of the Royal Australasian College of Surgeons and I are delighted to have the opportunity of joining with the mother university of Australia in paying tribute to one of her greatest sons.

PART I
EVOLUTION OF MAN

I SIR GRAFTON ELLIOT SMITH AND THE EVOLUTION OF MAN

Raymond A. Dart

Introduction

My great privilege today (and I can hardly express appropriately my appreciation of the favour to have it entrusted to me by my fellow-alumni) is to commemorate the achievements of Sir Grafton Elliot Smith with respect to the subject of our consideration, i.e. his great contribution to our knowledge of the evolution of man.

Should we not try at the outset to think of the era, 1871-1937 in which he lived? Firstly, let us recall that his birth synchronized not only with the publication in England of Charles Darwin's *The Descent of Man*, but also with Sir Edward B. Tylor's *Primitive Culture*. That year also marked Schliemann's excavational attack in the hill of Hissarlik in Asia Minor, which along with Mycenae and Tiryns in Greece during the following decade, translated Troy's mythology into historical fact. In the Hall of Mirrors at Versailles on 18 January 1871 William I of Prussia was proclaimed German Emperor after the siege and defeat of Napoleon III and the French in the 1870 war. Nationalism was becoming rampant.

Those were certainly exciting times to live in. In the heart of Africa on 19 November 1871 also, Stanley greeted Livingstone at Ujiji, south of Kigoma on Lake Tanganyika in Central Africa with those immortal words: 'Dr Livingstone I presume'. That following on the discovery of diamonds in south Africa led to the scramble for Africa.

When I was in secondary school from 1906-9 and was introduced to ancient history, I was taught that history began with the foundation of Rome *c.*753 BC; that although some things must have happened on earth before that time the only records we had were tales that poets told: myths to be taken with a grain of salt; that according to the Irish archbishop, James Usher (or Ussher) the earth had been created in 4004 BC; and that in any event the only authentic account of what had happened on earth earlier than the events Greek and Roman authors recorded were those found in the Old Testament of the Bible.

A quarter of a century earlier most people of European descent were emphatic about these matters but the coming of mass education and the writing of Darwin and Huxley in England and of Haeckel in Germany had provoked a revolution in biology and alarm in most other fields of thought.

The Australian Years

Elliot Smith was a second son, named Grafton by his parents; and his father was the schoolmaster of that northeastern New South Wales town. Beran Wolfe (1932, p. 57) author of that popular psychiatrical work of 40 years ago *How to be Happy though Human*, wrote that:

> the second child, having a pacemaker ahead of him, is usually *aggressive and rebellious*. The second child, if not discouraged by the progress of the first-born, is in an unusually good position. The trick is to keep him from being a professional *iconoclast*, who wants to uproot power for the sake of uprooting it. The aggressiveness of the second-born is a perfect foil to the conservatism of the first-born, who having tasted the uniqueness of power, knows how to conserve it. (italics mine)

Elliot Smith's elder brother ultimately became the Director of Education for New South Wales. His younger brother became medically qualified and was a Demonstrator in Anatomy when I was at this University. Through doing some work for him at Louis Schäfer's request it was my good fortune to become associated with him and Professor J. T. Wilson.

This day of our symposium in honour of Sir Grafton Elliot Smith is appropriately devoted to what became his central pursuit: understanding human mental evolution and communicating that understanding to humanity as widely as possible.

It would be foolish to imagine that objective as having arisen spontaneously; it emerged and crystallized gradually. His father had come from the heart of a London he loved. He had sold artists' materials for Winsor & Newton in London at the time of Lyell (1797-1875), Owen (1804-92), Darwin (1809-82) and T. H. Huxley (1819-85), but enrolled as a student under the famous art critic John Ruskin (1819-1906), in the Working Men's College he started in Queens Square with E. D. Maurice, T. Hughes and several of the new school of painters in 1854. His father's ship took six months in sailing to Australia but his attainments earned him a teaching post in Sydney and later that of headmaster at Grafton, New South Wales, where presumably his second son, named Grafton was born.

His facility in drawing with pen and pencil Elliot Smith attributed rightly to his father's love of art and Landseer's drawings, especially dogs that he copied; but his industry therein was maintained by local competitions and prizes. A smaller book on elementary physiology awoke a new vision of science. His elder brother following his father's footsteps, had attended the training college for teachers in Sydney, and had brought home the book. From that time no carcass of a shark found on the beach during seaside holiday visits, only 25 to 30 miles away, was safe from his penknife dissections: more especially of the mystifying collections of tricks represented by their brains and nerves.

Whether that 'second-child' situation in what Wolfe termed 'the family constellation', influenced the future of Sir Grafton Elliot Smith you must judge for yourselves. It is certain from his own writings that he was thrilled by the evolutionary iconoclast T. H. Huxley's *Lessons in Elementary Physiology* (1866), not only because of its lucidity and information, but also by the world of science his aggressive biology had opened up after Charles Darwin's *Origin of Species* had been published. But the man who opened Elliot Smith's eyes in 1894 to the virginal state of the comparative anatomical world that the brains of monotremes and marsupials might illuminate, was Dr (the late Sir Charles) James Martin, CMG, FRS. Martin at that time was his colleague in the Physiology Department here in Sydney, and later became Director of the Lister Institute and Professor of Experimental Pathology, in the University of London.

In 1894 Dr Eugene Dubois brought the *Pithecanthropus* remains to Europe. Haeckel's (1866) 25-year-old prophecy had materialized in Java. Evolution was inescapable! How was it that Elliot Smith so readily fell in with this, of all things, working directly on brains? Firstly, because as a high school student in Sydney he had been attracted to medicine by that outstanding physiological personality Dr (later Sir) Thomas Peter Anderson Stuart, whom all of my generation will remember not only for his artificial larynx, but as founder, and the first and most distinguished Dean of the Faculty of Medicine. Professor Stuart gave a public course of lectures on physiology which Elliot Smith had seen advertised. Stuart had also organized incidentally a visit of his audience to the young medical school he was founding and building. Elliot Smith had already dissected sharks' brains but here Professor Stuart was showing them human brains, which they were allowed to handle; and there too he showed them C. Aeby's illustrated treatise written in German on skull form in man and the apes, and with pictures of human brains and ape brains; and he told them about their convolutions and *'that nobody knew them all'*. As Elliot Smith wrote in his own brief biographical note many years later, he formed then and there silently the vow that he would be 'the one exception to that statement'.

Secondly, from the very first year of his medical study when awarded a prize for natural history he chose Ferrier's *Localization of the Brain*; he had also subscribed to the new medical journal *Brain*. Thirdly, on graduation in 1893 in his twenty-second year he had started learning with Dr (later Sir) Almroth Edward Wright, KBE, FRS, Principal of the Institute of Pathology, St Mary's Hospital, London but then his colleague in the Physiology Department, the neurological techniques in histology essential for doing surgical experimental work on the thalamus of cats and the sensory paths thereto. So the brain, the organ we think with, had become the dominating plan of his life from adolescence. The only thing that became changed was his line of approach. Pasteur and Lister were the greatest figures in medicine; he would be a surgeon!

Dr Martin told him that was stupid! People all over the world had cats to work upon, and neurologists among them would give anything they had, to have the opportunity to work upon Australia's unique monotremes and marsupials. So he started off with J. P. Hill, his and Professor J. T. Wilson's zoologist friend (and later also an FRS) collecting bandicoots and the like, and became the world's leading comparative neurologist, as it were overnight. He would find out whether brains as well as their skull-boxes and muscles evolved and if so, how did they do it.

The curious fact is that Professor J. T. Wilson was working simultaneously on the marsupial mole, *Notoryctes*. But he had been analysing its musculature, and was prevented by that generation's lack of comparative data (and also the physiological data that Sherrington (1857-1952) and also W. B. Cannon (1871-1915) were soon to collect) about the musculature. He was thus blocked from being able to show in what respects man's unique bipedal posture had evolved from that of the lower vertebrates.

No such handicap faced Elliot Smith in studying brains, i.e., the central nervous system, simply because at that time so little was known about the detailed form of brains in both mammals and lower vertebrates. Their comparable cranial nerves of course were known and also the fact that they had brains, but their fundamental parts were not innumerable as were the names of muscles. There were only three: the fore-brain, the hind-brain and the mid-brain.

So he started off with the fore-brain of these Australian creatures and was instantly struck by the vivid anatomical contrast between the commissures connecting the two halves of their fore-brains in higher mammals, such as both cats and human beings on the one hand, and monotremes and marsupials on the other. He communicated this dramatic discovery immediately to the Linnean Society in Sydney in that very year—1894, when he was only twenty-three years old. The following year he had presented his beautifully illustrated MD thesis on the monotreme fore-brain to this university and had also sent off monthly, as it were, in this twenty-fourth year, a barrage of five shorter papers arising from these comparative mammalian brain studies to Germany to appear in the *Anatomischer Anzeiger*; a sixth paper on their overall implications to the *Journal of Anatomy and Physiology* in England; and a seventh to the Royal Society of South Australia on the fore-brain of the virtually blind, marsupial mole, whose muscles Professor J. T. Wilson had been patiently studying.

Shortly after Elliot Smith's death in 1937, Professor J. T. Wilson wrote about this amazing scientist in his early twenties as follows:

Once he had entered upon the selected avenue of his first serious research, he was emphatically an independent worker. His originality of mind was impressive and I can even now recall the somewhat disconcerting impact of his fresh reading of some anatomical features of brain structure upon my own perhaps more traditional outlook.

This quality of mind became conspicuous in the *very first* of his memoirs on brain structure published in the *Proceedings of the Linnean Society of New South Wales* as early as 1894.

His brilliant insight in the twenty-third year of his life which Flechsig's myelinization sequences stimulated, was founded upon separating the rhinencephalon (that part of the fore-brain dominated by the sense of smell) in mammals from the remainder, which he perceived had been informed and modulated by later information coming in from all the other senses. This latter portion ultimately became distinguished and named by him, the *neopallium*. This demarcation revolutionized brain morphology by indicating how mammalian fore-brains had evolved. His paper was soon hailed by the world's premier comparative neurologist at the other end of the world, in Frankfurt, Germany, Ludwig Edinger, as a 'classic'.

Pursuits and Discoveries at Cambridge, Cairo and Manchester

Elliot Smith went with an overseas scholarship to England and was admitted to St John's College, Cambridge in 1896, his twenty-fifth year. Four years later, after he had been elected a Fellow of that college in 1899, and had completed his next classical study of the brains in the Edentates, the most primitive mammals of South America, he was recommended for the Anatomy Chair in Cairo, by Professor Macalister of Cambridge in 1900 (the first year of this century) and his twenty-ninth year. The following year his summarizing paper 'The natural subdivision of the cerebral hemisphere' (1901) was published. Having also completed that year the descriptive and illustrated catalogue of the reptilian and mammalian brains in the Royal College of Surgeons, the next year witnessed the appearance of his correspondingly classical work on the hind-brain entitled 'The primary subdivisions of the mammalian cerebellum' (1902).

Finally to crown this intense six years of comparative brain study in Australia and England he found in 1903 among Egyptian human brains, one whose critical back end (or occupied lobe concerned with vision) was so similar in the pattern of its *lunate sulcus* to the 'Affenspalte',—or ape fissure, as German anatomists had called it in living anthropoids—that he immediately sent off his eleventh, and in many respects crucial comparative evolutionary missive entitled 'The so-called "Affenspalte" in the human (Egyptian) brain', to the *Anatomischer Anzeiger*.

By the end of that year this, his favourite foreign journal had published no less than thirteen papers from his pen; a further five or eighteen in all before he got back to Manchester in 1909 and had ready access to *Nature*. By then he had already published in all over 100 papers. His reputation as the world's leading comparative neurologist and an authority on mammalian as well as primate cerebral evolution thus became established throughout both Old World and the New.

What was done and who did it over sixty years ago is more than our own modern textbooks have space to record. What I wish to stress at this juncture however, is that if all this basic work by Elliot Smith on the evolution of the primate, anthropoid and human fore-brains had not been executed, accepted and so become 'old hat' scientifically and colloquially speaking by 1925, it would have been impossible for me twenty-two years later to identify the transitional nature of *Australopithecus* by means of that same 'affenspalte', or *lunate sulcus*, landmark. The increased separation of that sulcus from the parallel sulcus in the infantile Taungs *Australopithecus* enabled me to assess and also to demonstrate to anybody familiar with brains the triple degree of expansion that had taken place in australopithecine psychology through this associational brain matter within the crucial parietal brain region. This posterolateral intra-parietal expansion was situated between the primary areas for vision, hearing and tactual body sensibility (particularly of the hands and feet) as compared with that of the chimpanzee and gorilla. Therefore it was the clearest possible evidence of the improvement the australopithecine brains had achieved in practising and performing much more skilled body movements with both their more dextrous hands and more competent footwork.

Elliot Smith not only corroborated the conclusions I had drawn from the endocranial cast, he even amplified them by drawing attention to the greater resemblance of its orbital margin to that found in *Pithecanthropus*. Nor did he minimize as others did, the ecological facts of their inhabiting the temperate zone of South Africa nearly two thousand miles away from the tropical forests, and the consequent dietary inevitabilities that a savannah and even desertic habitat necessitated for such an advanced humanoid stock.

But we must return to his staggering nine-year (1900-9) stay in Egypt. For seven years (five of them singlehanded) Elliot Smith had brought 60/100 students unfamiliar with the English language, annually up to the Conjoint Board's standard of anatomical knowledge from a state of biological ignorance. Then during the last two years assisted by F. Wood Jones and later by D. E. Derry, he compiled the data on the thousands of burials of predynastic Egyptians (some 6,000 skeletons and mummies in the first season's campaign alone) then being excavated by G. D. Reisner in Upper Egypt as a result of the 1907 elevation of the Aswan Dam Wall. That fieldwork enabled him to publish his authoritative book on *The Ancient Egyptians and Their Influence upon the Civilisation of Europe* in 1911. He and Wood Jones also jointly initiated the new scientific studies of Human and Comparative Palaeopathology.

A Chronological Survey of Publications

'There were times when, to those about him, he (Elliot Smith) seemed to be completely idle and disinclined for work' wrote Professor Wood Jones, but his 'periods of apparent idleness were those which, in reality, made possible his vast output of considered and completed contributions to science.'

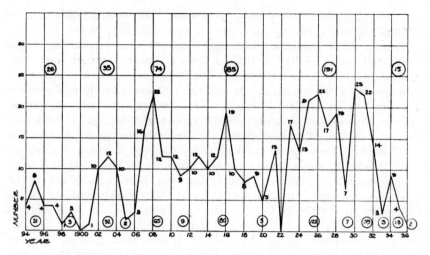

Figure 1.1 A numerical chart of the published works of Sir Grafton Elliot Smith.

The formidable total of 434 works including at least eight books published by him and listed in Warren R. Dawson's *Sir Grafton Elliot Smith: A Biographical Record by His Colleagues* show that a six-fold and cumulative periodicity of this sort characterized that immense output over its 43 years. The 20 papers that appeared in the first four-year period (1894-7), were followed by 5 only during the following fallow three-year period (1898-1901), during which he had also become married (1900) and had gone to Cairo (see Figure 1.1).

The second, or Egyptian upsurge of 32 papers in the three-year period (1902-4) dropped again to 5 during another but shorter, less active two-year or reflectional period (1905-6). Then there came the third outburst. This, having begun in Egypt with the mummification and pre-dynastic populational investigations, climaxed in the 62 papers that came during the four-year Cairo-Manchester transition period (1907-10). Next came a purely comparative recession period of only a year with 9 publications in 1911, and was then immediately followed by another six-year (1912-17) or fourth explosion of 80 papers which peaked in 1916, to form a second major Manchester outpouring, which subsided to 5 in 1920 during the comparative relaxational period of only 22 papers between 1918 and 1920 during transference from Manchester to London.

It was during this relatively slack period that I was fortunate enough to become associated with him personally. I appreciate now from examining the chart that I have drawn up that his fourth surge had probably synchronized with the added significance to his Egyptian physical and cultural research that Wilfred Jackson's studies on shells and W. J. Perry's insight into the distribution of gold-mining and pearl-seeking probably supplied in confirming his primary concept of Egypt's place in cultural diffusion, founded directly on mummification.

Among the 'Associations with and impressions of Sir Grafton Elliot Smith' (*Mankind*, 8 No. 3, 1972) I have recounted already how other Australians, i.e., the late Dr Joseph Shellshear of Sydney University and subsequently Professor of Anatomy in the University of Hong Kong, and also the late Dr H. H. Woollard of Melbourne University and subsequently Professor of Anatomy in the universities first of Adelaide and later of London, at St Bartholomew's Hospital, also joined the staff of the Anatomy Department at University College, London during the 1919-20 year. It was a period marked not only by Elliot Smith's transference from Manchester to London, but also by the visit of the Rockefeller Foundation's representatives and the subsequent grant of £1,205,000 to University College and its Medical School as a mark of appreciation of the contributions of British medical science to the wellbeing of mankind during the 1914-18 World War I. The late Professor H. A. Harris described this gift as 'the largest single benefaction to any educational institution in Great Britain' (Ch. 7 in *Sir Grafton Elliot Smith*, W. R. Dawson (ed.)).

Retrospect over these first four output periods shows that the first in Australia was dominated by the primitive mammalian brain; the second given over to ratifying evolution in mammalian brains in general, and demonstrating it by primate brains, in particular. The latter two outputs that really fuse into one mark his transition to, or concentration upon demonstrating human thinking, firstly by anatomical and physiological illustrations, and secondly by psychological issues most especially.

In his search to explain the dominant motives in human beings, mummification and burial customs with all that they implied in the rituals, doctrines, buildings, clothing and ornaments of mankind, whether living or dead, were additional clues for our human understanding, just as inescapable as brain evolution and bodily evolution had been.

As J. B. Stopford puts it (Dawson, p. 162)

> His distinguished position as a scholar enabled him to speak with authority and he had an unusual power of gathering together the essential facts and then interpreting them in such a clear way that all could follow the argument. Sometimes he was distinctly provocative and he could be very severe when criticising the conclusions of others; these phases acted as a savoury and often added to the pleasure of his audience. Such outbursts were in striking contrast to his usual demeanour on these occasions . . . He invariably spoke easily, simply and without much preparation. . . . When taking part in discussions before learned societies he was commonly unrestrained and would at times hit hard and treat opponents and critics of his views with the greatest severity.

How can one depict the frustration with which he was surrounded on his return to England and the gigantic nature of the revolution he was instrumental in carrying out both in the teaching of anatomy and in bridging the gap between zoology and psychology through his mastery of comparative primate neurology in the settled England of Edward VII and George V before and during World War I.

His previous basic work on the fore-brain and the hind-brain enabled him to concentrate in his Arris and Gale Lectures in 1910 on the part played by the thalamus, or mid-brain in producing the neopallium. He had thus exposed how evolution had proceeded in all three: fore-, mid-, and hind-parts of the brain and had made the several fundamental stages in primate anatomy of the brain intelligible to all biologists for the first time. The facts underlying the evolution of human intelligence thus became demonstrable to the scientific world through his amazing ability for exposition. The seemingly inextricable multiplicity of the human brain's convolutions faced in his adolescence had been reduced to five preliminary stages in its evolution: *firstly*, from the generalized smell-dominating insectivore stage of the jumping shrew through *secondly*, from the vision-dominated and expanded cortex of the tree shrew, to *thirdly*, the more acutely visioned, leaping, toe-clinging and manually-dexterous and basically double-eyed or binocular, Tarsius-type of arboreal primate; and *fourthly*, from the stage of an enhanced mastery of the limbs or agility, balance, hearing and vocalization of the monkeys had become adapted to any and every type of arboreal life; and *fifthly*, through the anthropoid stage of creatures with partially freed hands worked by inquisitive brains controlling powerful bodies and capable of exploring the forests for both plant and animal food to that of human beings themselves.

That evolutionary picture of mammalian and human evolution he presented to the British Association for the Advancement of Science in 1912 and thus paved the way for his friend Broom's presentation of the South African mammal-like reptilian story in his Croonian Lecture to the Royal Society and to the same public in 1913. Then in 1914 he, Elliot Smith, came to Australia with the British Association and here in Sydney participated in congratulating Professors Edgworth David and J. T. Wilson on the discovery of Australia's first fossil human skull from Talgai.

The Contemporary Scene Before and After World War I

It is easy enough for modern eyes to follow those steps in brain and body evolution after they have been predigested for us in his lectures to the British Academy (1916) and the Royal Institution (1924) and published in his *Evolution of Man: Essays* (1924). Those teachings have been abstracted and incorporated so completely and for so long in time in everyone's concepts about the primates ever since, that their cerebral source in his life work is as forgotten as World War I itself.

At the end of the first decade of the twentieth century these ideas which are basic to modern comparative ecological and psychological studies of primates and ourselves were revolutionary. Who attributed thought to primates? That only came in after World War I was over with Köhler and Yerkes. Similarly with evolution: interesting as a theory, sure; but who really believed it then in England or America in 1909?

What proportion of the world's 3,000 million people in 1972 do the members of our audience here today imagine to be actually realizing that human beings have been evolving physically over the last few millennia, evolving artistically over the last few hundreds of years and evolving technologically during the last few scores of years?

The proportion of believers in evolution is minimal because human lives are so short and the great majority of human beings are still bereft of the mental education for which those hundreds of millions of years of evolution prepared their brains. Evolution made their posture erect, and freed their clever hands to work under the direction of their sight, hearing and bodily control, i.e., this improved their understanding of the appearance, sounds and movements of everything around them during the last five million years. But the mills of God grind slowly. Human brains have failed to conquer the skill they have also fostered to kill and destroy one another while following their collective pursuits.

However small the percentage of informed believers in an evolving humanity may be today it was insignificant in the first decade of the twentieth century throughout the western world. As a theory of course it had been entertained by the intelligentsia, but who amongst them really believed it? Only such crazy coots as Darwin, or science fanatics like Huxley?

Of course there was that contentious ape-man brought to Europe by Dubois, the fanciful Dutch surgeon from Java in 1894. But Virchow, the father of pathology and most eminent doctor in Berlin was the Leader of the Opposition in the Reichstag, and thus doughty political antagonist of Prince von Bismarck himself. He denied this *Pithecanthropus* discovery.

This was the same formidable man who 37 years earlier had diagnosed Neanderthal Man in 1857 as a 'rachitic idiot affected with arthritis'. Now in 1894, his 74th year, he declared that the thigh bone from Java was human, osteophytic and modern; that the skull was that of an ape, a big gibbon, and had nothing to do with the thigh bone! Of the 12 professors present at the congress in Leyden, 2 others aligned themselves with Virchow and the ape concept, 3 opposed that view, they considered the remains human and 6 agreed with Dubois about its transitional nature. So opinion was divided! Dubois attended several further congresses in France, England and Germany, but what could he do except to hide both himself and the remains? The attacks he encountered embittered him so deeply that he locked away in Leyden all the collections he had made in Java.

There they were not seen by anyone until 1921. Then he showed them to Henry Fairfield Osborn, Director of the American Museum of Natural History, who the previous year had described 'Hesperopithecus' or the Western Ape, the first anthropoid primate claimed as found in America. This claim was based on two molar teeth found in Nebraska.

They were ultimately diagnosed to be not primate but those of a peccary, but they were still being accepted in America as potentially anthropoid when *Australopithecus* was discovered and published in 1925.

That was one of the many reasons why it was important to emphasize the southern source of *Australopithecus*. *Hesperopithecus* was still being discussed by Elliot Smith in his *Evolution of Man: Essays* (2nd edn, 1927, pp. 6-10) and its position was retained (in Fig. 2 'A tentative scheme of relationships of the Order Primates). It is therefore appropriate to draw attention at this centenary to his remarks

> I refer to it (i.e. *Australopithecus*) now to suggest that its position in the Order Primates might be tentatively indicated if it were put in the place of the questionable *Hesperopithecus* in Figure 2, but of course removing its stem of origin below the human rank. (pp. 10-11)

Clearly, therefore, the differences between Elliot Smith's interpretation of the facts and mine were negligible. Even the gap in brain dimension between the australopithecine brain and that of *Eoanthropus* (as long as the hoax was undetected) had been bridged by *Pithecanthropus* and that bridge was soon reinforced by its cousin form *Sinanthropus*. Today of course we await the additional light that Lantian Man on the one side and the australopithecine types like *Meganthropus* from Java and the Gigantopithecines of both China and India, are bound to throw on human evolution.

The later evidence in support of the ancestral nature of the australopithecines fortunately did not start accumulating until the end of World War II. Not until the first Pretoria Museum Monograph was published in 1946 by the late Dr Robert Broom and Dr G. W. H. Schepers, Professor of Anatomy in the University of Pretoria (and also a past student of the University of the Witwatersrand) had the neglect of that evidence by overseas become invidious. The late Professor (later Sir Wilfrid) Le Gros Clark visited South Africa late the same year and supported independently in England and America the claims made about their proximity to humanity. The following year the discovery of australopithecine pelvic remains at both Sterkfontein and Makapansgat led to Sir Arthur Keith's generous public admission in *Nature* (1947) that he had been wrong and Dart had been right. The next year witnessed the publication of his penultimate book *A New Theory of Evolution* (1948) in which he accepted fully their significance but terming them preferentially 'Dartians'. I cannot imagine that the evidence that both Professor Le Gros Clark and Sir Arthur Keith had found irresistable in 1947 would have been rejected by Sir Grafton Elliot Smith had he been alive.

The Fatal Decade (1922-32)

What had become of far greater importance to Elliot Smith with the devastating deaths of his chief life-long friend, Dr W. H. R. Rivers in

1922, and then of John Hunter in 1923 whom he loved like a son, was to complete their unfinished labours; and to fashion the newly established Institute of Anatomy into the fountain-head of information about human structure, prehistory, and an understanding of human bodily and mental activity, such as a properly rounded anatomy department in a modern medical school and a university of the future should be.

The Pacific Ocean responsibilities that fell upon Australia after World War I, led to the second congress of the Pacific Science Association in Melbourne and Sydney in 1923. W. J. Perry represented Elliot Smith there. From it arose the five-year grant of the Rockefeller Foundation of some $15,000 a year for Human Biology; the journey of Elliot Smith to Australia in 1924; the founding of the Department of Anthropology in Sydney University in 1925; and Professor A. R. Radcliffe-Brown's appointment thereto in 1926. Elliot Smith returned to Australia after attending the Pacific Congress in Java in 1929; and the story of his subsequent intervention in 1933 to preserve the continuation of the Department of Anthropology has also been recorded fully by A. P. Elkin in *The Oceania Monographs, No. 16* (1970).

The stupendous work forced upon Elliot Smith simultaneously by the Rockefeller generosity to University College and to Sydney, and by the deaths had no true relaxation in the total absence of publication in 1922, the year of Dr Rivers's death, or of only 7 in 1929. Between the peak years of 1921-8 papers, he produced the fantastic number of 122 publications and the 59 works of 1930-2, of 191 publications altogether, one of which was his unrivalled last book *Human History* (1930) dedicated to his friend and collaborator W. J. Perry. The seizure he suffered in December 1932 to my mind was the inevitable result of that terrific strain of 191 compositions without adequate relaxation; that incessant demand that not even his normally strong physical frame and placidity of outlook, but deep sensitivity, could withstand. The deaths of Davidson Black in 1934, and his youngest son, Stephen, early in 1936, as well as his wife's accident soon afterwards took their additional toll and brought his own life to its unseasonable early close at the all too early age of sixty-six, on New Year's day in 1937: a grievous shock to all his admirers, who encircled the globe. To me it brought not only pain like a bolt from the blue, for I had no prior warning of these effects upon his health, but later another unexpected surprise, for in his will he had bequeathed his entire library to me. Subsequently shipped out to South Africa that unexpected trust was incorporated forthwith: part in the Witwatersrand Medical Library then under the care of my wife and part in the Central Library of the University of the Witwatersrand. Each book carries within it a book-plate recording his bequest to myself and thence to the library concerned. So every inquisitive reader of his books in Johannesburg has been and will continue to be aware of the friendship underlying their privilege in reading each of those books.

Epilogue

Life was far kinder to his old friends J. T. Wilson and J. P. Hill as well as Robert Broom (1866-1951) and Sir Arthur Keith (1866-1955). There are doubtless many other figures to recall, but four of his older and honoured medically-qualified contemporaries whose life tracks I find interesting to compare with his because their approaches to the study of the nervous system and human mentality were parallel and also realistic and had outstanding but divergent effects upon his era being physiological or clinical. Thus Walter B. Cannon (1871-1945) of Harvard, who war born in the same year but studied particularly the emotional reactions of the autonomic nervous system in *Bodily Changes in Pain, Hunger, Fear and Rage*, and lived into his seventies. Sir Charles S. Sherrington (1857-1952) of both Cambridge and Oxford, author of *The Integrative Action of the Nervous System* was fourteen years older than both of them and only five years from attaining his own centenary when he passed away. Two others come to mind as clinical and long-lived contemporaries whose influence was more widely spread socially. Sigmund Freud (1856-1939), the psychologist who introduced psychoanalysis was born three years before *The Origin of Species*. He dealt directly with mental behaviour and ultimately shocked his own colleagues into confronting the mentalities of all their patients. The other is Havelock Ellis (1859-1939), who survived Elliot Smith by two years, but Ellis was coeval with *The Origin of Species*. His *The Nationalisation of Health* (1892) was a remarkable anticipation of modern British health services while the popularity of *Man and Woman* (1894), which compared the physiological differences between the sexes led to his seven-volumed *Studies in the Psychology of Sex* (1897-1928). The first volume's claim to being a scientific study was ruled by the judge 'a pretence, adopted for the purpose of selling a filthy publication' and the other volumes published in the United States until 1935, were legally available only to the medical profession. This stifling of sex discussion for nearly 40 years did not prevent Freud from adopting terms that Ellis had used. Long before Freud wrote on interpreting dreams Ellis started detailed records of his own dreams; and he regarded Freud's emphasis on sex excessive (*Encyc. Brit.*, 1969 edn).

So did Elliot Smith: for him man's *will to live* was the over-riding or dominant motive. But this contemporary world of 1972 and mankind's future living is concerned very immediately with the problems of sex and of world population as well as their emotional resultants in human individual and mass behaviour. For our understanding of what the central nervous system contributes to that behaviour individually, phylogenetically and culturally humanity is deeply indebted to Sir Grafton Elliot Smith. His status Robert S. Goodman and George Johnston's *The Australians* have (1966, p. 188) recently recognized as 'a monolithic figure among anatomists and anthropologists'. At some centenary in his honour, maybe in 2071 or 3071 if humanity succeeds in adapting itself to the self-knowledge that Elliot Smith and his contemporaries spent their lives in revealing, the relative importance of the contributions made by each individual may be better understood; or the computors of those future days may be able to unravel such mysteries automatically. For our days of celebration, it is perhaps enough to say that only by including under that term 'anthropologists' all the fields of human activity that he embraced in his perspective, will we fully comprehend Elliot Smith's particular contributions to mankind.

REFERENCES

BROOM, R., (1914) 'On the origin of mammals' (Croonian Lecture), *Phil. Trans. R. Soc.*, B. 206, 1-48.

BROOM, R. & SCHEPERS, G. W. H., (1946) *The South African Fossil Ape-Men, The Australopithecinae*. Pretoria, *Transvaal Museum Memoir, No. 2.*

DART, R. A., (1925) '*Australopithecus africanus*: the man-ape of South Africa', *Nature*, 115, 195-9.

——, (1972) 'Associations with and impressions of Sir Grafton Elliot Smith, *Mankind*, 8, 3, 171-5.

DARWIN, C., (1859) *The Origin of Species by Means of Natural Selection*, Murray, London.

——, (1871) *The Descent of Man and Selection in Relation to Sex*, Murray, London.

DAWSON, W. P. (ed.), (1938) *Sir Grafton Elliot Smith: a Biographical Record by His Colleagues*, Cape, London, 272 pp., illustrations.

ELKIN, A. P., (1970) 'The Journal of Oceania: 1930-1970', *The Oceania Monographs*, No. 16.

ELLIS, H., (1894) *Man and Woman: A Study of Human Sexual Characters*, Walter Scott, London.

——, (1897-1928) *Studies in the Psychology of Sex*, Heinemann, London. (Medical Books) 7 vols.

FREUD, S., (1913) *The Interpretation of Dreams* (transl. by A. A. Brill from *Die Traumdeutung*, 1900).

GOODMAN, R. S., & JOHNSTON, G., (1966) *The Australians*, Rigby, Sydney, 292 pp., illustrations.

HUXLEY, T. H., (1866) *Lessons in Elementary Physiology*, Macmillan, London.

KEITH, SIR A., (1947) 'Australopithecinae or Dartians', *Nature*, 159, 377.

——, (1948) *A New Theory of Human Evolution*, Watts, London, 451 pp.

SMITH, G. E., (1894) 'A preliminary communication upon the cerebral comissures of the Mammalia with special reference to Monotremata and Marsupialia', *Proc. Linn. Soc. N.S.W.*, 2nd ser., 9, 635-57.

——, (1895) *Anatomy and histology of the cerebrum of the neoplacental mammal.* MD thesis, University of Sydney.

——, (1903) 'The so-called "Affenspalte" in the human (Egyptian) brain', *Anat. Anz.*, 24, 139-41.

——, (1911) *Ancient Egyptians and Their Influence upon the Civilisation of Europe*, Harper, London.

——, (1924) *Evolution of Man: Essays*, Milford, London, viii, 159 pp., illustrations.

TYLOR, SIR E. B., (1871) *Primitive Culture*, John Murray, London.

WOLFE, W. B., (1932) *How to be Happy though Human*, Routledge, London, xiv, 374 pp.

2 THE BRAIN AND EVOLUTION OF LOWER MAMMALS

J. R. Simons

Sir Grafton Elliot Smith attained such rank and fame as an anthropologist that people seem surprised when a mere zoologist expresses an admiration for the man and his work. They tend to forget that he began his professional career as an anatomist and that his early publications, as well as some of his later ones, were concerned with the structure of the central nervous system of vertebrate animals. In those early years, he dissected and examined the brains of reptiles, birds and an extraordinary number of mammals. Not only were the facts which he gleaned from his prodigious activity significant contributions to the storehouse of zoological knowledge but his speculations and interpretations of them illuminated our understanding of the evolution of the mammalian brain.

Among his many important contributions that one might discuss are: the increasing significance of vision in the primate series; the development of nervous pathways between the cerebellum and the cerebral hemispheres of the higher vertebrates and the subservience of the cerebellum to cortico-pontine control in them, but the thing which is most likely to ring the bell of memory for any zoologist is Elliot Smith's teaching that the evolution of the mammalian brain involved the elaboration of an entirely novel layer of grey matter over the surface of the hemispheres of the fore-brain together with connecting pathways between them. That is to say, he advanced the view that the evolution of the mammalian brain is essentially the story of the elaboration of the cerebral cortex and its large commissure of connecting nerve fibres, the corpus callosum. As my contribution to this commemorative symposium I should like to discuss in general terms, these two parts of the brain in conjunction with what we know of the evolution and behaviour of the Australian marsupials and monotremes.

When in 1894, the young Grafton Elliot Smith published his first paper on the cerebral commissures of mammals, there was already a generally accepted theory about the evolution of the vertebrate brain. Some nine years before the German anatomist, Edinger, had published a book (1885) in which he explained the general form of the mammalian brain as the result of the evolution of what he called the neo-encephalon (i.e. new brain). This he defined as the hemispheres of the fore- and hind-brains. These he interpreted as additions to the palaeoencephalon

39

or old-brain. The first signs of the neo-encephalon were to be seen in the fore-brain of fish. In the successive evolution of the amphibians, reptiles and birds, the neo-encephalon progressively enlarged and, in the mammals came to form the most prominent part of the brain. At its highest development the neo-encephalon included parts of the hind-brain as well as constituting most of the fore-brain.

Elliot Smith queried this view and pointed out that the important characteristic feature of the mammalian fore-brain is that it is composed of a phylogenetically old part concerned with olfaction which is always divided off from a phylogenetically new covering of grey matter. He called this new covering the neo-pallium, a term which incidentally, is still used by zoologists although it is much more commonly called the cerebral or neo-cortex by non-zoologists.

All mammals possess the neo-pallial covering of the cerebral hemispheres but, as Elliot Smith indicated, the nervous pathway connecting the pallia of the right and left sides is not the same in all cases. In the higher mammals (the placentals), such as a cat there is a broad and thick band of nerve fibres, the corpus callosum, which passes between the two halves of the fore-brain connecting the two pallia. In marsupials such as a possum this broad band is absent and although there are connecting pathways between the hemispheres these pass through the regions of the anterior and hippocampal commissures.

The lowest grade of mamals are the monotremes: the platypus and the echidnas. In their brains, as in those of the marsupials, there is no corpus callosum and the interconnecting pathways are restricted to pass through the region of the anterior commissure (Figure 2.1).

In Elliot Smith's view the corpus callosum is a phylogenetic replacement of the more primitive commissures—the hippocampal one in particular. Because of its dorsal position it can undergo extensive elaboration without interfering with the more basal and phylogenetically older parts of the fore-brain.

By virtue of the neo-pallium and the corpus callosum the capacity in mammals for voluntary adaptive behaviour is thus increased and the fore-brain becomes, in his words, 'the instrument that makes it possible to compare new experience with what has happened before and to modify behaviour in the light of such knowledge. We can indeed', he continued, regard the arrangement 'as fulfilling all the conditions of the *"sensorium commune"* which Aristotle and many generations of philosophers have sought during more than twenty centuries'.

This view will, I think, be familiar to anyone who has read any of the innumerable modern elementary texts of zoology or psychology. They will look in vain, however, for a mention of the name of its originator.

Turning to authors who have more recently considered the evolution of the mammalian brain, I would refer rather briefly to two, Rensch and Pribram. Rensch (1954) reviews and discusses certain interesting palaeontological evidence, while Pribram (1958) offers a view of brain structure and function that amplifies the inferences that Elliot Smith drew.

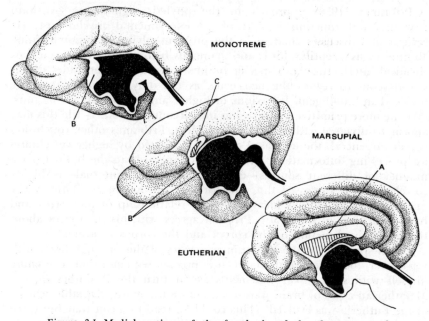

Figure 2.1 Medial sections of the fore-brain of the three types of
mammals. The structures referred to in the text are (A) the corpus
callosum, (B) the anterior commissure and (C) the dorsal commissure
('corpus callosum') of the kangaroo/wallaby brain (after Wood Jones).

A characteristic feature of the fossil record of mammals is the progressive increase in the size of the brain case. Allowing for allometric
considerations, the absolute size of the brain case of placentals has
increased with the passage of time. The same seems to be true for
marsupials, although not to the same degree. No doubt a similar trend
will be seen in the monotremes if, and when, we find their fossils.

The increase is in the main due to the expansion of the fore-brain
rather than the other parts. This is particularly demonstrated in those
fossils which not only constitute an almost linear series from the earliest
to latest, but also have been formed in conditions that have allowed
endocranial details to be preserved. The series from *Hyracotherium*,
(Eohippus) the Eocene ancestor, to *Equus* the modern horse shows this
particularly well, but a similar evolutionary trend can be demonstrated
for other groups of mammals—a familiar example for anthropologists
would be the hominid series. As Rensch points out, increase in size
means not only that there is an increase in the surface area of the neo-
pallium but an even greater increase in the volume of white matter.
That is, because of surface area/volume relationships, the larger brain is
characterized not only by an increase in cortex but an even greater
increase in the number of internal connections to which the corpus
callosum makes considerable contribution.

Pribram's (1958) approach to the phyletic significance of brain structure and function is that of an experimental psychologist. He reviews and discusses changes in the problem-solving or lesson-learning abilities of fish, reptiles, birds and mammals before and after surgical or chemical interference with specific brain structures. He concludes that it is erroneous to regard the neo-cortex as the only significant structure involved in 'intelligent' behaviour in higher animals, but that one must take the more primitive brain region into account as well. While this may appear to disagree with Elliot Smith's ideas, Pribram's other conclusion is that in general, the increased capacity exhibited by higher vertebrates for processing 'information' arriving simultaneously to the brain from a number of different sources—external as well as internal—is highly correlated with increased differentiation of the fore-brain. Thus, while qualifying Elliot Smith's ideas about the relationship of the cortex and basal structures of the brain, Pribram agrees with his inferences about the associative function of the cortex and the corpus callosum.

When speaking of the evolutionary stages of the brain, Elliot Smith was never too categorical about the precise sequence but contented himself with such broad statements as 'in turn the Prototherian and Metatherian types of brain were tried before the more adaptable scheme of the Eutheria was evolved'. This could be read to mean that the three types were evolved one from the other, in succession, or alternatively that they could all have been coexistent, with the Eutherian or placental type eventually winning the evolutionary race. Today I think we can be more certain because we know a lot more about the history of mammals, particularly the Mesozoic forms. We can also infer more about the evolution of Australian marsupials despite a continuing scarcity of pre-Pleistocene fossils.

About twenty years ago the total amount of fossil material of very early mammals known from all the world would not have weighed more than a few pounds. Following the inspired searchings of Kermack and his colleagues during the 1950s we now possess several hundredweight of them. This considerable quantity of material shows that during the Jurassic period there were at least six separate lines of small animals that had crossed the reptile-mammal boundary. The interrelationships of the six lines have been only very recently agreed on, and the consensus is that there were two groups. One group—the theria—contained the lines evolving towards the marsupials and placentals. The second group—the non-theria—contained three fairly closely related forms; the Docodonts from which were derived the Triconodonts, and a group, the Multi-tuberculata, which probably had a common ancestor with the Docodonts among the mammal-like reptiles. The Multituberculata persisted the longest and became widespread throughout the world. The modern monotremes were, in all probability, derived from them (Kermack & Jaworowska, 1971) (Figure 2.2).

Whatever the exact relationship may be between all these non-theria it is fairly evident that the brain of a modern platypus or echidna

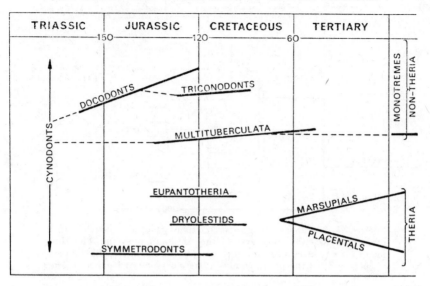

Figure 2.2 The occurrence in geologic time of fossil and modern mammals (solid lines). The probable evolutionary relationship of the non-therian types to each other are indicated by dashed lines. Age indicated in millions of years (data from Kermack).

cannot be regarded as the prototype of the placental brain. They have each had their separate evolution for a considerable time.

F. Wood Jones (1925) in his classic *Mammals of South Australia* comments with a discernible air of puzzlement on the monotreme brain. 'It cannot be said' he wrote, 'that the monotremes are deficient in the extent of their cerebral hemispheres—indeed they are mysteriously well endowed with cerebral cortex'.

There is a certain amount of anecdotal information about the behaviour of both the platypus and the echidna in captivity as well as in the wild (Burrell, 1927; Troughton, 1946). Controlled studies with adequate numbers are unfortunately, completely lacking. There is however, a very interesting recent paper by Saunders, Chen and Pridmore (1971) dealing with Habit-Reversal Learning in three specimens of the echidna, *Tachyglossus aculeatus*—the common species of eastern Australia.

Habit-reversal learning I might explain has been used by psychologists over the past ten years or so as a method of comparing the 'intellectual' capacities of different types of animals.

It may be too early to generalize about the monotremes as a whole but it is a pleasure to relay the information that despite having brains lacking a corpus callosum the three echidnas tested by Saunders and his colleagues performed well up to mammalian standards—as well as rats, in fact. I don't think Wood Jones would have been too surprised at the result, but perhaps Elliot Smith would have been.

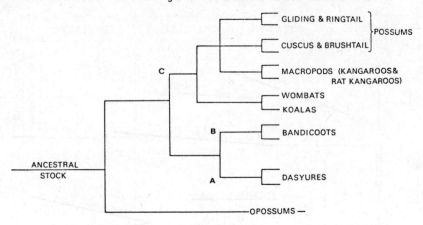

Figure 2.3 Probable phylogenetic relationship of the more familiar marsupials to each other and to the American opossum. The three major lines referred to in the text are: (A) the Dasyurids, (B) the perameloids and (C) the phalangeroids (diagram modified from Ride after Kirsch).

Turning our attention to the evolution of marsupials in Australia we might note that serological work by Kirsch (quoted by Ride, 1968) tends to support very strongly the account which previously had been inferred from comparative anatomy and a rather scanty fossil record. This means that although there are uncertainties about the times involved the interrelationships seem reasonably certain and sound (Ride, 1968, 1971).

Australian marsupials can be regarded as a radiation of three major lines from a common ancestor (Figure 2.3). The three lines are: the dasyurids, represented by the native cats, Tasmanian devils, numbats and the marsupial mice; the perameloids, represented by the bandicoots and finally, the phalangeroids, comprising the wombats and koalas, the various possums, as well as the kangaroos and rat-kangaroos. The common ancestor, reaching Australia about the end of the Cretaceous, was also the ancestor of the modern American opossum and probably looked something like it.

The phalangeroids are a distinctive Australian grouping which includes, as I have just mentioned, the macropods—the kangaroos, wallabies, euros as well as their much smaller cousins, the rat-kangaroos. Ride (1971) is of the opinion that the macropods split off as a distinct line probably early in Eocene times. At some later time they differentiated into kangaroo-wallabies, on the one hand, and the rat-kangaroos on the other.

A striking feature of the brain of the large macropods (Figure 2.1) is that 'part of the neo-pallial commissure lies dorsal to the anterior commissure in the form of a true corpus callosum' (Ariëns Kappers, 1936). The interesting question is, to what extent does this structure supplement or replace the connections through the anterior commissure? Martin (1967) has shown that in the opossum *(Didelphys virginiana)* all the corresponding areas of the right and left neocortices are linked through the anterior commissures. Presumably the same is true of all our marsupials and perhaps even the monotremes. If this is so then the macropod corpus would seem to be supplementary. However, whatever the relationship is, one concludes that the condition evolved in the kangaroo-wallaby line after it separated from that of the rat-kangaroos because in the latter the structure does not occur.

The macropod corpus callosum is not derived from or related to that of the placentals. The two structures have been evolved quite independently in very distantly related stocks and at very different times. The placentals must have had theirs shortly after the time of the common ancestor of themselves and the marsupials—that is, sometime towards the close of the Cretaceous. The macropod corpus could not have appeared before the Eocene. We are dealing here then with what appears to be an interesting case of convergent evolution in which the beginnings of the evolution of two similar structures are separated by at least 15 million years.

In turning to consider how the Australian marsupials might rank in 'intelligence' either among themselves or in comparison with placental mammals, we are handicapped by disappointing gaps in our knowledge. There is recent work by Russell and Pearce (1971) on the reactive behaviour of various marsupials to novel objects. Russell (1970) has also published a study of agonistic behaviour of a group of red kangaroos, but while these studies demonstrate that marsupials exhibit the same varieties of behaviour as is seen among placentals they are ambiguous as evidence of comparative intelligence. On the other hand, there is a fair amount of anecdotal evidence about our marsupials and one of the more pertinent points is the contention, which is maintained fairly consistently, that kangaroos and wallabies make the most satisfactory pets. Now, the criterion here is that these are creatures which respond to, take notice of and form attachments to their human owners, and while there is so to speak, a fair element of customer satisfaction in this evaluation, I do not think one need be too hasty in dismissing the idea that it could be a rough and ready way of rating the intelligence of the creatures. In descending order, wombats rank second favourites while opossums, despite all the charm of the smaller ones, rank poor thirds. Interestingly this ranking does not conflict with the controlled study of Munn (1964) on habit-reversal learning in the grey kangaroo. Comparing them with rats, Munn's results show that the best performance among his kangaroos was well above rat average although not as good as the best rat performance. At the other end of the scale, the poorest kangaroo performance was not as bad as the weakest performance among the rats. In the same paper Munn quotes a personal communication of Jeeves who indicated that in similar tests, which apparently remain unpublished, opossums (species unidentified) performed below the level of kangaroos. Jeeves himself (1965) was of the opinion that in simple discrimination learning tests 'opossums, the kangaroo and bandicoot . . . are all as bright as cats' but, according to psychologists, these tests are not as useful as tests of habit-reversal learning in ranking 'intelligence'.

If we assume the better performance of kangaroos to be a real phenomenon that reflects a general quality among the large macropods, could it perhaps to due to their possession of the additional dorsal commissure in their fore-brain? It may well be that this is so, but I do not think it could be argued very convincingly at present because not only do we lack information about what happens to a kangaroo's behaviour if the commissure is cut but also in studies of placentals whose corpus callosum is bisected—the so-called 'split-brain' studies reviewed by Sperry (1968) or Young (1971)—it has been found that although specific abilities may be affected, general performance is not necessarily impaired.

The general interpretation (Jeeves, et al., 1965) is that there are alternative pathways in the placental brain that take over the function of the bisected callosal tracts. The kangaroo has the alternative pathways very well developed, and, in all probability, they are still more important than the dorsal set, so even when someone does get round to cutting the dorsal commissure one guesses that the effect is going to be even less obvious than in the case among placentals. But even so, such is the logic of science, this should not be a reason for not doing the experiment.

The disappointingly few studies of marsupial learning behaviour have depended upon certain specific abilities of the animals, such as the ability to discriminate between two visual patterns, and while the results are interesting one is always left wondering about what exactly they do tell us. Quite apart from difficulties of trying to match the significance of a particular set of cues for one species of animal with its significance for another, there is the wider question of whether such techniques do tell us anything about the general overall quality of the brain. Can the quality be accounted for by adding up, so to speak, all the results for different abilities or is the whole somehow greater than the sum of the constituent parts? I suspect, as in the case of other biological phenomena, it is.

The implications of Elliot Smith's or Pribram's ideas about the significance of the neo-cortex and its connections concern an increased capacity for voluntary adaptive behaviour, but because of an almost complete lack of information about marsupial brain structure and its correlation with behaviour we are hardly in a position to say anything really convincing about this capacity in them, let alone consider questions of whether it may be the expression of whole brain function or a simple addition of specific abilities. However, as an alternative, I should like to mention an aspect of macropods I find interesting and which, it could be argued, indicates that they at least possess some capacity for voluntary adaptive behaviour.

Everyone is aware these days that kangaroos are extensively hunted for their meat and skins, but despite the very heavy pressures of commercial shooters and the countless numbers of so-called sportsmen there are, according to authorities such as Calaby, *et al.* (1971), greater numbers of euros, red kangaroos and, it would seem, grey kangaroos than have ever existed in this country at any previous time. How are their numbers maintained in the face of such heavy predation? Part of the answer lies in the effects of protective legislation, but it is possible that adaptive behaviour also contributes significantly by making things just that much more difficult for hunters.

The ethnologist, F. D. McCarthy, who I am glad to see is taking part in this symposium, noted in his contribution to the Record of the Arnhem Land Expedition of 1948, that when he accompanied Aborigines on kangaroo hunts they told him that the creatures would, sooner or later, become aware that they were being hunted and would then move away from the area. This kind of response may be no more than a simple 'flight following fright' reaction, but in the context of present day commercial hunting something more seems to be involved. The hunting is done towards dusk and at night with the aid of spotlights and rifles. The animals do not usually flee the area, but according to farmers and hunters I have spoken to, appear to have become more wily than they used to be. They do not move out from cover as early in the evening as was their habit, but wait until dusk is well advanced. Furthermore, few animals will sit more than a moment or two when they are picked out by the hunters' spotlight.

If there has been a change in the kangaroos' behaviour in these respects an interesting question arises. Is it to be explained as an instance of voluntary adaptive behaviour?—that is, something learned by individuals who then alter their behaviour accordingly—or is it a case of the operation of a selection process? that is, the altered behaviour being due not to learning by individuals but to the kangaroos being the offspring of individuals that in past generations had the same kind of behaviour, as an innate response, and because of it were more successful at eluding the hunters and thus leaving descendants. I do not know which of these explanations is true—or indeed whether there may not be another, but personally, I feel that an explanation in terms of individual learning and voluntary adaptive behaviour would be the more probable.

To summarize; it is apparent from the evidence of the palaeontological record that the brains of the three extant types of mammals have evolved separately for a considerable time. In the case of the monotremes the separation extends from the very beginning of mammalian evolution whereas in the case of the marsupials it reaches back to the upper Cretaceous. The anatomical similarities of a well developed neo-cortex with interconnecting pathways in the region of the anterior commissures of the brain of the three types may therefore be considered to be the result of the parallel evolutionary elaboration of structures which were incipient in the ancestral stocks of mammal-like reptiles. The elaboration of an additional complex of dorsally placed interconnecting nerve fibres, the corpus callosum, probably began in the placentals not long after they had separated from the marsupials in the later Cretaceous. A similar structure appeared as a convergent character in the large macropod marsupials, probably after Eocene times.

Because of a dearth of experimental data with a consequent heavy dependence on anecdotal material, attempts to correlate the stage of evolutionary development of the brains of lower mammals with their behavioural capacities cannot be currently described as satisfactory. However, the indications are that Monotremes and the larger macropods are both as 'intelligent' as at least one variety—the laboratory rat—of a very successful placental type.

It is interesting that these two groups of lower mammals are, despite the pressures of Man and his industrial-agricultural activities, thriving surprisingly well. The case of the kangaroos has been discussed, but it is also true that the unlikely echidna is more common, even in Sydney, than most people realize while the platypus has recovered from what was, not so long ago, thought to be the point of virtual extinction to become so numerous in many areas that periodically suggestions are made about removing it, for at least part of the year, from the list of totally protected fauna. Protective legislation no doubt predominantly explains the present good fortunes of monotreme and macropod, but I am sure that the possibility of explaining it, even partially, in terms of the significance of their brain structure would have appealed to Sir Grafton Elliot Smith.

REFERENCES

ARIENS KAPPERS, C. U., (1936) 'The Mammalian Telencephalon', in *The Comparative Anatomy of the Nervous System of Vertebrates*, Vol. 2, Ariens Kappers, C. U. *et al.*, MacMillan, New York.

BURRELL, H., (1927) *The Platypus*, Angus and Robertson, Sydney.

CALABY, J. H., NEWSOME, A. E. *et al.*, (1971) Papers and discussions in 'Kangaroos and Men', a symposium of the Roy. Zool Soc., *N.S.W. Aust. Zoologist*, 16, 17-98.

EDINGER, L., (1885) *Zehn Vorlesungen über der Bau der Nervösen Zentralorgane*, Vogel, Leipzig.

JEEVES, M. A., MEYERS, R. E. *et al.*, (1965) Papers and discussions in 'Functions of the Corpus Callosum', a symposium of the Ciba Foundation. Study Group No. 20. Churchill, London.

KERMACK, K. A. & JAWOROWSKA, Z. K., (1971) 'Early Mammals', a symposium for the Linn. Soc. Lond., Academic Press, London.

MARTIN, G. F., (1967) 'Interneocortical connections in the Opossum', *Anat. Rec.*, 157, 607-11.

MUNN, N. L., (1964) 'Reversal learning in kangaroos', *Aust. J. Psychol.*, 16, 1-8.

PRIBRAM, K., (1958) 'Comparative Neurology and the Evolution of Behaviour', in *Behaviour and Evolution*, Roe & Simpson (eds), Yale University Press, New Haven.

RENSCH, B., (1954) 'Relation between Evolution of Central Nervous Function and the Body Size of Animals', in *Evolution as a Process*, Huxley, Hardy & Ford (eds), Allen & Unwin, London.

RIDE, W. D. L., (1968) 'Past, present and future of Australian mammals', *Aust. J. Sci.*, 31, 1-11.

——, (1971) 'On the fossil evidence of the evolution of the Macropodidae, *Aust. Zoologist*, 16, 6-16.

RUSSEL, E. M., (1970) 'Agonistic interactions in the red kangaroo (*Megaleia rufa*)', *J. Mammal.*, 51, 80-8.

RUSSELL, E. M. & PEARCE, G. A., (1971) 'Exploration of novel objects by marsupials', *Behaviour*, XL, 312-22.

SAUNDERS, J. C., CHEN, C. S. & PRIDMORE, P. A., (1971) 'Successive habit-reversal learning in monotremes', *Animal Behaviour*, 19, 552-5.

SMITH, G. E., (1894) 'The cerebral commissures of the Mammalia, with special reference to the Monotremata and Marsupialia', *Proc. Linn. Soc., N.S.W.*, 9, 635-57.

SPERRY, R. W., (1968) 'Brain bisection and mechanisms', in *Brain and Conscious Experience*, Eccles (ed.), Springer, Berlin.

TROUGHTON, E., (1946) *Furred Animals of Australia*, Angus and Robertson, Sydney.

YOUNG, J. Z., (1971) 'Divided brain and the problem of consciousness', in *An Introduction to the Study of Man*, Oxford University Press.

3 GRAFTON ELLIOT SMITH'S CONTRIBUTION TO VISUAL NEUROLOGY AND THE INFLUENCE OF THOMAS HENRY HUXLEY

P. O. Bishop

Huxley and Elliot Smith belonged respectively to the beginning and end of an era and it is fascinating to uncover the many similarities and points of contact between the careers and achievements of the two men. Both were medical graduates who, very early in their careers, deserted the strict confines of medicine and ranged far afield into disciplines remote from medical practice; both spent very important formative years in parts of the world relatively distant from the centres of scientific activity. Huxley became a world-renowned zoologist as a result of his five year voyage (1846-50) to Australia and Melanesia in H.M.S. *Rattlesnake*. Also in Sydney it was Elliot Smith's very early contacts with the relatively new Medical School that first attracted him to neuroanatomy, an attraction that was later to be confirmed when, in 1894, he became a demonstrator in the Department of Anatomy at Sydney University. Still later, Elliot Smith was to spend nine very important years as Professor of Anatomy in the University of Cairo from 1900 to 1909. These experiences led him from comparative neuroanatomy to Egyptology and thence to physical and cultural anthropology.

Curiously, it was during the voyage to Australia that Huxley, while in Sydney, met his future wife Henrietta Heathorn. She lived in Newtown not far from the Darlington home that the Smith family were to occupy many years later. By a curious coincidence also, Elliot Smith's London home in Regent's Park was in the same street where Huxley lived for a large part of his married life.

Both Huxley and Elliot Smith were great expositors of broad themes in biology and both wrote and lectured with great clarity and vigour. Both were very able popular lecturers and were much sought after on that account. Indeed, very many of their papers particularly in their later years were first prepared as lectures.

Though the two never met—Huxley died in 1895 while Elliot Smith was still in Sydney—there is no doubt that Huxley's work and writings had a profound influence on the young Elliot Smith and on the direction that his investigations were to take. In an autobiographical fragment,

Elliot Smith recalls his excitement as a schoolboy on being introduced to Huxley's book *Elementary Lessons in Physiology*. Later on it was a remark of Huxley's that suggested to Elliot Smith the theme of his first scientific paper 'A Preliminary Communication upon the Cerebral Commissures of the Mammalia, with Special Reference to the Monotremata and Marsupiala' that was published in the *Proceedings of the Linnean Society of New South Wales* in 1894. Elliot Smith acknowledges his indebtedness by beginning his paper with a quotation from Huxley. The quotation stresses the importance of the corpus callosum as a key to the understanding of the vertebrate brain. It is interesting to note that, not only his first paper but also the second last that he was to write before he died should be directly concerned with Huxley. In 1935 Elliot Smith gave the Huxley Memorial Lecture on *The Place of Thomas Henry Huxley in Anthropology* and it was published later that year (Elliot Smith, 1935).

In a sense Elliot Smith's contribution to comparative neuroanatomy can be regarded as completing the work that Huxley had started nearly half a century earlier. The half century that began in the early 1850s and ended in the early 1900s saw the real beginning and the virtual completion of the systematic and detailed comparative description of the cerebral convolutions and fissures of the primate brain. The work, begun by Owen, Huschke, Gratiolet and Huxley, was brought to a close by men such as Cunningham, Retzius and Elliot Smith. The completed publication of Retzius' atlases in 1906 marks the end of the era of the macroscopic descriptions of the cerebral convolutions and fissures. By then these morphological features had the macroscopic descriptions and names familiarly recognized in modern neuroanatomy. The new era that was opening was to be devoted to microscopic and neurophysiological investigation, an era that still continues on into the present day.

The early work on the comparative morphology of the primate brain was enormously stimulated by Darwin's *Origin of Species* and it was the storm of controversy that greeted its publication in 1859 that led directly to Huxley's involvement in the study of the brain. The aspect of Darwin's work that rankled most was, of course, the proposition that man had evolved from an ape-like creature, a proposition that directly opposed the view, held by church and laity alike, that man occupied a unique position in nature. Since it is his mental attributes which most strikingly distinguishes man from the apes, it was to be expected that attempts would be made to discover in what way man's brain is different from that of other mammals, and particularly that of the apes. As we shall see, Huxley was attracted to this problem, but the understanding of primate neuromorphology at that time did not allow of a proper recognition of homologous structures in the brains of the various species. A brief statement of Huxley's views as they were in 1874 is included as a supplement to the second edition of Darwin's *The Descent of Man and Selection in Relation to Sex* (Huxley, 1874). Many years later it was Elliot Smith's great contribution to trace the phylogenetic development of the important brain structures, recognizing in particular, the homologies in the primate series (Elliot Smith, 1902a,b).

Let us return to 1859—Sir Richard Owen, the leading comparative anatomist of the day, opposed the new Darwinian theory and attempted to get rid of the assumed similarity between man and the apes by claiming that the brains of each had certain features that were lacking in the other, creating an impassable gulf between them. In his Rede lecture in 1859 Owen claimed that both the backward projection of the cavities of the brain into the posterior horn, and the *hippocampus minor* were structures specific to man. The hippocampus minor is a curved elevation on the infero-medial wall of the posterior horn. It is known today by the name *calcar avis*, so-called because of its supposed resemblance to a bird's claw. Both terms, hippocampus minor and calcar avis, were, however, in current use in Owen's day. The term hippocampus minor is of some interest because of the famous 'hippocampus episode' that Elliot Smith was fond of retelling. Charles Kingsley wrote an amusing satire on Owen's claims in his book *Water Babies*, the hippocampus minor being referred to as the *hippopotamus major*. The affair was also parodied in the pages of *Punch*. Elliot Smith used to speak of Owen in disparaging terms but it was a strange twist of fate that Elliot Smith, in his first scientific papers, should have shown that Owen was right in claiming that non-placental mammals have no *corpus callosum*. The corpus callosum appears for the first time in the placental mammals and increases progressively with the phylogenetic development of the neo-pallial cortex.

It was Owen's claim that certain structures in the human brain had no counterpart in those of the higher apes that first involved Huxley in the defence of Darwin. It also focused Huxley's attention on the posterior part of the cerebral hemisphere. He subsequently revised the anatomy of the occipital lobe, giving the *calcarine sulcus* its permanent name and separating it from the hippocampal fissure. Huxley also did away with the term hippocampus minor, used by Owen, and confirmed the use of calcar avis. It was, of course, from calcar avis that Huxley derived the adjective calcarine. In its deep anterior part, the calcarine fissure indents the whole thickness of the medial wall of the cerebral hemisphere, the protrusion into the posterior horn of the lateral ventricle being the calcar avis.

Huxley published his observations on the occipital lobe in 1861 (Huxley, 1861a, b). At that time he did not have the advantage of the knowledge of the location of specific functions in the cerebral cortex. The concept of localization of function in the cerebrum was first experimentally established by the work of Fritz and Hitzig (1870) and Ferrier (1873). In particular Huxley was unaware that the main cortical area for visual functions was centred on the calcarine fissure. Munk (1890) was the first to locate the visual area in the occipital lobe though it remained for Henschen (1893) to demonstrate that the visual area was actually centred on the calcarine fissure.

Many years later Elliot Smith was to take over where Huxley left off. It came about in this way. When Elliot Smith arrived in England in 1896 one of the first persons he called upon was Professor G. B. Howes who had succeeded Huxley as Professor of Zoology at the Royal College of Science, London (afterwards renamed Imperial College of Science). Howes became a warm friend and it was his advocacy that was responsible for the publication by the Linnean Society of London of Elliot Smith's classical work on the origin of the *corpus callosum*. Elliot Smith's reference to Huxley in his first scientific paper published in 1894 while he was still in Sydney (see above) induced Howes to show Elliot Smith the scientific notes that Huxley had left at the Royal College of Science. Among Huxley's papers were notes on the brain of the African anteater *(Orycteropus)* and Howes suggested to Elliot Smith that he should complete this work for publication. The paper, *The brain in the Edentata*, duly appeared in the *Transactions of the Linnean Society of London* in 1899.

Huxley had made much use of the Museum of the Royal College of Surgeons and when Elliot Smith began using the Museum collection himself, the College invited him to prepare a second edition of the catalogue of their collection of reptilian and mammalian brains. It was this study that provided Elliot Smith with his unrivalled grasp of the comparative morphology of the brain. It also led to an investigation of the calcarine region of the occipital lobe which had been Huxley's last subject of study in the Museum. It is a curious coincidence that the first edition of the *Catalogue of the Physiological Series of Comparative Anatomy* contained in the College Museum had been prepared by Sir Richard Owen in the years 1833-8, when he was assistant curator of the collection.

Elliot Smith transformed the catalogue into a great monograph of comparative neurology, containing comments, often very detailed, on about 700 specimens and illustrated by over 200 figures (Elliot Smith, 1902c). Subsequently Elliot Smith wrote of his work on the catalogue in these words.

> The study of the collection of brains in the Museum of the Royal College of Surgeons led me step by step from the lowliest mammals up to man, and at last to the discovery that certain features, Affenspalte, until then assumed to be distinctive of the Apes, were also present in the human brain, as I have explained in *The Evolution of Man*. The investigation of this demonstration led me to the appreciation of the meaning of the calcarine area and the significance of high visual discrimination in the development of man's distinctive qualities (Elliot Smith, 1935)

In 1892 Cunningham had taken the important step of dividing the calcarine sulcus into anterior and posterior parts. It is the anterior calcarine sulcus that is the true calcarine sulcus in the sense that it is responsible for the ventricular elevation of calcar avis. When he went to Cairo in 1900 Elliot Smith had the opportunity of examining a large number of brains. In a series of studies on the occipital lobe (Elliot

Smith, 1902, 1904) he confirmed Cunningham's analysis. He then went on to define the primary receptive area of the visual cortex giving it the name *area striata* and distinguishing it from the parastriatal and peristriatal areas which approximately correspond to Brodmann's areas 18 and 19 (Elliot Smith, 1907a). Because of the sharpness of the intracortical medullary striations (stria of Gennari) the boundaries of the striate area can be precisely defined even in sections of the fresh brain.

Elliot Smith remained in Cairo till 1909 and he continued to publish neuroanatomical papers throughout this period, including his celebrated topographical survey of the whole of the human cerebral cortex (Elliot Smith, 1907b). Using fresh brains and only a razor and hand lens he was able to map the human brain into 28 areas distinguishable by their intracortical medullary differences. Throughout this period he was, however, also becoming increasingly involved in studies of Egyptology and anthropology and when he returned to England in 1909 to take up the Chair of Anatomy at Manchester he had largely ceased to be active in neurological research. He summarized his studies on the evolution of the brain in his Arris and Gale Lectures (Elliot Smith, 1910) and thereafter only published one further original neurological investigation—a paper on the corpus striatum and the origin of the neopallium (Elliot Smith, 1919).

Throughout the remainder of his life, however, Elliot Smith retained his absorbing interest in neurology. Reading widely and keeping abreast of fresh discoveries, he wrote extensively, expressing novel ideas on a wide variety of neurological topics. A whole generation or more of medical students and students of neurology throughout the English-speaking world learnt their neuroanatomy from Elliot Smith's section in 'Big Cunningham', as Cunningham's *Textbook of Anatomy* was always known to us as medical students. It was in 1911 that Elliot Smith undertook the onerous task of rewriting the section on the Central Nervous System for the fourth edition of this famous textbook and he was to revise the section in three further editions, the last being the seventh published in 1937. Throughout the whole of this period he remained a dominant figure in British anatomy and together with Wood-Jones and Arthur Keith formed a triumvirate whose interplay livened the anatomical scene. I still have vivid memories of coming to neurology for the first time as a medical student in the 1930s and reading the striking word pictures these men painted in bold sweeping strokes. They discussed the origin of man and the evolution of the brain in such a novel and exciting way that it seemed to us that we were on the threshold of an understanding of the mind itself.

One of the constantly recurring themes in the writings of Wood Jones (1916, 1928) and Elliot Smith (1927, 1930) was the overwhelming importance of the progressive development of the visual system for transforming the ape-like creature into a human being and for conferring upon him 'the distinctive attributes of mind and skill which are the outstanding tokens of his humanity' (Elliot Smith, 1930). They particularly emphasized the development of the stereoscopic powers of binocular vision by which we see objects in depth and appreciate the third dimension in space.

In a lecture delivered to the Royal Institution and subsequently published in *Nature*, Elliot Smith (1930) brought together in one short essay the complex interplay of evolutionary changes that have led to the development of stereoscopic vision in man. I shall briefly retell the essence of this essay since the story of the evolutionary development of stereoscopic vision is surely one of the most intriguing in the whole of the evolution of the brain.

In the course of the evolution of certain mammalian lines such as the carnivores and primates there has been a gradual recession of the snout and a movement of the eyes from a lateral sideways-looking position to a frontal binocular location. Since stereopsis depends upon the discrimination of the slight differences in the images in the two eyes it could not have developed unless there was a considerable overlap in the visual fields of the two eyes. In addition, an essential requirement for stereoscopic vision is that the two eyes must be carefully yoked together, moving at all times in precise register one with the other. The evolution of this pattern of eye movements was doubtless greatly assisted by the development, in the carnivores and primates, of a regional specialization within the retina. In the primate retina there is a fovea, which is a centrally-located region highly specialized for making the finest visual discriminations. The fovea would be of little use without a precise control of the extraocular muscles, so directing the eye that the image of the object of regard always falls accurately on the specialized region. Furthermore, the binocular co-ordination of the movements of the eyes could hardly have been possible without a precise monocular control of these movements in the first place.

Coupled with the changes I have already outlined there were equally important developments within the brain. Stereoscopic vision depends not only on the binocular overlap of the visual fields of the two eyes but also upon the sorting of the optic nerve fibres at the chiasma whereby those conveying impulses from corresponding regions of the two retinas are carried to the same region in the brain. This is brought about by a large proportion of fibres remaining uncrossed at the chiasma. The incomplete decussation enables optic nerve fibres from corresponding regions of the two retinas to come into a fairly precise topographical register. Coupled with these changes in the primary visual pathway there was a massive reorganization of the visual centres in the brain. In the sub-mammalian vertebrates the main visual centres lie in the mid-brain. During the course of mammalian evolution there was a gradual development of a new pathway through the lateral geniculate nucleus up to the cerebral cortex, and, with these changes, a relative reduction in the importance of the mid-brain centres. The lateral geniculate nucleus became complexly laminated and there was a marked growth in the area of the cerebral cortex devoted to vision.

The evolutionary changes that I have briefly outlined were correlated with another very important advance, namely the development of eye-hand co-ordination. The adoption of the upright posture freed the hands from their role in postural support and enabled the development of manipulative skills under visual guidance. The evolution of binocular vision was undoubtedly a major factor in bringing these manual skills to their highest level of performance in man. Under normal viewing conditions, the quality of stereoscopic vision improves as the objects regarded are brought closer to the eyes, up to the point where the ability to focus begins to fall off. There is maximal benefit, therefore, for close work involving delicate eye-hand co-ordination.

In the last few years methods of recording the electrical activity of single cells in the brain have brought about major new advances in our understanding of the neutral basis for stereoscopic vision but these quite recent developments are not part of our present story (Bishop & Henry, 1971).

It has been repeatedly observed that the work of great men is frequently so fully incorporated into the generally-accepted or standard literature that we cease to recognize the source from which it was derived. This is certainly the case with much of Elliot Smith's work. We remember the work but the man himself has tended to be forgotten. We should all be grateful to the organizers of this symposium for bringing to mind again Grafton Elliot Smith the man.

REFERENCES

BISHOP, P. O. & HENRY, G. H., (1971) 'Spatial vision', *Ann. Rev. Psychol.*, 22, 119-60.

HUXLEY, T. H., (1861a) 'On the zoological relations of man with the lower animals', *Nat. Hist. Rev.*, 1, 67-84.

——, (1861b) 'On the brain of *Ateles paniscus*', *Proc. Zool. Soc. Lond.*, 247-60.

——, (1874) 'Note on the Resemblances and Differences in the Structure and Development of the Brain in Man and Apes', in *The Descent of Man and Selection in Relation to Sex*. Darwin, C. R., 2nd edn. London.

SMITH, G. E., (1894) 'A preliminary communication upon the cerebral commissures of the mammalia, with special reference to the Monotremata and Marsupiala', *Proc. Linn. Soc. N.S.W.*, 9, 635-57.

——, (1899) 'The brain in the *Edentata*', *Trans. Linn. Soc. Lond.* (*Zool.*), 7, 277-394.

——, (1902a) 'On the homologies of the cerebral sulci', *J. Anat. Physiol.*, 36, 309-19.

——, (1902b) 'On the morphology of the brain in the Mammalia, with special reference to that of the lemurs, recent and extinct', *Trans Linn Soc. Lond.* (*Zool.*), 8, 319-432.

——, (1902c) *Descriptive and Illustrated Catalogue of the Physiological Series of Comparative Anatomy contained in the Museum of the Royal College of Surgeons of England*, 2, 2nd edn, Taylor and Francis, London.

——, (1904) 'The morphology of the occipital region of the cerebral hemisphere in man and the apes', *Anat. Anz.*, 24, 436-51.

——, (1907a) 'New studies on the folding of the visual cortex and the significance of the occipital sulci in the human brain', *J. Anat. Physiol.*, 41, 198-207.

——, (1970b) 'A new topographical survey of the human cerebral cortex, being an account of the distribution of the anatomically distinct cortical areas and their relationship to the cerebral sulci', *J. Anat. Physiol.*, 41, 237-54.

——, (1910) 'Some problems relating to the evolution of the brain', Arris and Gale Lectures, *The Lancet*, 1-6, 147-53, 221-7.

——, (1919) 'A preliminary note on the morphology of the corpus striatum and the origin of the neopallium', *J. Anat.*, 53, 271-91.

——, (1927) *Essays on the Evolution of Man*, 2nd edn, Oxford University Press, London.

——, (1930) 'New light on vision', *Nature*, 125, 820-4.

——, (1935) 'The place of Thomas Henry Huxley in Anthropology', *J. Royal Anthropological Institute of Great Britain and Ireland*, 65, 199-204.

WOOD JONES, F., (1916) *Arboreal Man*. Edward Arnold, London.

WOOD JONES, F., & PORTEUS, S. D., (1928) *The Matrix of the Mind*. University Press Assn, Honolulu.

The following references were among those consulted both for biographical details and for other general information.

ABBIE, A. A., (1959) Grafton Elliot Smith. *Bulletin of the Post-Graduate Committee in Medicine, University of Sydney*, 15, 101-50.

ARIENS KAPPERS, C. U., HUBER, G. C. & CROSBY, E. C., (1936) *The Comparative Anatomy of the Nervous System of Vertebrates, Including Man*. Macmillan, New York.

DAWSON, W. R. (ed.), (1938) *Sir Grafton Elliot Smith, a Biographical Record by his Colleagues*. Jonathan Cape, London.

EARL WALKER, A., (1970) 'Grafton Elliot Smith (1871-1937)', in *The Founders of Neurology*. Haymaker, W. & Schiller, F. (eds), Charles C. Thomas, Springfield.

MEYER, A., (1971) *Historical Aspects of Cerebral Anatomy*. Oxford University Press, London.

POLYAK, S., (1957) *The Vertebrate Visual System*. University of Chicago Press, Chicago.

SHELLSHEAR, J. L., (1937) 'Obituary: Grafton Elliot Smith', *Med. J. Aust.*, 1, 307-10.

WOLLARD, H. H., (1938) 'An outline of Elliot Smith's contribution to neurology', *J. Anat.*, 72, 280-94.

4 SOME ASPECTS OF THE ANATOMY OF THE TRIGEMINAL NERVE: AN EXAMPLE OF CHANGING CONCEPT SINCE ELLIOT SMITH'S DAY

G. Selby

Elliot Smith's scientific career was dedicated to cerebral morphology, anthropology and human palaeontology. Though essentially a neuro-morphologist with little personal inclination towards clinical or experimental enquiry, much of his work reveals a continued and absorbing interest in neurology.

The clinician is apt to forget his debt to anatomy and may even come to regard it as a 'dead' science, descriptive and topographical and with little prospect of value for research into causes and treatment of nervous disease. A study of the neural mechanisms concerned with pain perception serves as an example of the progress in anatomical research, achieved by an interdisciplinary approach and by the use of new experimental methods which were made possible by technological advance.

Elliot Smith did not concern himself particularly with the trigeminal nerve. Pain is such a primitive function that comparative anatomy and anthropology would have little to contribute to its study. With the tools at his disposal he could have studied only the gross morphology of the nerve and of its central connections, and this had already been done by many anatomists. At the time of his graduation from Sydney University several surgeons (Rose, 1890; Ferrier, 1890; Horsley, *et al.*, 1891; Hartley, 1892) had attempted section of trigeminal primary divisions or excision of the Gasserian ganglion in the treatment of trigeminal neuralgia. It was not until 1937, the year of Elliot Smith's death, that Sjøqvist (1938) first performed trigeminal tractotomy. This operation, though often successful, was based on anatomical premises which subsequently proved not to be entirely correct.

The neurologist's interest in the anatomy of the trigeminal nerve derives from his concern with the pathogenesis of trigeminal neuralgia, and more particularly with the question how paroxysms of severe facial pain can be provoked by tactile and proprioceptive stimuli.

The sensory part of the trigeminal nerve has the important function of protecting the head, the seat of the brain and of the special sense

58

organs, from local injury. This functional significance is reflected in the dense network of cutaneous sensory receptors of the face, the size of the Gasserian ganglion—the largest sensory ganglion in man—and in the complexity of the central connections of the sensory trigeminal pathways.

In Elliot Smith's day it was known that fibres from the ophthalmic, maxillary and mandibular divisions of the trigeminal nerve maintained a topographical organization at least as far as the nucleus of the descending trigeminal tract. It was then accepted, evidently without much dissent, that touch and pain were mediated by different fibres and had distinct terminations in the principal and descending nuclei of the trigeminal pathway.

Recent studies have confirmed that a somatotopic organization is maintained in the centripetal axons of the pseudo-unipolar cells of the Gasserian ganglion. In spite of extensive anastomoses between fibre bundles from different divisions (Ferner, 1970; Gudmundsson, et al., 1971), the mandibular fibres occupy a postero-lateral position throughout the course of the sensory root from ganglion to pons, the ophthalmic fibres are dorso-medial, and the maxillary fibres lie in an intermediate position. Aberrant sensory rootlets frequently arise from the pons, separately from the main sensory root (Jannetta & Rand, 1967), and most of these join the root fibres from the ophthalmic division. There is no anatomical evidence, however, that these accessory rootlets are concerned with only a single modality of sensation.

On entering the pons almost half of the fibres of the sensory trigeminal root divide into an ascending branch ending in the main sensory nucleus, and a descending branch which terminates in the nucleus of the spinal tract. Olszewski (1950) has shown that the nucleus of the spinal tract can be subdivided into three regions which differ in cytoarchitectonics, and are called the nucleus caudalis, interpolaris and oralis. Within each of these nuclei different subgroups can further be distinguished, suggestive of a functional differentiation of various parts of the nucleus of the spinal tract.

The longheld concept that the ophthalmic fibres extend most caudally, while the maxillary and mandibular fibres are disposed successively more rostrally in the spinal tract and nucleus has been challenged by recent studies. Kerr (1963), in cats and monkeys, found that the spinal tract terminates at the mid-point of the second cervical level, and that both in the spinal tract and nucleus the ophthalmic fibres lie ventro-laterally, the mandibular fibres dorso-medially, and the maxillary fibres occupy an intermediate position. The fibres from each division remain segregated with little or no overlap. Some third division fibres leave the spinal tract and enter the nucleus of tractus solitarius, suggesting that the trigeminal nerve may contain some visceral afferent fibres from glands and vascular structures from the nose, mouth and teeth, and some which could be concerned with taste.

The termination of fibres in the main sensory nucleus shows the same dorso-ventral somatotopic organization as in the spinal tract and nucleus (Kerr, 1963). Emmons and Rhoton (1971) could not discover a component of the posterior root that projected specifically to the main sensory or spinal trigeminal nucleus, and dispute the concept that the main sensory nucleus is concerned with touch, and the spinal nucleus with pain and temperature sensation.

Apart from primary trigeminal sensory fibres, the spinal tract contains some afferent fibres from the intermediate, glosso-pharyngeal and vagus nerves, as well as dorsal root fibres from the upper cervical roots. There are also fibres which pass from the nucleus caudalis to the more rostral nuclei, including the main sensory nucleus.

All the subdivisions of the spinal nucleus, as well as the main nucleus, receive descending fibres from the primary sensory cortex and from the reticular formation, which appear to be concerned with presynaptic inhibition of trigeminal impulses relayed by these nuclei (see Brodal, 1969 for references).

The ascending connections from the trigeminal nuclei to the thalamus and somato-sensory cortex are complex and have not yet been fully elucidated. Current concepts include a largely crossed, but partly uncrossed projection from all cells of the main sensory nucleus, ascending close to the dorso-medial portion of the medial lemniscus, to the medial part of the posterior ventral nucleus (VPM) of the thalamus. Fibres arising from cells in the oralis and interpolaris part of the spinal nucleus also cross and ascend with the medial lemniscus to VPM. The central projection from the nucleus caudalis differs from that of the other three nuclei; it is a bilateral projection, ascending partly with the medial lemniscus and partly with the reticular formation, and ending in some intralaminar thalamic nuclei, in the magnocellular part of the medial geniculate body, and to a lesser extent in the VPM. Some somatotopical pattern in the VPM has been described. From a number of physiological studies it is generally accepted that the projection to VPM is concerned with tactile stimuli. There is good evidence for a thalamo-cortical projection from VPM to all three somatosensory areas of the cortex (SI, SII, SIII), but the functional relationships of the three regions are not clear. The thalamo-cortical projection transmits tactile sensation and retains a somatotopic organization. There are cortico-fugal fibres from the sensory cortex to VPM, presumably concerned with inhibition (for references see Brodal, 1969).

While there is reasonable agreement on the maintenance of a somatotopic organization from cutaneous fields to the somatosensory cortex, the anatomical pathways concerned with specific modalities of sensation remain a subject of controversy.

We have more precise information about the transmission of tactile information from the face than we have about the anatomical tracts and physiological mechanisms concerned with pain. In the pathways transmitting touch the degree of convergence at successive synaptic levels is limited by both pre- and post-synaptic inhibitory mechanisms, which help to maintain a sharp spatial and temporal 'image' of the location and duration of the peripheral tactile stimulus. These include pre-synaptic 'surround' inhibition, as well as a cortical inhibitory feedback, both acting on the relay cells within the brain stem trigeminal nuclei (Darian-Smith, 1965). There is evidence also of a positive feedback mechanism of post-synaptic facilitation from the somato-sensory cortex on neurones in the trigeminothalamic (lemniscal) projection (Wiesen-danger, et al., 1970).

Neurophysiological studies have shown also that units responding to tactile stimuli are present not only in the main nucleus, but in all subdivisions of the spinal nucleus (Darian-Smith, 1966). Only cells in the nucleus oralis of the spinal trigeminal nuclear complex, however, were found to respond to cutaneous vibratory stimuli applied to the face. These cells have the capacity to relay to the thalamus information about the intensity of a tactile stimulus with only negligible loss of accuracy, whereas no gradation of stimulus intensity is possible from the limited information relayed by cells in the nucleus caudalis.

Although physiological studies have failed to demonstrate neurones responding specifically to pain (Grubel, 1970), it is assumed from the clinical results of medullary tractotomy that cells in the nucleus caudalis are the second order neurone concerned primarily with transmission of pain from the face. On the basis of degeneration studies in monkeys, and of experiences derived from stereotactic operations in human patients, Hassler (1970) states that pain fibres from the caudal trigeminal nucleus terminate in the parvicellular basal and medial part of VPM, nucleus limitans and in the intralaminar thalamic nuclei. While VPM projects to the sensory cortex, the intralaminar nuclei and nucleus limitans have no cortical connection, but may project to the external pallidum, which has links with the reticular substance. He postulates two distinct trigeminal pain pathways, one cortical (VPM to cortex), the other subcortical (limitans and intralaminar nuclei to external pallidum), which interact with each other. If the cortical pathway is interrupted, the subcortical pathway may become released from inhibition.

Further evidence of the complexity and significance of facilitation and inhibition, and of the anatomical basis for these antagonistic functions was recently provided by Denny-Brown and Yanagisawa (1970). They found that trigeminal anaesthesia resulting from section of the descending tract at the first cervical segment, in the monkey, could be abolished by the administration of subconvulsive doses of strychnine. Differential section of the dorsal part of the lower descending tract produced a sensory loss similar to that following total section. In contrast, section of the ventral part of the tract failed to produce anaesthesia, but resulted in an expansion of the area of both trigeminal and vagus skin sensation, corresponding to the increase in area caused by strychnine. These observations suggest that the dorsal part of the descending tract is concerned mainly with facilitation, while the ventral part is concerned with inhibition, which can be abolished by strychnine. A similar situation applies to the medial (facilitatory) and lateral (inhibitory) segments of Lissauer's tract in the spinal cord. Further observations after additional section of the upper three cervical dorsal roots permit the assumption that the descending tract of the fifth nerve provides a mechanism for intersegmental sensory facilitation between the trigeminal and upper cervical segments. Interstitial cells at all levels, sending axons up and down the tract, are the anatomical substrate for this mechanism.

From a series of recent physiological experiments, Young and King (1972) propose the hypothesis that the direct relay of sensory information from the face, including painful stimuli, may occur mainly in the rostral parts of the spinal trigeminal nuclei, and that one of the functions of the nucleus caudalis is to modulate the transfer of information through these rostral nuclei.

It may then be postulated that pain reactions are elicited by a massive spatial and temporal summation of many impulses from the primary nuclei on deeper, presumably second order, neurones. Surgical section of the descending spinal tract can abolish pain by reducing this integrated maximum discharge, while touch sensation is preserved.

All the studies cited in this brief review were undertaken during the last few years and were chosen to illustrate the changes in scientific methods since Elliot Smith's day. The anatomist now has new tools at his disposal, such as the electron microscope, and can rely on the experimental physiologist and neurochemist to support his morphological observations. Concepts of pre- and post-synaptic facilitation and inhibition and the functional subdivisions of the somatosensory cortical areas were proposed and proven only in recent times. The foundation for these concepts, however, was laid by Elliot Smith's pioneer work on the anatomy of the brain and nervous system.

REFERENCES

BRODAL, A., (1969) *Neurological Anatomy*. Oxford University Press, New York, pp. 411-29.

DARIAN-SMITH, I., (1965) 'Tactile Sensory Pathways from the Face', *Proc. Aust. Assoc. Neurol.*, 3, 27-39.

———, (1966) 'Neural mechanisms of facial sensation', *Int. Rev. Neurobiol.*, 9, 301-95.

DENNY-BROWN, D. & YANAGISAWA, N., (1970) 'The descending trigeminal tract as a mechanism for intersegmental sensory facilitation', *Trans. Amer. Neurol. Ass.*, 95, 129-33.

EMMONS, W. F. & RHOTON, A. L. JR., (1971) 'Subdivision of the trigeminal sensory root. Experimental study in the monkey', *J. Neurosurg.*, 35, 585-91.

FERNER, H., (1970) 'The Anatomy of the Trigeminal Root and the Gasserian Ganglion and their Relations to the Cerebral Meninges', in *Trigeminal Neuralgia. Pathogenesis and Pathophysiology*. Hassler, R. & Walker, A. E. (eds), Saunders, Philadelphia, pp. 1-6.

FERRIER, D., (1890) 'Discussion of paper by Rose', *Trans. med. Soc. Lond.*, 14, 38-9.

GRUBEL, G., (1970) 'The Physiology of Single Neurons of the Trigeminal Nuclei', in *Trigeminal Neuralgia. Pathogenesis and Pathophysiology*. Hassler, R. & Walker, A. E. (eds), Saunders, Philadelphia, pp. 73-7.

GUDMUNDSSON, K., RHOTON, A. L. JR, & RUSHTON, J. G., (1971) 'Detailed anatomy of the intracranial portion of the trigeminal nerve', *J. Neurosurg.*, 35, 592-600.

HARTLEY, F., (1892) 'Intracranial neurectomy of the second and third divisions of the fifth nerve. A new method', *N.Y. med. J.*, 55, 317-19.

HASSLER, R., (1970) 'Dichotomy of Facial Pain Conduction in the Diencephalon, in *Trigeminal Neuralgia. Pathogenesis and Pathophysiology*. Hassler, R. & Walker, A. E. (eds), Saunders, Philadelphia, pp. 123-38.

HORSLEY, V., TAYLOR, J. & COLMAN, W. S., (1891) 'Remarks on the various surgical procedures devised for the relief or cure of trigeminal neuralgia (tic douloureux)', *Brit. med. J.*, ii, 1139-43, 1191-3, 1249-52.

JANNETTA, P. J. & RAND, R. W., (1967) 'Gross (mesoscopic) description of the human trigeminal nerve and ganglion', *J. Neurosurg.*, 26 (Suppl.), 109-11.

KERR, F. W. L., (1963) 'The divisional organization of afferent fibres of the trigeminal nerve', *Brain*, 86, 721-32.

OLSZEWSKI, J., (1950) 'On the anatomical and functional organization of the spinal trigeminal nucleus', *J. comp. Neurol.*, 92, 401-13.

ROSE, W., (1890) 'Removal of the Gasserian ganglion for severe neuralgia', *Trans. med. Soc. Lond.*, 14, 35-40.

SJØQVIST, O., (1938) 'Studies on pain conduction in the trigeminal nerve. Contribution to surgical treatment of facial pain', *Acta psychiat. neurol. scand.*, (Suppl.) 17, 1-139.

WIESENDANGER, M., HAMMER, B. & HEPP-REYMOND, M. C., (1970) 'Corticofugal Control Mechanisms of Somatosensory Transmission in the Spinal Trigeminal Nucleus of the Cat', in *Trigeminal Neuralgia. Pathogenesis and Pathophysiology*. Hassler, R. & Walker, A. E. (eds), Saunders, Philadelphia, pp. 86-9.

YOUNG, R. F. & KING, R. B., (1972) 'Excitability changes in trigeminal primary afferent fibres in response to noxious and nonnoxious stimuli', *J. Neurophysiol.*, 35, 87-95.

PART II
EARLY MAN

5 RECENT DEVELOPMENTS IN UNDERSTANDING THE RELATIONSHIP BETWEEN THE NEANDERTHALS AND MODERN MAN

T. D. Stewart

Introduction

Only a little more than 200 years has elapsed since Linnaeus (1758) assigned modern man to the genus *Homo*, species *sapiens*, in the order Primates; and only a little more than 100 years has elapsed since Schaaffhausen (1858) reported the discovery in Germany of the first skeletal remains of a different and presumably ancient form of man. The latter was soon designated *Homo neanderthalensis* (King, 1864). The mid-nineteenth century is famous also for Darwin's publication (1859) of his evolutionary theory, which helped explain the German discovery and in turn was supported by that discovery. It was not until 1886, however, that clear evidence was found of Neanderthal man's prehistoric age. Exploration that year in the Spy cave, Belgium, revealed for the first time Neanderthal skeletons in association with Mousterian artefacts and extinct animal bones (de Puydt & Lohest, 1886).

These facts are mentioned here because only ten years after the discoveries at Spy, Elliot Smith, the man whose birth centenary we are celebrating, left Sydney for Cambridge, England, to pursue a career in anatomy. Thus his arrival in Europe followed immediately upon a series of anthropological developments there which opened up an exciting vista of man's physical evolution. As it happened also, he came under the influence of famous English anatomists who were at the same time outstanding physical anthropologists, most notably from the standpoint of the subject under discussion, Sir Arthur Keith. In such an environment Elliot Smith could not avoid becoming involved in the study of human evolution. And this involvement intensified when in 1900 he accepted the chair of anatomy in Cairo, Egypt. For some ten years thereafter he was exposed to the glamor of Egyptian antiquities and the salvage work of the Archaeological Survey of Nubia.

Egypt was far away, of course, from the European area where Neanderthals then were being discovered. Yet there can be little doubt that

Elliot Smith watched these and other new developments in palaeo-anthropology. This follows from the fact that in 1916, after returning to England and the professorship at Manchester, he delivered a discourse at the British Academy on 'Primitive Man'. The views set forth therein regarding the Neanderthals—the only part that concerns us here—understandably include the then current opinions about their body-posture and taxonomic classification; opinions which were strongly influenced by Boule's description (1911-13) of the skeleton from La Chapelle-aux-Saints. What probably caught Elliot Smith's attention in Boule's cited publication was a contrasting pair of profile drawings of an Australian Aboriginal skeleton and the reconstructed La Chapelle-aux-Saints skeleton. Since the latter included an unusually complete spinal column, Boule had represented it as incompletely erect. The resulting 'uncouth and repellent' appearance, to use Elliot Smith's words, is best expressed in the following statement from his discourse:

> [Neanderthal man's] short, thick-set, and coarsely built body was carried in a half-stooping slouch upon short, powerful, and half-flexed legs of peculiarly ungraceful form. His thick neck sloped forward from the broad shoulders to support the massive flattened head, which protruded forward, so as to form an unbroken curve of neck and back, in place of the alternation of curves which is one of the graces of the truly erect *Homo sapiens*. The heavy overhanging eyebrow-ridges and retreating forehead, the great coarse face with its large eye-sockets, broad nose, and receding chin, combined to complete the picture of unattractiveness, which it is more probable than not was still further emphasized by a shaggy covering of hair over most of the body. The arms were relatively short, and the exceptionally large hands lacked the delicacy and nicely balanced co-operation of thumb and fingers which is regarded as one of the most distinctive of human characteristics. (1916, p. 470)

In 1924, after Elliot Smith had moved to London, he reprinted the British Academy discourse in a little book of essays entitled 'The Evolution of Man'. A revised edition of the book appeared in 1927. The wording of the above quotation is the same in all three places. Also, in all three places the statement about Neanderthal man's appearance precedes the following important taxonomic commentary:

> The contemplation of all these features emphasizes the reality of the fact that the Neanderthal Man belongs to some other species than *Homo sapiens*.
> Many writers have been puzzled to account for the great size of his brain, seeing that the average capacity of the Neanderthal cranium exceeds that of modern European. But . . . the development of the brain of Neanderthal Man, was partial and unequal. That part of the organ which plays the outstanding part in determining mental superiority was not only relatively, but actually, much smaller than it is in *Homo sapiens*. The large size of the Neanderthal brain was due to a great development of that region which was probably concerned primarily with the mere recording of the fruits of experience, rather than with the acquisition of great skill in the use of the hand and the attainment of the sort of knowledge that comes from manual experiment.

The discovery of this species thus revealed the former existence of a type of mankind which, in spite of its great size of brain, is clearly on a lower plane than its successors whom it is customary to include within the genus [sic] *sapiens*. (1916, pp. 470-1)

Incidentally, Elliot Smith took note (1916, pp. 477-8) of the fact that the aboriginal Australians present a number of primitive structural features which have suggested to some observers that their affinities are with the Neanderthals. He had a different explanation, namely, that the earliest members of the species *sapiens* shared with the Neanderthals a good many features derived from the parent stock from which each had sprung and that the observers were seeing in the Australians an unusual example of the persistence of these shared features.

During the same year—1927—in which Elliot Smith was maintaining in print that the Neanderthals are a species distinct from *Homo sapiens*, Hrdlicka (my predecessor in the Smithsonian Institution) was stating a contrary opinion in his Huxley Memorial Lecture in London. Although Hrdlicka admitted that 'Neanderthal man is of a primitive physique, appears to have ended by a sudden and complete extinction, and to have been replaced by *H. sapiens*', he could see no explanation for the order of succession except through 'the evolution of the Neanderthalers into later man'. He concluded, therefore, that 'there appears to be less justification in the conception of a Neanderthal *species* than there would be in that of a Neanderthal *phase* of Man' (p. 273).

If Elliot Smith did not hear Hrdlicka give his lecture, he must have read the text as distributed (1928) in the *Journal of the Royal Anthropological Institute*, because in 1928 he published in *Nature* a rebuttal in the form of a thinly-disguised book review. For the purpose of this review he chose the second part of G. M. Morant's 'Studies of Palaeolithic Man' (1927). Of this work he said in part:

> [Morant] informs us that the available measurements of the skulls associated with the Mousterian phase of culture in Europe and Palestine indicate a remarkable homogeneity of type, between which and all modern types there is a distinct hiatus, which may be taken to indicate a specific difference . . .
>
> The only justification for re-opening the problem of the status of Neanderthal man would be afforded by new evidence or new views, either of a destructive or constructive nature. I do not think Dr. Hrdlicka has given any valid reasons for rejecting the view that *Homo neanderthalensis* is a species distinct from *H. sapiens*. Dr. Morant's important memoir comes at a very appropriate time to buttress the generally accepted view against such criticisms as Dr. Hrdlicka's. (p. 141)

Perhaps Elliot Smith felt called upon just at this time to rebut Hrdlicka's unorthodox argument because he was in the process of bringing out a new book entitled *Human History* (1930). In any case, he contended still in this second book that Neanderthal man is a species distinct from *Homo sapiens* and described him again as an 'uncouth creature'. So far as I can discover, Elliot Smith and Hrdlicka did not give up their different opinions on this subject during the rest of their lives. Accordingly, now—35 years after Elliot Smith's death, and 29 years after Hrdlicka's death—the following related questions may be asked: Have subsequent archeological discoveries shed new light on the relationship between the Neanderthals and modern man? Do anthropologists still believe that Neanderthal man was as primitive looking as Boule pictured him? Are Neanderthal man and modern man still classed as different species? In other words, how omniscient in these respects was Elliot Smith? Let us look at the record since 1937.

The Finds at Mount Carmel, Palestine

Already before Elliot Smith's death in 1937 the British and American Schools of Prehistoric Archaeology had spent five years (1929-33) in collaborative exploration of the Skhūl and Tabūn caves at Mount Carmel just south of Haifa in the northern coastal region of present-day Israel. During that time they encountered twelve skeletons (ten at Skhūl and two at Tabūn) and numerous isolated bones. Not until 1939, however, did McCown and Keith's volume on the recovered skeletal remains appear in print. Apparently these authors realized that the main impact of their report resided in their conclusions, because they placed them at the beginning (Ch. 2). For present purposes it will suffice to paraphrase the main points of their argument.

Although initially they were inclined to believe that the Mount Carmel collection represented two distinct types of humanity (Tabūn and Skhūl), eventually they decided that the two types were extremes of a single highly variable population. The Tabūn type appeared to them as a continuation of the Neanderthal type of Europe, whereas the Skhūl type appeared to them to pass towards a Neanthropic form such as that found at Cromagnon. In explanation of this divergence they ruled out miscegenation and instead embraced the idea of the Mount Carmel population being in 'the throes of evolutionary change'. As such, however, they could not grant it a supporting role for Hrdlicka's theory of a Neanderthal phase of man.

Having ruled out miscegenation and evolutionary transformation, a new theory was called for and this McCown and Keith proceeded to supply. They started with the assumption that in mid-Pleistocene times western Asia was the homeland of the proto-Caucasian. From this they went on to assume further that the Mount Carmel people were not the ancestors of the Cromagnons but Neanderthal collaterals or cousins of the ancestors of that type. Then, to dramatize this theory, they characterized Europe after mid-Pleistocene times as 'the "Australia" of the ancient world' and to liken the people who colonized it and extinguished its Neanderthal inhabitants—Caucasians from western Asia—to the whites who 'are now ousting the "blacks" of Australia'.

Finally, McCown and Keith felt that the accummulated knowledge about early man called for a revision of the nomenclature used in his classification. Consequently, following Bonarelli's lead (1909), they recommended using *Palaeoanthropus* as 'a generic designation for all forms of humanity which show a predominance of Neanderthal characters'.

Comments on most of the points in this argument must await the presentation of subsequent developments. Here I will note only that McCown and Keith went beyond Elliot Smith taxonomically; they made Neanderthal man not only a different species from that of modern man, but a different genus.

Taxonomic Revisions

McCown's and Keith's uncritical acceptance of Bonarelli's generic name for the Neanderthals added fuel to a spreading fire of dissatisfaction among zoologists regarding the way in which anthropologists were ignoring international rules of zoological nomenclature. Among those who at this time saw the need for more care and simplification in this matter was the renowned paleontologist G. G. Simpson of the American Museum of Natural History in New York. The way he tackled the problem was to publish his opinions in the part of a new classification of mammals (1945) relating to the primates. Because of his respected position in the field, his classification soon became the accepted standard. In this arrangement man is classed (p. 68) essentially as follows:

Super fam. Hominoidea Simpson, 1931
> Fam. Hominidae Gray, 1825
>> Genus *Homo* Linnaeus, 1758. Pleistocene-Recent; world wide. Men (including all living races and also Heidelberg man, Neanderthal man, Rhodesian man, and other prehistoric races).

In defense of this sort of simplification Simpson stated:

> All specimens of fossil hominids that differ in any discernible way from *Homo sapiens,* and some that do not, have at one time or another been placed in different genera. Almost none of these anthropological 'genera' has any zoological reason for being. All known hominids, recent and fossil, could well be placed in *Homo.* (p. 188)*

Re-examination of Neanderthal Posture

In 1956 a group of American anthropologists celebrated the centenary of the discovery of the first Neanderthal skeleton by presenting a symposium on the status of Neanderthal studies at the annual meeting of the American Association for the Advancement of Science. This is mentioned here because one of the papers in the symposium (Straus & Cave, 1957) criticizes and corrects the 'uncouth and repellent' image of Neanderthal man created by Boule and perpetuated by Elliot Smith as already outlined. Unbeknownst to Straus and Cave at the time they

* Simpson had not yet accepted the australopithecines as hominids.

made their study, Arambourg (1955), and perhaps also Patte (1955), had just concluded independently that Neanderthal man was far less primitive-looking than generally believed. I will disregard this complication, however, and continue the account of the Straus and Cave study.

It seems that while attending the Sixth International Anatomical Congress in Paris in 1955, they took the opportunity to examine the Neanderthal skeletal specimens in the Musée de l'Homme. The thing that most attracted their attention was the amount of osteoarthritis in the vertebral column of the skeleton from La Chapelle-aux-Saints. Their careful observations on the individual segments led them to conclude that this particular individual probably had had a pathological kyphosis, and if so, his spine could not be used to provide 'a reliable picture of a healthy Neanderthalian'. They thus denied to Boule his only 'valid reason for the assumption that the posture of Neanderthal man of the fourth glacial period differed significantly from that of present-day man' (p. 358).

I will have occasion later to mention newer evidence on this subject.

The Finds at Shanidar, Iraq

The Neanderthal studies thus far outlined represent the state of knowledge in this field when I first became actively involved therein. Put in another way, up to this point I have been outlining some of the Neanderthal problems reflected in the views of Elliot Smith; whereas in the present section I will review my own experience in dealing with the same problems when confronted with new finds. In favouring myself space-wise I hope for forgiveness, if only on the grounds that it is useful to have the widely scattered references assembled in one place.

It was in 1957—just one year after the Neanderthal centenary—that Ralph Solecki, then one of my colleagues in the Smithsonian Institution, discovered the first adult skeletons in association with Mousterian artefacts in the Shanidar cave in northeastern Iraq. Most of the initial publicity attendant on the finds (Solecki, 1957a and b) focused on a more or less extended and articulated skeleton (No. I) with a broken but seemingly restorable skull encountered at a depth of approximately 14 feet below the cave floor. In addition, however, a flattened skull (No. II) had been removed from a wall of the excavation at around 24 feet below the cave floor, and a lot of unidentified bone fragments (actually skeleton No. III) had been removed from near No. I and at about the same level (Solecki, 1960). Since these specimens had to remain in Baghdad, Solecki asked me to go to that city in the latter part of 1957 to carry out the work of restoration. I wondered, naturally, as I started on this mission whether the Shanidar skulls would turn out to be of the Tabūn type or of the Skhūl type, and in any case, whether any parts of the skeleton would throw new light on the relationship between the Neanderthals and modern man.

I spent most of the three months I was in Baghdad putting together what remained of the skull of No. I and striving for a satisfactory restoration of the missing parts (Stewart, 1958). Most of the post-cranial bones of No. I, and especially the long bones of the legs, were incomplete and therefore only partially restorable. No time was spent on the skull of No. II on this occasion. Right from the beginning, however, it became evident that skeleton No. I (a male around 40 years of age) had a skull of the Tabūn type. Especially impressive in the restoration—at least to one who has worked mainly with modern man, as I have—is the massiveness and fullness of the mid-facial region. The degree of facial grossness present in this specimen just does not exist in any of the modern skulls I have seen. Associated with it is a marked descent of the nasal floor behind the external nasal orifice. Surmounting this unusual mid-face are more pronounced brow ridges than occur in modern man, whereas inferiorly a proportional massiveness continues through a distinctive lower jaw, which nevertheless exhibits only a moderately receding chin. On each side posteriorly, on the other hand, there is a contrast in size between the mastoid process and the occipitomastoid crest, the latter far exceeding the former and at the same time being separated therefrom by a very large digastric fossa. Here again is a combination of features rarely, if ever, found to such a degree in modern man (cf. Stewart, 1961a). Significantly, too, the same is not true of the Skhūl type.

Shanidar skeleton No. I has two additional unusual features in its post-cranial bones. One of these, the sulcus dorso-axillaris of the scapula, has been known since 1912 when Boule reported its presence in the first Neanderthal skeleton from La Ferrassie (Stewart, 1962b). It is present also in a number of other Neanderthals, including the original specimen from Germany and Tabūn I. As the name implies, this feature consists of a sulcus on the dorsal side of the axillary border. In modern man the sulcus dorso-axillaris has been replaced by a sulcus ventro-axillaris. An intermediate condition has been reported for early *sapiens*-like types, including Skhūl V. This finding strengthens the distinction between the Tabūn-Shanidar type on the one hand, and the Skhūl type on the other.

The other unusual post-cranial feature of Shanidar I occurs in the pelvis (Stewart, 1960). The most delicate part of this complex of bones is the pubis, and damage here restricts the possibility of sexing and ageing the individual. For this reason I made a special effort to recover and restore as much as possible of the pubic bones. In doing so I was struck by the fact that the superior ramus is much more flattened in the vertical direction than is the case in modern man. McCown and Keith had found the same thing in Tabūn I and been completely unable to explain it, because in the only other skeletons in which this part is preserved—Skhūl IV and IX—the superior ramus has the modern thicker configuration. Thus again the distinction between the Tabūn-Shanidar and Skhūl types is strengthened.

Besides this array of strange-looking but normal features, the skeleton of Shanidar I presents an unusually large number of pathological features.

Most notable is the absence of all of the bones of the right forearm, along with the distal end of the right humerus. Also, the remaining part of the shaft of the right humerus has a diameter ranging in size between only 8 and 15 mm (as compared with that on the left, which ranges between 18 and 22 mm). The terminal part of the humerus, which seems to be at the level where the shaft begins to widen to form the elbow joint, is pointed medially and flattened antero-posteriorly. About 8 cm above this end point is an irregularity of the shaft representing an old healed fracture. Seemingly, the line of fracture has passed diagonally downward from the lateral side of the medial side and resulted in slight over-riding of the fragments and some medial displacement of the lower fragment in the medial direction, with eventual side-to-side union at the site of fracture. The head of this abnormal humerus was not recovered, but the only convincing restoration is one of small size.

The right clavicle, most of which was recovered, is noticeably smaller in size than its counterpart on the left. This is true also of the right scapula. One can argue from all this that the bones so affected either had atrophied from the normal state represented on the left or had failed to develop normally. Thus far the medical authorities with whom I have consulted have tended to favour one or the other of two possible causes for this condition: (1) damage to the brachial plexus at birth (Erb's palsy), and (2) poliomyelitis of the right arm in youth. In either case it is necessary to assume that some time after the right arm was paralyzed it was injured, possibly twice, and certainly once to such an extent as to require deliberate amputation. The likelihood of some sort of injury having occurred long before death is indicated by healed scars on the skull vault, deformation of the lateral side of the left orbit, deformation of the left tibia, and by advanced arthritic changes in the right ankle joint.

This is not the place to present arguments for or against the diagnostic aspects of this remarkable example of palaeopathology. I will say only that, if further study supports the idea that a deliberate amputation was performed in this case, it will go far toward destroying whatever remains of the concept of Neanderthal man as lacking compassion, intelligence, and manual dexterity. Yet, the fact that this early man survived such physical handicaps and lived to an adult age probably equal to his normal life expectancy is in itself evidence of 'man's humanity to man' at the Neanderthal cultural level. Thanks to the recovery of charcoal in close association with Shanidar I and the availability since 1951 of the radio-carbon test, this cultural level at Shanidar has been dated at 46,000 ± 1,500 years BP (GRO 2527; Solecki, 1960).

I went back to Baghdad in the summer of 1960 for the purpose of working in the museum on the skull of No. II and then accompanying Solecki to the cave where he planned to excavate the post-cranial bones of No. II. Unfortunately, the first part of this mission had only limited success because the cranial bones had undergone much compression

(Stewart, 1961b). However, I was able to show that the skull type of No. II was similar to that of No. I. In the process of doing so I separated from the skull most of the left scapula and 12 more or less complete vertebrae (seven cervical and five thoracic). At the cave I was equally unfortunate as regards this individual because, in spite of extensive searching, the only post-cranial parts recovered were seven vertebrae (three thoracic and four lumbar), parts of three ribs, and the practically complete left tibia and fibula (Stewart, 1961b). I will have further comments on some of these specimens later.

After exhausting the possibilities at the cave of recovering more of No. II, I turned my attention to the site of No. III and succeeded in finding more fragmentary bones there. While thus engaged, skeleton No. IV was discovered on the same lower level as No. II. The bones of this skeleton were riddled with fracture lines caused by the weight of the superimposed deposits. For this and other reasons, including the flexed position of the skeleton, removal *en bloc* was decided upon. As it turned out, however, the construction of the box around the skeleton could not be carried out satisfactorily because of the close proximity of the latter to the bones of another individual underneath. Only a few parts of the latter individual were recovered, but they were designated No. VI since in the meantime the badly damaged remains of skeleton No. V had been found near the sites of Nos I and III in the upper level. The point is that the field season of 1960 yielded three more adult Neanderthal skeletons, but all in bad condition. This brings the total to six, of which three (Nos I, III and V) are from the upper level (46,000 years ago), and three (Nos II, IV and VI) are from the lower level (guess-dated at 60,000 years ago).

After returning to Washington from Baghdad in 1960 I received an invitation to contribute an article to the *Festschrift* honoring Adolph H. Schultz on the occasion of his seventieth birthday. Having been a student of his at the Johns Hopkins Medical School and knowing of his interest in the spinal column of the primates, I accepted the invitation and selected as the subject of my contribution (Stewart, 1962a) the cervical vertebrae of the Shanidar skeletons Nos I and II. As a result of this study I found that in practically all respects the spinal segments of the neck are within the range of modern man. At the most, certain features, such as a long spinous process on C5 and horizontal spinous processes on C5-7, tend to be more common in Neanderthals than in modern man. These findings support the contention of Straus and Cave, already referred to, that Elliot Smith was mistaken in describing Neanderthal man's body as being 'carried in a half-stooping slouch'.

The need to study the Shanidar specimens recovered in 1960 necessitated my return to Baghdad for a third time in 1962. This time my efforts were directed mainly at developing as much information as possible from skeletons III, IV and VI. Most of the results need not concern us here since they pertain to anatomical details of minor significance (Stewart, 1963). I will direct attention only to those observations relating to skull type, pubis type, and bone pathology.

The only further evidence on skull type comes from the left half of the lower jaw of No. IV, probably a male. All of the observable features of this jaw fragment match those of Nos I and II and suggest therefore that all three skulls conform to the Tabūn type.

Included among the loose bone fragments collected at the time the block of earth containing skeleton No. IV was boxed for transport from the cave to Baghdad was a piece of the horizontal ramus of a left pubis. Judging from size, this belonged to No. IV rather than to No. VI, probably a female. In any case, the ramus shows the same unusual form reported for Tabūn I, Shanidar I, and Shanidar III (Stewart, 1960). The fact that four examples of this unusual pubic conformation have now been reported gives added weight to the idea that these sites yield a single primitive type of Neanderthal.

Shanidar skeleton No. III had suffered such extreme damage, perhaps from a fall of rock from the cave ceiling, that most of the major bones were unrecognizable (Stewart, manuscript). Yet one of the ribs survived to bear witness to what may have been the cause of death. This rib, which is perhaps the ninth on the left side, has a sharply-defined, parallel-sided, artificial groove or cut posteriorly in its upper border. The outer edges of the cut are very slightly raised, but the inner edges are irregularly raised nearly 2 mm, suggesting the inward displacement of cortical fragments caused by the passage of a blade-like object entering between the ribs and at a right angle to their axes. If this is so, the unrecovered rib next above must have had a corresponding cut. A radiograph of the recovered rib shows increased bone density around the cut. This combination of findings means, of course, that the individual suffered a penetrating wound in life and survived long enough for some bone-healing to have taken place. Not unlikely the penetration was deep enough to have punctured the lung and caused pneumothorax.

The sharply-defined, parallel sides of the cut provide a clue as to the nature of the blade. The edges of a Mousterian stone blade are wedge-shaped and must have produced a correspondingly-shaped cut upon entering bone. Metal was not in use at that time. This leaves only bone, ivory, and wood as possibilities. However, bone and ivory can be ruled out because the only way that a cut in bone can remain open and sharply defined while undergoing healing is with the blade in place. Failure to recover the blade in this case can only mean that it was made of perishable material: hard wood.

Support for such an interpretation comes from a wound with similar characteristics described by McCown and Keith (1939, pp. 74-5) in the Skhūl IX skeleton. They noticed in preparing this skeleton for study that the left femur had its head fixed in the acetabulum of the pelvis in a flexed position. Further investigation revealed a sharply-defined artificial passage, quadrilateral in section, extending through both the femoral head and the wall of the acetabulum. The passage decreased regularly in size from the surface of the femoral head to the point where it opened into the pelvis. By filling the passage with plaster-of-Paris McCown and Keith were able to produce a cast of the space occupied by the embedded portion of the weapon and to demonstrate that its tapering sides would have ended 'at least an inch within the pelvic basin'.

As for the material from which the weapon had been made, McCown and Keith were not able to rule out stone, metal, ivory and bone from the shape of the passage and the presence of bone-healing. In fact, they say nothing about bone-healing, probably because the state of the bones did not permit its detection. I think they were correct, however, in deciding that the weapon must have remained in the bone after death, because otherwise the femoral head would not have remained locked in the acetabulum. The presence of the head of the weapon in the bones after death and its absence upon discovery millennia later indicate that the material of which the weapon was composed was perishable. Hence it could only have been wood.

The two wounds which I have dealt with in some detail constitute the only evidence thus far of the kinds of weapons made of wood by Neanderthal man. By bringing wood into the picture it becomes evident that man's culture at the Mousterian level extended beyond the objects for which imperishable materials provide evidence. This implies greater capabilities than formerly were attributed to him.

Indirect evidence of a quite different Neanderthal cultural practice came to light in 1968 when Arlette Leroi-Gourhan of the Musée de l'Homme in Paris reported her analysis of soil samples collected by Solecki from around Shanidar skeleton No. IV. Unexpectedly, this soil was found to be full of pollen and flower fragments from at least eight species, most of them small, brightly-colored wildflowers. The presence also of abundant pollen and wood fragments from a pine-like shrub suggested to her that the flowers and pine branches had been formed into a funerary tribute (see also Solecki, 1971, pp. 246-50).

Getting back to the wounds, it is apparent that the bearers of the Mousterian culture were no strangers to personal violence. Besides the two cases from Shanidar and the one from Skhūl, there is also one from Germany—the first Neanderthal skeleton to be found. Not too well known is the fact that the original Neanderthal skeleton shows a long-standing deformity of the left elbow probably representing a fracture of the ulna (Stewart, 1964). When it is recalled that all of these specimens were collected from caves, one wonders whether these Neanderthal men had sought protection there. If so, were they hiding from modern man?

Additional Finds in Israel

Since so many of the Neanderthal studies of the last quarter-century have been based on finds in the Near East, it is desirable to comment on two recent reports of finds in Israel, namely, those from caves at Amud (Suzuki & Takai, eds, 1970) and Qafzeh (Vallois & Vandermeersch, 1972) in the general region of Mount Carmel. The Amud report deals mainly with skeleton No. I and the Qafzeh report deals only with skull No. VI, each the most complete of the specimens recovered. Also, the order of publication of these two reports is the reverse of the order in which their respective specimens were discovered: Qafzeh in 1934 and Amud in 1961. For present purposes, however, the date of publication is more important than the date of discovery, because only when the anatomical details become available can the evolutionary significance of the specimens be evaluated.

Coming along at different intervals of time after the reports on the Mount Carmel and Shanidar finds, these new reports tend to be anti-climactic; i.e., their findings simply confirm what is already established. Thus, the Qafzeh skull No. VI exhibits many of the *sapiens*-like characters that make up the Skhūl type. And on the other hand, the Amud skull No. I is only a little less primitive-looking than those from Tabūn and Shanidar. Also, like the Tabūn and Shanidar skeleton, the Amud skeleton No. I has a sulcus dorso-axillaris of the scapula and a superior pubic ramus that is flattened in cross-section. At the present time, therefore, the dichotomy of types noted in the Mousterian populations of the Near East remains intact.

Resumé and Discussion

The general focus of this paper, as its title makes clear, is on the continuing efforts of anthropologists to understand the relationship between Neanderthal man and modern man. Within this field the views held by Elliot Smith in his later years have been singled out to serve as a sort of marker from which to measure changes of viewpoint since his day. The views in question revolve around the then-current concept of Neanderthal man's appearance and capability. Largely because Elliot Smith accepted Boule's reconstruction of the skeleton of La Chapelle-aux-Saints as stoop-shouldered and bent-kneed, he imagined Neanderthal man to be an uncouth creature of limited intelligence, incapable of standing fully upright, and lacking in manual dexterity. Accordingly, he felt that it was proper to assign Neanderthal man to a different species from that of modern man.

In the mid-1950s anthropologists began to express doubts about Neanderthal man being as primitive-looking as usually represented. Since that time descriptive references to him gradually have become more flattering, although none has surpassed the now-classic image created by Straus and Cave (1957, p. 359): 'if [a Neanderthaler] could be reincarnated and placed in a New York subway—provided that he were bathed, shaved, and dressed in modern clothing—it is doubtful whether he would attract any more attention than some of the other denizens'.

The growing acceptance of the idea that Neanderthal man was not very different from us aided the efforts of the taxonomists to simplify the classification of fossil men. In Elliot Smith's time the genus *Homo* included very little more than modern man and the Neanderthals.

Now it includes the pithecanthropines *(Homo erectus)* and possibly certain of the much more primitive hominids being recovered in East Africa *(Homo habilis)*. This raises questions, such as: Did Neanderthal man differ enough from both *Homo sapiens* and *Homo erectus* to warrant a different species name *(Homo neanderthalensis)*? Or was he so close to our kind that he is better regarded as a variant of our species *Homo sapiens neanderthalensis)*?

At the present time the Neanderthal finds from the Near East that I have reviewed here supply the most useful guidelines for answering these questions. Unfortunately, the available pithecanthropines are far less complete and hence do not supply comparable data, except for the skull and lower jaw. I noted this fact at the VIII International Congress of Anthropological and Ethnological Sciences in Tokyo in 1968 (Stewart, 1969b) and pointed out that several mandibular features show a continuum through the pithecanthropines and Classic Neanderthals (including the Tabūn and Shanidar specimens) and then changed abruptly in modern man (including the Skhūl specimens) . Suzuki 1970, pp. 166-8) has shown that Amud man follows the pattern of the Classic Neanderthals in this regard.

Cranial capacity is another feature, of course, that can be compared between these groups. Here we find a marked difference between the pithecanthropines and the combined Neanderthal and modern-man groups. On the average, the difference probably amounts to somewhat more than 500 cc. And strange as it may seem, as Elliott Smith noted, the average for the available Neanderthals is above that of modern man.

Earlier I cited Morant's (1927) metrical study of Neanderthal skulls and Elliot Smith's comment that the measurements 'indicate a remarkable homogeneity of type, between which and all modern types there is a distinct hiatus'. The results of this metrical study are at variance, however, with the morphological evidence from the recent discoveries in the Near East, as I have pointed out in some detail. Now, thanks to W. W. Howells (1969) , two of the newer specimens from the Near East (Shanidar I and Skhūl V) have been compared metrically both with modern man and with two of the European Neanderthals (La Chapelle-aux-Saints and La Ferrassie). Also, a newer and better method of analysis has been used: discriminant functions rather than coefficients of racial likeness.

Of the four ancient specimens tested in this way, Skhūl V is much more like modern man than Shanidar I and the two European Neanderthals and, in Howell's opinion, 'is unlikely to be a simple hybrid between Neanderthals and any modern type of man'. On the other hand, of the latter three, Shanidar I differs least and La Ferrassie most, from modern man. Indeed, to quote Howell further, 'The Upper Paleolithic and later Europeans seem more clearly distinguished than ever [by this sort of comparison] from their Neanderthal predecessors'. From all such evidence he concludes 'that modern man did not develop from Neanderthal man in Europe . . . or in the Near East'.

Howell's conclusion goes far toward finally setting to rest Hrdlicka's idea of a Neanderthal phase of man. I welcome it because it reinforces the argument which I advanced at the Tokyo congress in 1968 (Stewart, 1969b) and which was intended to counter a revival of the Hrdlicka viewpoint. Loring Brace (1964) is responsible for this revival. He contends that Neanderthal man and modern man differ significantly only in the larger face of the former and therefore a reduction in Neanderthal man's face size for any reason would transform him into modern man. He equates a large face size with big teeth and claims that a reduction in Neanderthal man's tooth size resulted when the latter began making better tools and thereby removed the selective pressure for large teeth. In the Near East there was only about 11,000 years between the Tabūn-Shanidar and Skhūl occupations for this change to have taken place. Besides, Neanderthal man, in my opinion, did not have such large teeth, nor was he subjected to such cultural change, as Brace claims. Moreover, any pressure governing face size is unlikely also to have eradicated the differences which have been noted as distinguishing the scapula and pubis of Neanderthal man from those of modern man.

It follows from what I have just said that evidence for a Neanderthal phase of man is lacking at present. Where then did modern man come from? I mentioned in connection with the Mount Carmel finds McCown's and Keith's theory about the ancestors of the Cromagnons coming from western Asia. This has not been borne out by subsequent finds. Indeed, the failure to find anywhere solid evidence of the existence of the modern form of man before 35,000 years ago is the strongest argument for the Neanderthal phase theory. To my knowledge, the only find of this sort is that made in 1967 by Richard Leakey in the Omo region of Ethiopia. In this case three skulls were found weathering out of slopes, which, unfortunately, makes their dating problematical. The geologist Karl Butzer, who studied the sites, believes that the remains are older than 35,000 years BP and possibly as old as late Middle Pleistocene (Butzer, 1969). Michael Day, who studied the skulls, says only that at whatever time these individuals were living in East Africa 'there were early representatives of Homo sapiens whose range of variation, at least in terms of skull characters, was every bit as wide as that known for Upper Pleistocene sapiens from other parts of the world' (Day, 1969, p. 1,138).

Taking all this into account, but especially the evidence that Neanderthal man approaches modern man morphologically far more closely than he does Homo erectus, I feel that there is strong justification for joining in the growing practice of including both modern man and Neanderthal man within the species Homo sapiens, but distinguishing them as subspecies (i.e., Homo sapiens sapiens and Homo sapiens neanderthalensis, respectively).

Although this would seem to complete the answer to the question, asked at the end of the Introduction, about Elliot Smith's omniscience regarding the relationship of Neanderthal man to modern man, proof that he was entirely wrong is not yet complete. The same applies to

Keith and Hrdlicka, not to mention many others. Apparently, few subjects are more prone to misinterpretation than the interrelationships of the remains of fossil man. This being the case, it is less important that scholars with backgrounds lending weight to their opinions are sometimes wrong, than that these scholars have had sufficient courage to point out where they think the available evidence leads. Elliot Smith was such a scholar and his ideas have served as stimulating guidelines for further research.

REFERENCES

ARAMBOURG, C., (1955) 'Sur l'attitude, en station verticale, des Neanderthaliens', *Comptes-Rendus de Académie des Sciences, Paris,* 240, 804-6.

BONARELLI, G., (1909) 'Palaeanthropus (n.g.) Heidelbergensis (Schoetensack)', *Rivista Italiana di Paleontologia, Perugia,* n.o. 19.

BOULE, M., (1911-13) 'L'homme fossile de la Chapelle-aux-Saints'. *Annales de Paléontologie, Paris,* 6, 109-72; 7, 21-56, 85, 192; 8, 1-67.

BRACE, C. L., (1964) 'The fate of the "Classic" Neanderthals: a consideration of hominid catastrophism'. *Current Anthropology,* 5, 3-43.

BUTZER, K. W., (1969) 'Geological interpretation of two pleistocene hominid sites in the lower Omo Basin', *Nature,* 222, 1133-5.

DARWIN, C., (1859) *The Origin of Species.* London.

DAY, M. H., (1969) 'Omo human skeletal remains', *Nature,* 222, 1135-8.

HOWELLS, W. W., (1969) 'Mount Carmel man: morphological relationships', *Proceedings of the VIII International Congress of Anthropological and Ethnological Sciences (Tokyo and Kyoto, 1968)* , 1, 269-72.

HRDLICKA, A., (1928) 'The Neanderthal phase of man (The Huxley Memorial Lecture for 1927)', *Journal of Royal Anthropological Institute of Great Britain and Ireland,* 57, 249-74.

KING, W., (1864) 'On the reputed fossil man of the Neanderthal', *Quarterly Journal of Science,* 1, 88-97.

LEROI-GOURHAN, A., (1968) 'Le Neanderthalien IV de Shanidar', *Bulletin de la Société Préhistorique Française, Comptes-Rendus des Séances Mensuelles,* 65, 79-83.

LINNAEUS, C., (1758) *Systema Naturae.* 10th edn.

McCOWN, T. D. & KEITH, SIR A., (1939) *The Stone Age of Mount Carmel: II The Fossil Human Remains from the Levalloiso-Mousterian.* Oxford.

MORANT, G. M., (1927) 'Studies of palaeolithic man. II', *Annals of Eugenics,* 2, 318-81.

PATTE, É., (1955) *Les Néanderthaliens: Anatomie, Physiologie, Comparaisons.* Paris.

PUYDT, M. DE & LOHEST, M., (1886) 'L'Homme Contemporain du Mammouth à Spy, Province de Namur (Belgique)', *Compt-Rendu de Congres de Namur.*

SCHAAFFHAUSEN, D., (1858) 'Zur Kenntnis der ältestes Rassenschädel'. *Archiv für Anatomie, Physiologie und wissenschaftliche Medicin, Leipzig,* pp. 453-78.

SIMPSON, G. G., (1945) 'The principles of classification and a classification of mammals', *Bulletin of the American Museum of Natural History, New York,* 85.

SMITH, G. E., (1916) 'Primitive Man', *Proceedings of the British Academy, 1915-16,* pp. 453-504. (Reprinted in *The Evolution of Man,* London 1924, 2nd edn, 1927) .

——, (1924) *The Evolution of Man.* London (2nd revised edn, 1927) .

——, (1928) 'Neanderthal man a distinct species', *Nature,* 121, 141.

——, (1930) *Human History.* London.

SOLECKI, R. S., (1957a) 'Shanidar Cave', *Scientific American,* 197, 158-64.

SOLECKI, R. S., (1957b) 'The 1956-57 season at Shanidar, Iraq: a preliminary statement', *Quaternaria*, 4, 23-30.

——, (1960) 'Three Adult Neanderthal Skeletons From Shanidar Cave, Northern Iraq', *Annual Report of the Smithsonian Institution for 1959*. pp. 603-35.

——, (1971) *Shanidar: The First Flower People*. New York.

STEWART, T. D., (1958) 'First views of the restored Shanidar I skull', *Sumer*, 14, 90-6. (Reprinted in 1959 with slight changes under the title 'The Restored Shanidar I Skull' in the *Smithsonian Report for 1958*, pp. 473-80.)

——, (1960) 'Form of the pubic bone in Neanderthal man', *Science*, 131, 1437-8.

——, (1961a) 'A Neglected Primitive Feature of the Swanscombe Skull', in *Homenaje a Pablo Martínez del Rio en el XXV Aniversario de la Edición de Los Orígenes Americanos*. Mexico. pp. 207-17.

——, (1961b) 'The skull of Shanidar II, *Sumer*, 17, 97-106. (Reprinted in 1962 with minor changes in the *Smithsonian Report for 1961*, pp. 521-33.)

——, (1962a) 'Neanderthal cervical vertebrae', *Bibliotheca Primatologica*, 1, 130-54.

——, (1962b) 'Neanderthal scapulae with special attention to the Shanidar Neanderthals from Iraq', *Anthropos*, 57, 779-800.

——, (1963) 'Shanidar skeletons IV and VI', *Sumer*, 19, 8-26.

——, (1964) 'The scapula of the first recognized Neanderthal skeleton', *Bonner Jahrbuch*, 164, 1-14.

——, (1969a) 'Fossil evidence of human violence', *Trans-action*, 6, 48-53.

——, (1969b) 'The evolution of man in Asia as seen in the lower jaw'. *Proceedings of the VIII International Congress of Anthropological and Ethnological Sciences (Tokyo and Kyoto, 1968)*, 1, 263-6.

——, (no date) 'Sanidar III', Manuscript.

STRAUS, W. L. JR & CAVE, A. J. E., (1957) 'Pathology and the posture of Neanderthal man', *Human Biology*, 32, 348-63.

SUZUKI, H., (1970) 'The Skull of the Amud Man', in *The Amud Man and His Cave Site*, Suzuki, H. & Takai, F. (eds), Tokyo. pp. 123-206.

SUZUKI, H. & TAKAI, F. (eds), (1970) *The Amud Man and His Cave Site*. Tokyo.

VALLOIS, H. V. & VANDERMEERSCH, B., (1972) 'La crane Moustérien de Qafzeh (Homo VI) ; etude anthropologique'. *L'Anthropologie, Paris*, 76, 71-96.

6 EARLY MAN AND THE DOG IN AUSTRALIA

N. W. G. Macintosh

The most intractable problem facing anatomical and archaeological analysis in Australia over the last twenty years has been the dating of those human fossil relics which we did possess. It is now clear that it is at the best speculative to contrast two fossils of apparently different morphology and very different contour, and theorize that the more rugged and so presumptively more archaic predates the more gracile and so presumptively more recent. Subsequent archaeology might unearth a gracile skull from an older level and the temptation then could be to reverse the theory and predicate a presumptively archaic population invading an already established more recent-looking people. That indeed was being advocated, at least verbally, following the Lake Mungo excavation by Bowler, *et al.* (1970) of the fragmented cremated remains of two individuals, apparently young females, from occupational levels dated from 25,000 to 32,000 BP.

A third eventuality might be the contemporary status of the gracile and rugged morphology at one or more time levels. We can now say this is approximately the case with the Keilor and the Talgai crania. The former provides a collagen date from its femur of 12,900 ± 120 y BP (Rafter N.Z. R 4074/B). The latter is minimally dated between 14,000 and 16,000 years BP from soils and nodules (Hendy, *et al.*, 1972); samples to narrow that range are still being processed. Given such a result, a theory of a bimodal population might be put forward, if examples of intermediate morphological range are not available.

Mulvaney (1969, pp. 156-65) made a valiant attempt to interpret what various workers in this fossil field were saying and meaning. I have only one minor criticism. He says (p. 160) 'Macintosh may imply two races were involved'. I would agree that my paper of 1965, which he quotes, stressed the contrast between the morphology of Keilor and that of the Talgai, Cohuna and Mossgiel fossils. But subsequently, Macintosh (1967), while still referring to two contrasting groups, Green Gully-Keilor-Tartanga and Cohuna-Talgai-Mossgiel, drew attention to the work of Larnach and Macintosh (1966) in which a series of Aboriginal skulls from coastal New South Wales were analysed. They provided a continuous range within which all the fossils mentioned and the Tasmanian were contained. I said 'The subjective impression of two separate types is not confirmed by this type of analysis'; furthermore using that same formula we had found that *H. erectus* and Solo man fell outside the Aboriginal range of variability, Solo even further than *H. erectus*.

Larnach and Macintosh (1970, 1971) extended the statistical analysis to embrace Queensland crania, and Eastern Australian mandibles. The range of values for all the skulls of coastal N.S.W., Queensland, the Cairns Tableland, Cape York and Keppel Islands was found to separate them completely from Mongoloid and Caucasoid crania. The range of values for Queensland, Cairns Tableland and N.S.W. were practically identical, and we were unable to find a Negritic component in the Cairns Rain Forest skulls.

The Keppel Islands crania on visual inspection are unusually smooth and rounded for Aboriginal skulls, especially on the frontal bones of the males, and Klaatsch (1908) commented on certain characters at variance from continental Australians. They were studied separately (Larnach & Macintosh, 1972). They are unquestionably Australian Aborigines, yet exhibit certain traits which place them in a somewhat special position within the framework of the general Australians. This is the most striking instance we have seen of micro-evolution within the Australian Aborigines, and ascribe a similar position to the Tasmanian population in isolation for some 10,000 years. Macintosh and Barker (1965) advocated the view that skeletally, Tasmanians and Australians are similar people, that it was unreasonable to deny overlanding from the Australian mainland and subsequent isolation by rise of sea level. An earlier paper in which I explored the 'possibilities' of sea routes by-passing Australia became superfluous, once the flooding of Bass Strait was dated (Jennings, 1959, 1971) and once antiquity of man on the mainland some thousands of years before Tasmania was cut off had been established. There are very few workers who any longer deny the derivation of Tasmanians from the mainland. The analysis of many cultural traits now gives similar support; the point I make at the moment is the paramount importance of absolute chronology; without the modern techniques, denied to earlier writers, the endless and inconclusive speculations of how the Tasmanians got there would still afflict us.

Dr Eugene Giles formerly of Harvard using a weighted multivariate analysis method repeated all the Larnach and Macintosh observations on similar series of skulls and on expanded series from N.S.W. and Queensland, but additionally on the Tasmanians. We eagerly awaited his results, but to the best of our knowledge they have not yet been published although some four or five years have elapsed since he collected his data. At the last personal communication, it seemed likely that his N.S.W. and Queensland data and analysis agreed with ours. We had in the Queensland monograph analysed and separated New Guinean from Australian skulls on the scores for 12 traits.

Visually some of the Cape York skulls tend to support historical and other source evidence of Papuan infiltration, so a subsequent study was made (Larnach & Macintosh, 1972) using a larger series of New Guinea skulls. As a result I retract a statement (1965) that I could not see a physical relationship between Australian and New Guinean populations; because we have now demonstrated a north to south cranial cline from Cape York to the New South Wales coast. Australian crania show their maximum resemblance to New Guinean crania in the region (Cape York) which is closest to New Guinea (Sanghvi, et al., 1971 had pointed out that Cape York appeared to be genetically more distant from Central Australia than is suggested by linguistic studies).

From all this work we believed we had a very strong objective basis of recent Australian skulls, on which to make comparison and assessment of the fossil skulls. We now believe, although we have not yet published, that no Australian fossil skull falls outside the range we have established for our recent series.

To establish that proposition firmly will require a great deal of objective work. What is required is a large series of fossils continuing from considerable antiquity to the present. Australia is in the extraordinarily fortunate position that such a series is available, developed by Graeme Pretty and the large team of assistants he had trained since 1968.

Formerly it was thought that grave-goods were rare in Aboriginal Australia. Like so many other earlier beliefs, that is wrong as attested by Pretty's material, which shows an extraordinary range of burial posture, related to stratigraphy, and covering 18,000 to 4,000 BP by C_{14} analysis and continuing to mid-nineteenth century. New findings include shaft and status burials, the latter supporting my Lake Nitchie excavation (Macintosh, 1971). Also the pin-pointing of the antiquity of Treponematosis in Australia is possible and so will give time value to the study by Hackett (1963) and to his completed monograph, which now languishes for want of a publisher.

Cultural sequences of a physical nature including for example the inception of tooth avulsion (of which the earliest example to my knowledge is the Lake Nitchie specimen at 6,820 ± 200 y BP Rafter N.Z. R 2835/2b) will almost certainly be identified. Apart from all of which, the range of morphological variability at continuous time levels from 18,000 BP should be settled. Visually and subjectively the morphological range appears to me to embrace all our known fossil material. All that commentary arises from personal communication with Pretty, because, apart from report to the Australian Institute of Aboriginal Studies, he has commendably refrained from premature publication; but clearly his monumental work is quite unmatched in Australia, the nearest approach being the Edmund Gill and Sir Robert Blackwood salvage work relative to the proposed Chowilla Dam. The human antiquity span there however, is much more limited; (again personal communication) because their findings too are in course of preparation for publication.

The present time is an unhappy and difficult one in which to attempt a review of prehistoric man in Australia. Dozens of samples await date-processing; many workers have unpublished material; overseas publications are difficult to obtain or translate, and as will be seen this paper is sprinkled with the phrase, personal communication. However, in summary Larnach and I at present think it highly probable that from 18,000 BP onwards, Aboriginal skeletal material shows a range of morphological variability similar to recent range.

From one mile south of the Lake Nitchie excavation (Macintosh, 1971), a subsequently discovered cremated fragmented example has been collagen-dated at 15,300 ± 500 y BP (new T½) Rafter N.Z. R 4468/7, (personal communication, not yet published). Among the surviving fragments is a portion of occipital bone showing a massive occipital torus without a trace of external occipital projection. Tentatively, I regard this as balancing in morphological range the gracile female Lake Mungo remains.

Larnach and I then turned our attention to fossil material beyond Australia:

Homo erectus: A separate formula of 17 traits characteristic of all the *H. erectus* crania was applied to the Australian Aboriginal series and to five other races. The *H. erectus* crania gave a mean score of 49.0. Strikingly different are the Australians with a mean of 7.7 derived from a range of 4 to 20, New Guinea a mean of 4.7, Mongoloids 3.33 and Europeans 2.6. (Macintosh & Larnach, 1972).

While it may be said that there is a greater tendency for *H. erectus* traits to persist in Australians than in other modern racial groups, the overall persistence of the pattern is so thin as to be tenuous, and of course confirms and amplifies my former observation in 1967 that using a reverse procedure, i.e., applying the Australian formula to *H. erectus,* and Solo man, the latter two fell beyond the Australian range, Solo Man even more so than *H. erectus*. This tenuous persistence of *H. erectus* traits in modern populations is not surprising in view of the tremendous time difference of more than half a million years between the *H. erectus* fossils and the Australians with their maximum so far proven occupancy of the continent a mere 32,000 years.

The late Dr Louis Leakey shortly before his death in 1973 had been expressing in television features and popular articles his new view that *H. erectus* was not directly ancestral to *H. sapiens*. Some two months earlier his son Richard had reported to the National Geographic Society his discovery from Lake Rudolph of a 2.8 million-year-old fossil skull, morphologically large brained and very different from *Australopithecus* or *H. erectus*.

While this startling find is awaiting further elaboration, one is clearly in a quandary as to how the persistence of some elements, in varying frequencies, of the characteristic *H. erectus* morphological pattern, can occur if *H. erectus* is not in fact ancestral to *H. sapiens*.

I have already referred to the present time as an unhappy and difficult one in which to review prehistoric man in Australia itself; it becomes even more so in attempting to evaluate his possible derivation. No other alternative occurs to me than to state the remainder of our findings and leave it to the future to decide whether they are significant.

Some additional observations emerged from our *H. erectus* studies:

Firstly the *H. erectus* total differentiating pattern of 17 traits can be condensed into 3, i.e., a frontal, a mastoid and an occipital sub-pattern which are completely diagnostic.

Secondly, Weidenreich (1943, p. 236) wrote that 'a well defined frontal torus is rare in modern man, whereas an occipital torus, at least as far as the middle portion is concerned, may still be found in primitive races'. In our study, this is true for the Australian where an occipital torus occurs in 90 per cent and 70.3 per cent show no trace of an external occipital protuberance. Dr Jan Jelinek in a paper which he sent to *Homo* some four or more years ago and which I cannot locate took this a stage further and indicated that the frontal torus is less stable than the occipital (personal communication).

Thirdly in the light of this diagnostic pattern of anatomical characters, apparent contour similarities are of much less significance. I therefore retreat from the direction in which I was moving in my papers of 1965 and 1967 when on the basis of contours I said of the Australian fossil skulls they were 'reminiscent of' and had the 'mark of Java' on all of them (Talgai, Cohuna, Mossgiel and Keilor). I have stated this altered attitude (Macintosh, 1972) and added 'no example of *H. erectus* has been found in Australia and I suspect never will be'.

Fourthly, having been driven to appreciate that contour comparison can be beguiling, and further that the occipital bone is diagnostically a more stable and potent weapon than the frontal bone, Larnach and I completed a separate study of recession of forehead (not yet published).

Macintosh (1965) had mentioned an earlier paper (Macintosh, 1952) in which resemblance of the Cohuna frontal bone to the *Pithecanthropus* example of *H. erectus* was noted, as it has been by others also. Larnach has now pointed out that a low frontal curvature index, as occurs in Cohuna is not of itself an *H. erectus* trait; at least two other factors are necessary components of frontal recession commensurate with *H. erectus* comparison. These are (A) the position of the point of maximum curvature of the frontal, and (B) the tilt of the nasion-bregna chord relative to the basion-bregma height. In brief, in an extreme case it would be possible to have a low frontal curvature index without any frontal recession at all.

This was partly appreciated by Burkitt and Hunter (1922) when they pointed out that the more posteriorly the point of maximum curvature 'the more primitive is the *appearance* (italics mine) of the sloping forehead'. It was fully appreciated by the late Professor J. L. Shellshear who after the publication of my 1952 Cohuna paper, said to me 'you have not taken into account the high pre-bregmatic eminence'. As he did not elaborate, I missed the point, but perceive it now, and I agree with Larnach that recession of forehead in *H. erectus* cannot be diagnostically equated with Australian crania. Furthermore, Larnach researching past literature including papers by Karl Pearson in 1923, 1925, 1928 has extracted a series of 5 skulls of famous Europeans giving a frontal curvature index range of 12.0 to 23.6 and a mean of 18.69 compared with Sinanthropus II, III, X, XI, XII skulls which have a range of 14.8 to 18.6 and a mean of 16.4. The frontal curvature index of Australian skulls, therefore, falls within modern European ranges and can scarcely be a diagnostic trait for *H. erectus* derivation.

We then turned our attention to Solo Man. In my 1967 paper, again beguiled by contours, I thought I was seeing superficial resemblance to Solo man in certain fossil Australians, particularly in the Mossgiel specimen and in the skull described by Burkitt and Hunter (1922) called by them Neanderthaloid and subsequently claimed by Weidenreich to be better equated with Ngandong skulls.

As Larnach is presenting in this volume a separate paper on an analysis of Solo crania in comparison with Australian morphology, I confine myself to the statement that the Solo crania proved unique, completely discriminated not only from Aboriginal Australians, but also from *H. erectus*. After this work and at this overlate stage, I have recalled that the late Professor Shellshear, using 'Block Coefficient' (unpublished) had reached that conclusion 30 years ago. I have as an archive, Shellshear's drawings and calculations and perhaps at some future time, I may be able to edit those items. It is interesting also to speculate whether Weidenreich would have changed his view about Australian relationship had he lived to complete his Solo monograph. He had recorded the anatomical details which Larnach has welded into a morphological pattern.

As a final comment, much debate has related to the antiquity of Solo Man. Jacob has apparently excavated a Solo skull contemporary with *H. erectus* (personal communication) and so equally removed in time from the Australians. I believe a further revision of my 1972 paper (recent though it is) may be necessary, following communication with Professor Teuku Jacob. Jacob (1967) cleaned the Wadjak skulls as far as their condition permitted. I saw the Wadjak skulls in 1965 before they were cleaned, but not since. Jacob has not seen Keilor since its cleaning. Nevertheless he had noted some significant differences between the specimens, before cleaning, which were not recorded by earlier workers. Since the cleaning I suspect differences may have been accentuated, and therefore, comparison of Keilor and Wadjak needs repeating.

In 1965 I criticized the conclusion of Brothwell that the Niah skull was most clearly affined to a Tasmanian skull. I still think that was justified, but I now agree with Jacob's (1967) view that there are collectively some similarities in the Niah, Keilor, Wadjak, Tabon and Sampung skulls. Here we are back with the problem of diverse and uncertain or unknown antiquity. Keilor is securely dated at 12,900 BP; Niah is dated on charcoal only at 40,000; Wadjak cannot be dated indirectly because the site was destroyed (Stein Callenfels, 1936). Jacob refers to the Tabon skull as assumed to be 15,000, but it is now radio-carbon bracketted at 23,000 (Fox, 1970); the Sampung skulls are associated with the Mesolithic fauna of East Java. This somewhat similar morphology of items from Australia, Java, Borneo and Philippines ranges from 40,000 to 13,000 or less. To this collection must be added the pioneering archaeology of Dr Peter White in the New Guinea Highlands culminating in an occupancy date of 26,870 BP. His own paper appears in this volume, so it is sufficient to say that man in New Guinea must have been contemporary with man in Australia from some 30,000 years ago.

The first discovery of the actual bones of ancient man in the Philippines was made in 1962 by Dr Robert Fox. The most important relics are the fronto-nasal region of a skull, and a mandible, from the 22,000 to 24,000 BP levels of the Tabon Cave in Palawan.

The mandible was handed to me in January 1971, if possible to be cleared of crust and morphologically analysed. The crust ultimately proved to be practically pure guano and so had to be removed entirely by electric diamond drills under magnification. As the bone was extremely fragile, the care and time involved was great.

Using our analysis of eastern Australian mandibles (Larnach & Macintosh, 1971) for comparison, the Palawan mandible was easily identified as adult male and clearly could not be equated with our Mongoloid series, nor with any examples we possessed of Ainu, Andaman, Sulu, Solor nor Thai. In a trait by trait comparison with our Australian series, similarities were much more frequent than differences. As the Tabon mandible is not complete, I was only able to use 10 critical characters from our identificatory formula. These gave a mean score of 21.5 and a range of 17 to 27 for Australians; the Tabon mandible scored 25. Had this mandible been included unknowingly in an Australian series it would not have been detected as alien. But the cautionary comment is necessary that we know nothing whatever of the range of variation of mandibles in the ancient population at Tabon, nor the likely position of this one fossil mandible within that range.

A cast of the fronto-nasal skull bones was exhibited in Tokyo in 1968. From my examination of it then, some Aboriginal Australian traits were suggested, but it is impossible to describe the anatomical details hidden under an encrustation of guano. The relic constitutes an important and provocative item for future work, particularly as it and the mandible are associated with an upper palaeolithic flake industry. Within it the kuba (Tagalog) 'humpback' scraper and other tools are indistinguishable from Australian artefacts, and according to Dr Fox this industry is continuous between 45,000 and 9,000 BP in the Tabon Cave and forms a close link with Niah and northern Luzon. The Philippines may therefore be the link in morphology and in time span for interpretation of man and his migrations over the last 40,000 years relative to the somewhat comparable similarities in Niah, Wadjak, Keilor and other fossil relics as visualized by Jacob.

Dr Dale Stewart is presenting in this volume a review of comparisons and contrasts in the advent of man to the Americas and Australia. My views on that same topic are already stated (Macintosh, 1972). As he had that paper, and additionally we had discussions in 1968 in Tokyo, in 1970 in Washington and California and in October 1972 in Sydney, his present paper covers practically all the aspects I raised, and amplifies them thoroughly and admirably. As his delivery in this Commemorative Symposium preceded mine, it is only necessary for me to thank him for his masterly coverage and to add some brief comments on information not covered in my 1972 paper and not discussed between Dr Stewart and me.

First, an extraordinary paradox exists. Only a limited number of archaeological sites have been excavated in Australia, but the overwhelming majority are incontestably dated. We are able to say with conviction that man is firmly established at Lake Mungo 32,000 years ago and from the same site the skeletal remains at 25,000 BP, are the oldest recovered in Australia. These dates are at the apex of a broad pyramid of supporting dates; they are not raised on a solitary obelisk. To quote only the positive and more spectacular, there is the Lake Yantara camp fire at 26,200 ± 1,100 BP GAK-2121 (Dury & Langford-Smith, 1970); Malangangerr (Oenpelli region) 22,900 ± 1,000 BP, A.N.U. 77b where the oldest edge-ground axes so far found in the world occur (C. White, 1967); the Gallus site, Koonalda Cave, Nullabor Plain where man was mining for flint with torches and where art designs occur on the walls of this underground cavern 21,300 ± 350 BP, A.N.U.-71 (R. V. S. Wright, 1971); Burrill Lake, coastal N.S.W., 20,760 ± 800 BP, A.N.U. 137 for a land, marine and estuarine economy (Lampert, 1971). The younger sites are more numerous; among these Kenniff Cave, Queensland, 16,130 ± 140 BP, N.P.L. 68, flake tools sequence (Mulvaney & Joyce, 1965) is firmly dated, and what are apparently the second oldest human remains so far directly dated are from my cremation site at Lake Nitchie already mentioned as 15,300).

All these are in the eastern half of the continent so one can confidently predict higher antiquity yet to be established.

But the Americas with an infinitely greater number of archaeological sites, and a technology of multiple means of dating unparalleled yet in Australia, are only able to indicate about 12,500 BP on currently accepted hard evidence for man in both North and South America (Shutler, 1971).

Dr Stewart has presented a logical and meticulously argued case for the probability that man started moving out of Asia 'at the two available exits long before the last maximum lowering of sea level' and I have said (1972) that I have similar opinion.

Second, Stewart using the work of Hopkins (1967) suggests that migration from northeast and southeast Asia may have been around 50,000 years ago. He points out that early man could easily have negotiated Beringia because the interior of Alaska and adjacent Siberia were unglaciated in Pleistocene times; the more difficult problem is to identify an ice-free corridor from Alaska into America proper. Putting aside that latter problem, I want to refer to Stewart's comment that records from the field of human palaeontology for the whole of Asia are scanty (quite apart from the relative paucity of data from Alaska), and he has extracted all that is possible from extant relics. But neither of us have mentioned, and it is worth noting that the Russian archaeologists Alexejev and Dikov have excavated rich palaeolithic tool sites at Chukotskiy, Magadan and near Sopochnoye, all immediately west of Beringia (personal communication from Dr Jan Jelinek).

Third, Stewart's single stem arrow southeastward out of Asia (see his Figure 1) I would now convert into a broad reticulated network of exits embracing the northern and southern Philippines, and Borneo linked to Palawan, as well as Java.

Fourth, Stewart has stressed the need for further evidence of man's presence and a more concerted effort to get all such evidence dated. I want to stress the additional need for direct dating wherever possible of already existing material, notable instances being the Niah skull (similarly urged by Stewart and Jacob), and waste bone from Palawan.

The dog

The dingo could not have been introduced into Australia much before 12,000 BP when some links in the Bass Strait causeway were flooded because it did not get to Tasmania or the off-shore islands; and certainly not before 8,000 BP or probably 6,500 BP, the time range for separation of Australia from New Guinea, otherwise it would be found in New Guinea.

Jennings (1959, 1971) has shown that Torres Strait was flooded between 6,500 and 8,000 BP and Bass Strait between 12,000 to 13,500 BP; at glacial low sea level between 18,000 and 20,000 BP sea deeps up to 100 km wide existed between the Java-Flores arc, the Banda Islands arc, and Australia plus New Guinea and Tasmania. An alternative exit from Southeast Asia passing through the Philippines to the Celebes and Moluccas to the Banda Island arc and to New Guinea was interrupted by more than two, but shorter sea crossings.

The dingo had to be brought to Australia by man and in some sort of sea craft.

At Devil's Lair limestone caves in southwest Western Australia a single tooth of dingo was reported from a level of 8,500 BP, in 'disturbed' deposit (Dortch & Merrilees, 1971). I am extremely grateful to Dr Merrilees for responding to my request for loan of the tooth which he posted on 16 October 1972 and which I examined a few days later. It is a tooth of *Sarcophilus* with a slightly divergent crown shape.

At Mt Burr in South Australia fragments of teeth and jaw are stated to be dingo, charcoal bracketted to 8,000 BP. The excavators sent reports to the A.I.A.S. but died before writing up fair copies for publication. I think the time context of these items could be open to doubt and I have not been able to examine the fragments.

The almost complete skeleton of a male dingo, C_{14} dated at 3,000 BP from bracketting charcoal was excavated in South Australia (Mulvaney, *et al.*, 1964). Having cleaned and re-assembled it, I published an analysis and gave it a personal age at death of 23 to 27 weeks, stating that dingo morphological pattern has remained unchanged for 3,000 years, but that in total size the animal was small for its personal age (Macintosh, 1964). A revision of that analysis in the light of my subsequent work on dingo epiphyseal closure has shown that it was 18 weeks old at death and its size is similar to that of modern dingoes of that personal age.

We have this year worked out a cranial formula which separates dingo from domestic dog and shows also that the dingo is skeletally homogeneous across the continent.

I also conclude that the dingo was brought to Australia as a quasi companion, not in the true sense of a domesticated animal. Aboriginal association with the dingo reveals only minimal symbiosis.

I am unable to see the dingo as parent, offspring or cousin of the pariah dog, and in my opinion there are too many anatomical and behavioural differences, basic and plastic for the dingo to be a derivative of *C. lupus pallipes* (the Indian wolf).

Troughton (1971) postulated the New Guinea Highland dog *(C. hallstromi)* as the ancestor of the dingo. Archaeologically J. P. White (p. 148, 1972) indicates that the dog has been found only in the most recent highland levels, although he quotes F. J. Allen in personal communication saying the dog was on the south Papuan coast by 1,500 years ago; and of course he is right to add the caution that cultural aspects may have something to do with its archaeological Highland absence. Apart from that, my opinion is that morphology, metrical and non-metrical, separate *C. hallstromi* from dingo, and equate it with the Pacific Islands dog.

While the dingo's ancestry and affinities remain enigmatic, it constitutes an extremely important marker trait for Australia, and along the possible routes from Asia to Australia the only dingo-like animals I can locate are the recently extinct dog from the Tengger Mountains of Java, and possibly an existing dog of the Philippines.

I have tried to write this paper as a journal of endeavours to follow a variety of pathways, some based on the earlier and current work of others, some on my own earlier and current thinking and data. Some of my pathways proved to be misleading and have had to be abandoned; some have needed partial re-tracing; some remain obscure. Pathways that appear to have been traversed successfully include:

(1) the construction of a morphological range of recent skeletal Aboriginal material as a basic framework for comparison of the earlier fossil specimens from Australia and from regions beyond Australia;

(2) the apparently similar identification of earlier Australian morphological ranges;

(3) again derived from use of the basic framework, the realization that *H. erectus* traits, while represented with higher frequency in Australians than in 5 other modern races, are tenuous, which is reasonable with a time gap of half a million years dimension;

(4) the abandoning of Solo Man as an Australian ancestor;

(5) the successful dating of some fossil specimens which had seemed quite intractable;

(6) reasonable confidence that other fossils—Cohuna, Murrabit, Mossgiel as yet only tentatively or partially dated will be completed;

(7) the acknowledgment of revision or retraction as soon as the need was recognized.

REFERENCES

BOWLER, J. M., JONES, R., ALLEN, H. & THORNE, A. G., (1970) 'Pleistocene human remains from Australia: A living site and human cremation from Lake Mungo, western N.S.W.', *World Archaeology*, 2 (1), 39-60.

BROTHWELL, D. R., (1960) 'Upper Pleistocene human skull from Niah Caves', *Sarawak Mus. J.*, 9, 323-49.

BURKITT, A. N. & HUNTER, J. I., (1922) 'The description of a Neanderthaloid Australian skull', *J. Anat.*, 57, 31-54.

DORTCH, C. E. & MERRILEES, D., (1971) 'A salvage excavation in Devil's Lair, Western Australia', *J. Roy. Soc. Western Australia*, 54 (4), 103-13.

DURY, G. H. & LANGFORD-SMITH, T., (1970) 'A Pleistocene camp fire from Lake Yantara, northwestern N.S.W.', *Search*, 1 (2), 73.

FOX, R. B., (1970) 'The Tabon Caves', *Monograph 1*, Nat. Mus. Manila.

HACKETT, C. J., (1963) 'The human treponematoses', *Bull. W.H.O.*, 29, 7-41.

HENDY, C. H., RAFTER, T. A. & MACINTOSH, N. W. G., (1972) 'The formation of carbonate nodules in the soils of the Darling Downs, Queensland, Australia, and the dating of the Talgai Cranium', *Procs. 8th Int. Conf. on Radio-carbon Dating*, Wellington, N.Z., D107-D124.

HOPKINS, D. M. (ed.), (1967) *The Bering Land Bridge*, Stanford, California.

JACOB, T., (1967) *Some Problems Pertaining to the Racial History of the Indonesian Region*, Utrecht, pp. 162 ff.

JENNINGS, J. N., (1959) 'The submarine topography of Bass Strait', *Proc. Roy. Soc. Vict.*, 71 (1), 49-72.

——, (1971 'Sea level changes and land links', Ch. 1 in *Aboriginal Man and Environment in Australia*. Mulvaney, D. J. and Golson, J. (eds), A.N.U. Press, Canberra.

KLAATSCH, H., (1908) 'The skull of the Australian Aboriginal', *Rep. Path. Lab. Lunacy Dept*, N.S.W. Govt, 1 (3), 43-167.

LAMPERT, R. J., (1971) 'Burrill Lake and Currarong', *Terra Australis 1*, Dep Prehistory, A.N.U., pp. 86 ff.

LARNACH, S. L. & MACINTOSH, N. W. G., (1966) 'The Craniology of the Aborigines of coastal New South Wales', *Oceania Monographs*, No. 13, Sydney.

——, (1970) 'The Craniology of the Aborigines of Queensland', *Oceania Monographs*, No. 15, Sydney.

——, (1971) 'The Mandible in Eastern Australian Aborigines', *Oceania Monographs*, No. 17, Sydney.

——, (1972) 'The Keppel Islanders', *A.P.A.O.*, 7 (1), 8-14.

MACINTOSH, N. W. G., (1952) 'The Cohuna cranium: history and commentary', *Mankind*, 4 (8), 307-29.

——, (1964) 'A 3000 years old Dingo from Shelter 6, Fromm's Landing, South Australia', *Proc Roy Soc. Vict.*, 77 (2), 498-507.

——, (1965) 'The Physical Aspect of Man in Australia', in Berndt, R. M. (ed.), *Aboriginal Man in Australia*, Sydney, pp. 29-70.

——, (1967) 'Fossil Man in Australia', *Aust. J. Sci.*, 30 (3), 86-97.

——, (1971) 'Analysis of an Aboriginal skeleton and a pierced tooth necklace from Lake Nitchie, Australia', *Anthropologie*, 9 (1), 49-62, Moravske Museum—Ustav. Anthropos, Brno.

——, (1972) 'Radiocarbon dating as a pointer in time to the arrival and history of man in Australia and Islands to the north west', *Procs. 8th Int. Conf. on Radiocarbon Dating*, Wellington, N.Z., XLIV-LVI.

MACINTOSH, N. W. G. & BARKER, B. C. W., (1965) 'The Osteology of Aboriginal Man in Tasmania', *Oceania Monographs*, No. 12, Sydney.

MACINTOSH, N. W. G. & LARNACH, S. L. (1972) '*Homo erectus* traits in Australian Aboriginal Crania', *A.P.A.O.*, 7 (1), 1-7.

——, (1972) 'A cranial study of the Aborigines of Queensland with a contrast between Australian and New Guinea Crania', pp. 1-11 in *The Human Biology of Aborigines in Cape York*. Kirk, R. L. (ed.), Australian Aboriginal Studies No. 44, A.I.A.S., Canberra.

MULVANEY, D. J., (1969) *The Prehistory of Australia.* Thames & Hudson, London, pp. 276 ff.

MULVANEY, D. J. & JOYCE, E. G., (1965) 'Archaeological and geomorphological investigations on Mt. Moffatt Station, Queensland', *Procs. Prehist. Soc.*, 31, 147-212.

MULVANEY, D. J., LAWTON, G. H. & TWIDALE, C. R. (1964) 'Archaeological excavation of Rock Shelter No. 6, Fromm's Landing', *Proc. Roy. Soc. Vict.*, 77 (2), 479-94.

SANGHVI, L. D., KIRK, R. L. & BALAKRISHNAN, V., (1971) 'A study of genetic distance among some populations of Australian Aborigines', *Human Biol.*, 43, 445.

SHUTLER, R., JR (1971) 'Early Man in North America: new developments 1960-1970', *Arctic Anthropology*, 8 (2), 1-142.

STEIN CALLENFELS, P. V. VAN, (1936) 'The Melanesoid civilizations of Eastern Asia', *Bull. Raffles Mus.*, B, 1, 41-51.

STEWART, T. D., (1972) 'Perspectives on some problems of Early Man common to America and Australia'. Ch. 10 in this present volume.

TROUGHTON, E., (1971) 'The early history and relationships of the New Guinea Highland dog *(Canis hallstromi)*', *Proc. Linn. Soc. N.S.W.*, 96 (2), 93-8.

WEIDENREICH, F., (1943) 'The skull of *Sinanthropus pekinensis*', *Palaeontol. Sinica*, N.S., D, 10, 1-298.

——, (1951) 'Morphology of Solo Man', *Anthropol Paps Amer. Mus. Nat. Hist.*, 43 (3), 205-90.

WHITE, C., (1967) 'Early stone axes in Arnhem Land', *Antiquity*, 41, 149-52.

WHITE, J. P., (1972) '*Ol Tombuna*', *Terra Australis 2.* Department of Prehistory, A.N.U., Canberra, pp. 176 ff.

WRIGHT, R. V. S. (ed.), (1971) 'Archaeology of the Gallus Site, Koonalda Cave', *Australian Aboriginal Studies, No. 26*, A.I.A.S., Canberra. pp. 133 ff.

7 A COMPARATIVE STUDY OF SOLO AND AUSTRALIAN ABORIGINAL CRANIA

S. L. Larnach and N. W. G. Macintosh

In 1943 Weidenreich (p. 226) wrote: 'There is an almost continuous line leading from *Pithecanthropus* through *Homo soloensis* and fossil Australian forms to certain modern primitive Australian types.' He died before completing his monograph on the Solo skulls and we do not know whether his detailed study of these skulls would have led to a radical re-consideration of his earlier views. However, according to Birdsell

> Weidenreich orally expressed to the author (June, 1946) a much modified view. In it he considered the Australians to be related to the pithecanthropoids since they shared certain anatomical features in common, but he did not consider them to be derived solely from such a source . . . He apparently considered [the Australians] to be a blend between *Homo soloensis* and another unspecified racial group. (1967, p. 107)

In any event his earlier views have strongly influenced other anthropologists and the available evidence should be worth re-examining to see if Australians show any special resemblance to Solo man.

Superficially, at least, the Solo crania show strong resemblance to Australian Aboriginal skulls, especially to certain fossil Australian skulls. The most striking features seen in Solo crania are the strongly developed brow ridges, very retreating foreheads and powerfully developed ridge-shaped occipital tori. Similar, although not so strongly developed, brow ridges and ridge-shaped occipital tori can also be seen on some Australian skulls. Certain fossil Australian skulls, such as Cohuna and some crania from Kow Swamp in Victoria, show even more retreating foreheads than shown by Solo skulls. Measured on the cast with co-ordinate callipers the frontal curvature index is 17.9 on Solo VI, 14.7 on Solo V and 16.2 on Solo XI. The lengths of the frontal chords as determined by Jacob (1967) on the original crania were used. The forehead of Cohuna is even flatter with a frontal curvature of 13.8. The range for this index in 10 fossil Kow Swamp crania is 12.5 to 19 (Thorne, 1971). It can therefore be seen that although a retreating forehead may be characteristic of Solo man, it does not by itself distinguish Solo crania from some Australian fossil skulls. After consideration this trait was not used in our investigation.

Weidenreich (1951), in his monograph on the Solo crania, described a number of characters which distinguished them from those of modern man and from Neanderthal skulls. Among other traits Weidenreich mentioned a supplementary foramen ovale, which together with the main foramen ovale, opens externally into the floor of a pit. He regarded this supplementary foramen as 'the outlet for the smaller or motor root of the mandibular nerve of the trigeminal nerve' (Weidenreich, 1951, p. 282). Apparently unique to Solo man, this supplementary foramen ovale occurs 'in three of the four skulls'. Because it is not present in all, it has been omitted from the list of traits used here.

The Characteristic Traits

The final selection was made after a careful examination of the casts of Solo VI and Solo XI in the light of Weidenreich's (1951) description, and after it was quite clear that the traits were common to both crania. Other Solo casts were then examined to see which of these traits were present in those specimens not too fragmentary for the observations to be made. In this way it was hoped that the traits finally selected were those that might reasonably be claimed as characteristic of Solo man.

The following traits were finally selected and their values are indicated in the following list:

(1) The brow ridges are of the divided type: Distinct division = 3; division ambiguous = 1; no sign of division = 0. This type varies from a pseudo-torus, where the fused superciliary and trigonal elements almost produce a continuous supraorbital torus, to a condition where these elements are clearly separated by a somewhat deep groove crossing between them from the supraorbital notch. If a true continuous supraorbital torus is present there is, ipso facto, no division, or if the development of superciliary ridges is absent or very slight, even though there may be some prominence at the glabella, a value of 0 is given.

(2) A very large rounded zygomatic trigone (trigonum supraorbitale) is present. If its size is approximately equal to or larger than that seen on Solo VI it is given a value of 3; if its size is ambiguous it is given a value of 1; if definitely smaller its value is 0.

(3) A distinct ophrionic groove, which may be defined as the furrow sometimes seen immediately above the brow ridges, and showing a distinct supraglabellar fossa. It is very clearly seen in the La Chapelle skull. Obviously it can only be present if the brow ridges are sufficiently developed.

> Contrary to the conditions in *Sinanthropus*, the tori [of Solo Man] are not separated from the squama by a distinct sulcus supraorbitalis and glabellaris, but continue into the squama itself without any demarcating impression, except for the lateral halves of the supraorbital tori where they build the zygomatic process (Weidenreich, 1951, p. 251).

No ophrionic groove = 3; ambiguous = 1; present = 0. If the superciliary ridges (and consequently the ophrionic groove) are faintly developed the value is also given as 0.

(4) A suprameatal tegmen is present: Distinct = 3; ambiguous = 1; absent = 0.

(5) The long diameter of the external auditory meatus is horizontal = 3; ambiguous = 1; oblique or vertical = 0. (In contrast to the position of the long diameter in Solo man and in other specimens of *Homo erectus*, the specimen known as *Homo erectus leakeyi* has the long diameter vertical.)

(6) The tympanic is orientated horizontally and is convex below = 3; ambiguous = 1; not horizontal = 0. Weidenreich (1951, p. 275) has pointed out: 'In Solo man the [tympanic] plate is oriented in a horizontal plane; it is convex and covers the whole petrous portion.'

(7) The squamous suture is low, with practically no arch = 3; ambiguous = 1; arched = 0.

(8) The course of the squamo-tympanic fissure is transverse (i.e., not oblique to the middle line) = 3; ambiguous = 1; oblique = 0.

(9) The squamo-tympanic fissure is on the floor of the glenoid fossa = 3; ambiguous = 1; absent from floor = 0. Weidenreich (1951, p. 273) comments: 'In Solo man this fissure runs along the very floor of the fossa.'

(10) The postglenoid tubercle is absent = 3; ambiguous = 1; present = 0.

(11) Weidenreich's spina cristae petrosae is present = 3; ambiguous = 1; absent (vaginal crest present) = 0.

(12) The petrous portion of the petro-tympanic axis is clearly angled forwards in relation to the tympanic portion: Distinctly angled = 3; ambiguous = 1; absent = 0.

(13) The foramen ovale is situated at the bottom of an oval pit = 3; ambiguous = 1; the pit is absent = 0. Weidenreich (1951, p. 281) wrote that 'in contrast to conditions in modern man, in Solo man the foramen [ovale] is not a simple perforation of the skull base but is in the form of an outlet at the bottom of the ovale pit which is 3 to 6 mm deep'. (He then also points out that in three of the four skulls there is an accessory foramen ovale near the anterior end of the pit.)

(14) A juxtamastoid ridge: If present = 3; ambiguous = 1; absent = 0.

(15) A lambdoidal protuberance: If present = 3; ambiguous = 1; absent = 0.

(16) A large ridge-shaped occipital torus: If present = 3; ambiguous = 1; absent = 0. Weidenreich (1951, p. 255) commented: 'the lower margin of the torus forms a thick ridge that projects far out and overlaps the depressed upper areas of the nuchal planum on each side'.

(17) A strong external occipital crest emerging from the midline of the occipital torus and extending downward towards the foramen

magnum: if strong presence = 3; ambiguous = 1; absent = 0. Weidenreich (1951, p. 255) wrote: 'At the midline, where the external occipital crest emerges, the ridge is at its highest and broadest and is the equivalent of the protuberentia occipitalis externa of modern man.'

(18) A marked sulcus supratoralis is present = 3; ambiguous = 1; absent = 0. Although, as in Solo V, the sulcus supratoralis is extraodinarily conspicuous, nevertheless there are instances (e.g., in Solo VI) where a supra-iniac fossa interrupts the course of the sulcus supratoralis in the midline. In fact, Weidenreich (1951, p. 255) says that the 'varying appearance of the middle torus portion in the Solo series represents different phases of its disintegration'. He thought the 'irregular depressions' above the middle portion of the torus was 'the first indication of the process of reduction'.

The Morphological Pattern

The values of these traits were totalled to provide a score for each skull and the scores for crania of five racial groups are shown in Table 1.

Table 1. Scores for 18 cranial traits of Solo man

	Australian (207)	Mongoloid (20)	Caucasoid (26)	New Guinean (80)	Solo (2)
Mean:	9.9	6.5	7.4	8.2	54
Range:	4-19	3-10	3-14	1-16	54-54

If a comparison is made between the values of the mean scores for the 18 characteristic Solo traits as shown here in Table 1 with the mean scores for the 17 characteristic *Homo erectus* traits as given in Table 1 in the paper of Macintosh and Larnach (1972), it may be thought that Solo traits are actually better represented in modern races than are those of *H. erectus*. It may therefore be thought to follow that there is an even better reason to place Solo man than *Homo erectus* in the ancestral line of Australian Aborigines. There are at least three objections to this.

(a) Both Solo man and the Aboriginal Australian are probably at least half a million years later in time than *Homo erectus,* and resemblances of the former two groups to each other and to *H. erectus,* are almost certainly due to the common inheritance of some traits from the latter.*

(b) In comparing the scores for the Solo traits with those for the *Homo erectus* traits it should be remembered that the scores of each depend upon traits usually quite different from each other.

* Jacob (personal communication, 1974) has new evidence suggesting contemporaneity of *Homo Erectus* and Solo man.

(c)   The reasons for not accepting Solo man as ancestral to the Australian Aborigines are believed to be adequate and they will be
considered in detail later on in this paper.

The scores of the 18 traits were also determined from the casts of the
following fossil skulls:

H. erectus erectus	=	28
H. erectus pekinensis	=	28
H. erectus leakeyi	=	16
Rhodesian	=	18
La Chapelle	=	7
Steinheim	=	3
Skhūl	=	4

It can be seen at once that the scores of Solo man differ widely not
only from those of modern man but also from those of ancient fossil
skulls.

It cannot be stressed too much that differences between these scores
are not measures of any of these skulls from one another. If they are to
be taken as measurements at all, they are probably rough measurements
of the resemblance of these skulls to Solo man in so far as the 18
selected traits are concerned. The closeness in value of the score of one
skull to that of another does not necessarily indicate that these skulls
closely resemble each other. For example, two-thirds (12) of the score (18)
of the Rhodesian skull is made up of values for individual traits which in
H. erectus leakeyi only total a value of one. Conversely, more than half
the score (9) of the latter (16) is due to traits which are not present in
the former. This caution does not apply to the comparison of scores
with those of the Solo skulls themselves, for the traits were selected from
them and they are all present.

However, the scores for the 18 traits characteristic of Solo man clearly
help us in two respects:

(1)   they completely discriminate Solo crania from the other crania
used in this comparison; and
(2)   they identify Solo skulls specifically.

Comparison of Individual Traits

For the purpose of calculating the percentage frequencies of individual
traits, only those cases where a trait shows a very close resemblance to
its condition in Solo man are included. This eliminates all borderline
cases.

Table 2 lists the percentage frequencies of each of the eighteen
traits in Solo man, Australians, New Guineans, East Asian Mongoloids
and in Caucasoids. The small numbers of the latter two racial stocks
may have introduced sampling errors. Eleven of the eighteen traits
occur, and usually in very small percentages, i.e. eleven in Australians

99

and ten in New Guineans, but only six of the traits are recorded for East Asian Mongoloids and five for Caucasoids. The Caucasoid crania used comprised twelve European and fourteen Indian skulls. The latter were added to build up the series.

Table 2. Percentage frequencies of Solo traits

Solo characters	Australian (207)	Mongoloid (20)	Caucasoid (26)	New Guinean (80)	Solo (2)
(1) Brow ridges divided	98.1	94.1	100.0	86.2	100.0
(2) Very large rounded zygomatic trigone	0.4	0.0	0.0	0.0	100.0
(3) Absence of distinct ophrionic groove	84.5	50.0	50.0	62.2	100.0
(4) Suprameatal tegmen	0.0	0.0	0.0	1.2	100.0
(5) Long diameter of external auditory meatus is horizontal	0.0	0.0	0.0	0.0	100.0
(6) Tympanic is convex and orientated horizontally	0.0	0.0	0.0	0.0	100.0
(7) Low squamous suture; no arch	0.5	0.0	3.8	1.2	100.0
(8) Squamo-tympanic fissure is transverse	3.4	5.0	0.0	5.0	100.0
(9) Squamo-tympanic fissure is on floor of glenoid fossa	0.0	0.0	0.0	0.0	100.0
(10) Absence of postglenoid tubercle	0.0	0.0	0.0	0.0	100.0
(11) Spine of petrosal crest	0.0	0.0	0.0	0.0	100.0
(12) Angling of petrous to tympanic in petro-tympanic axis	1.9	0.0	0.0	5.0	100.0
(13) Foramen ovale pit	0.0	0.0	0.0	0.0	100.0
(14) Juxtamastoid ridge	83.1	85.0	100.0	81.2	100.0
(15) Lambdoidal protuberance	1.4	0.0	0.0	1.2	100.0
(16) Marked ridge-shaped occipital torus	3.4	0.0	0.0	0.0	100.0
(17) External occipital crest emerging from occipital torus	13.0	5.0	3.8	2.5	100.0
(18) Marked sulcus supratoralis	8.7	5.0	0.0	6.2	100.0

Discussion

On the basis of this study it is difficult to point to any particular racial group as a substantial inheritor of Solo genes. An examination of either Table 1 or Table 2 should convince the most sceptical anthropologist that there is a great morphological difference between Solo man and modern man. What is common to both may merely indicate a common inheritance.

Furthermore, it should also be noted that the Solo skulls possess traits which are apparently unique:

(1) The foramen ovale is located at the bottom of a pit which may be 3 to 6 mm deep. In 3 of the 4 skulls where the base is intact enough for the observation to be made there is an accessory foramen ovale in the pit.

(2) There is no postglenoid tubercle present. It can be seen in all other fossil human crania as well as in anthropoids. It is present in *Homo erectus* and is particularly well marked in *H. erectus leakeyi*.

(3) 'In Solo man this [squamo-tympanic] fissure runs along the very floor of the [glenoid] fossa . . . The posterior wall is formed for its full extent solely by the tympanic plate' (Weidenreich, 1951, pp. 273-4).

These traits must have appeared in Solo man after he evolved from *Homo erectus*, for they distinguish Solo man from *Homo erectus* no less than they do from modern man. If it is postulated that Australians are modified descendents of Solo men, then this hypothesis would require that during the transformation of Solo men into Australians these traits were lost and their sites then reverted to a similar state to that of *Homo erectus*.

Two hypotheses might be put forward to avoid this difficulty:

(a) The Solo crania available might represent an extremely localized genetical dead end which became extinct. Outside that population was a hypothetical main body of Solo-like people who may not have developed these peculiar characteristics. It would then be possible to postulate that Australians are descended from this latter people. Only by such an extreme device of postulation can descent to Australians be visualized.

(b) Alternatively, as suggested by Weidenreich himself during a conversation with Birdsell (1967, p. 107), Solo man [with or without his unique features] hybridized with some other unspecified racial group and it was from these hybrids that the Australians descended. In the process the unique traits were lost.

However, whatever hypothesis is put forward, and however close the superficial likeness of Solo and Australian skulls, it must be accepted that there is a great morphological difference between the Solo crania we know and the crania of any modern group.

Summary

(1) Eighteen traits, carefully selected as characteristic of Solo crania, were used in this study. The frequencies of these individual traits in certain racial groups, including Australians, were compared.

(2) The values of all the 18 traits were totalled to give the score for each skull.

(3) Both the frequencies of individual traits and the scores for each skull show that there is a very real morphological difference between Solo crania and the skulls of modern racial groups such as Australians, East Asian Mongoloids, Caucasoids and New Guineans.

(4) The scores completely and unequivocally discriminate Solo crania from those of the other racial groups used in this comparison and they identify Solo skulls specifically.

(5) The occurrence of traits unique to Solo man is considered and the difficulties they introduce to any hypothesis which would derive Australians from Solo man are discussed.

REFERENCES

BIRDSELL, J. B., (1967) 'Preliminary data on the trihybrid origin of the Australian Aborigines', *Archaeological and Physical Anthropology in Oceania*, 2 (2), 100-55.

COON, C. S., (1962) *The Origin of Races*. New York.

JACOB, T., (1967) *Some Problems Pertaining to the Racial History of the Indonesian Region*. Utrecht.

LARNACH, S. L. & MACINTOSH, N. W. G., (1966) *The Craniology of the Aborigines of Coastal New South Wales*. Oceania Monographs No. 13, Sydney.

——, (1970) *The craniology of the Aborigines of Queensland*. Oceania Monographs No. 15, Sydney.

MACINTOSH, N. W. G. & LARNACH, S. L., (1972) 'The persistence of *Homo erectus* traits in Australian Aboriginal crania', *Archaeological and Physical Anthropology in Oceania*, 7 (1), 1-7.

THORNE, A. G., (1971) 'Mungo and Kow Swamp. Morphological variations in pleistocene Australians', *Mankind*, 8 (2), 85-9.

WEIDENREICH, F., (1943) 'The skull of *Sinanthropus pekinensis*. A comparative study of a primitive hominid skull', *Paleontol. Sinica.*, N.S., D (10), 1-298.

——, (1945) 'Giant early man from Java and South China', *Anthropol. Papers Am. Mus. Nat. Hist.*, 40 (1), 1-134.

——, (1951) 'Morphology of Solo Man', *Anthropol. Papers Am. Mus. Nat. Hist.*, 43 (3), 205-90.

8 THE IDENTIFICATION OF ABORIGINAL TRAITS IN FORENSIC MEDICINE

T. H. G. Oettle and S. L. Larnach

The clinical specialities of medicine have often returned to the basic sciences for specialized knowledge applicable to a particular problem. The Department of Anatomy has fulfilled these needs in most of the postgraduate training of the various specialities. In one author's specialty of Forensic Medicine the Department has been no less helpful. It is interesting to note that Sir Grafton Elliot Smith whom we commemorate with this symposium, made a room and no doubt some of his vast knowledge available to Sir Bernard Spilsbury in University College London (Dawson, 1938). In the same tradition he has seen the Professor of Anatomy here provide anatomical expertise in a range of circumstances that varied from reminding an ex-graduate in court of the relations between pericardium and heart to his own experience where he has been made aware of the anatomical traits to be found in Aboriginal crania and skeletal remains.

In the state of New South Wales, whenever skeletal remains are found which by their extent imply the death of a person, the coroner is involved. His function is to enquire into the circumstances surrounding the death of that individual by holding an inquest. The practice, however, is that if skeletal remains are Aboriginal in origin and are likely to predate the European settlement, no inquest is held. It is of interest to note that at the time of the introduction of the coroner in Britain in the eleventh century, part of his function was to determine if the body was Norman or if it was Saxon.

In addition the police have files of missing persons. These, because of population distribution are mainly European. They have to be considered relative to the geographical area where the skeletal remains are found, and excluded if possible.

The traits used are those set out by Larnach and Macintosh in *The Craniology of the Aborigines of Coastal New South Wales* (1966) from which List 1 is taken. The criteria distinguish between Aboriginal on one hand and European and Mongoloid on the other. Each trait is assessed in terms of the value shown, varying from 0, 1, 2, and 3, with the high figures being those commonly found in the Aboriginal. These values are then totalled and the final score places the particular cranium under examination into the relevant racial group. In the series from which the twenty traits were worked out, Aboriginal skulls had totals of over 40, with the majority over 44, while the highest score showed by a European skull was 32.

Some of the values are non-metrical, e.g., (2), (3), (4), etc. To assist in assessing these, the Department of Anatomy of the University of Sydney has prepared a series of stable casts which demonstrate the maxima to be found in the mid-range of assessment.

In addition, sexing of the crania is made by the application of the seven characteristics described by Larnach and Freedman (1964) and are shown in List 2. In the same way the high values for each occur more commonly in males. The numbers are totalled in the same way and in this instance the cut-off level is 11, those below being female and those above male.

Where other parts of the skeleton are present, these are used to determine such characteristics as age at death, height and sex.

The facility with which these factors have been able to be used has been much appreciated by me, because my involvement in an under-staffed service division necessarily limits the time available for such studies. The range of their application and their value to the coroners of this state may be shown by the following three cases.

Case 1

A skeleton was found under a derelict water tank in the Coffs Harbour area by a fourteen year old youth who was chasing a blue tongue lizard. The lizard hid under the tank and entered the skull. Skull and lizard were taken by the boy who when nearing his parents camp, extracted the lizard and hid the skull in a plastic bag in the local rain forest. About three weeks later when in Sydney he told the police of his find, and skull and skeleton were sent to the Division of Forensic Medicine in Sydney.

The skeleton showed some fracturing of the ribs on the left side. The skull showed minimal soft tissue remains still present, remarkably poor dentition, and as can be seen in Plate 1, some Aboriginal characteristics. It had a total score above the upper limit for European and below that for Aboriginal, and was female. The skeleton showed characteristics of an adult, height about 160 cm, and aged about the 5th decade.

The police had on their records a missing person who was described as being a quarter caste female, aged about 45 years, height 157 cm, living in the area where the skeleton was found, and whose de facto husband had a long history of violence. This last characteristic of their relationship enabled an absolute identification to be made. Three weeks before her disappearance this woman had been hospitalized for fracturing of her ribs and possible fracturing of her skull. The routine X-rays taken of her head enabled a comparison to be made of her dentition

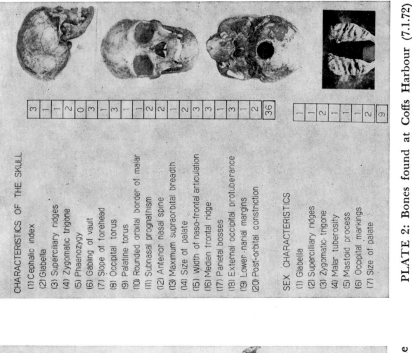

CHARACTERISTICS OF THE SKULL

(1) Cephalic index	1
(2) Glabella	1
(3) Superciliary ridges	1
(4) Zygomatic trigone	1
(5) Phaenozygy	1
(6) Gabling of vault	1
(7) Slope of forehead	1
(8) Occipital torus	1
(9) Palate torus	1
(10) Rounded orbital border of malar	3
(11) Subnasal prognathism	2
(12) Anterior nasal spine	3
(13) Maximum supraorbital breadth	1
(14) Size of palate	1
(15) Width of naso-frontal articulation	?
(16) Median frontal ridge	1
(17) Parietal bosses	1
(18) External occipital protuberance	3
(19) Lower narial margins	1
(20) Post-orbital constriction	3
	21

SEX CHARACTERISTICS

(1) Glabella	1
(2) Superciliary ridges	1
(3) Zygomatic trigone	1
(4) Malar tuberosity	1
(5) Mastoid process	
(6) Occipital markings	
(7) Size of palate	
	4

PLATE 1: Fragment of skull found at Engadine (8.4.72). X-rays of dentition

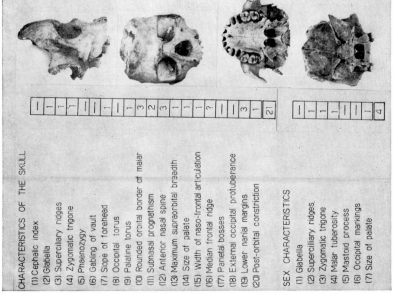

CHARACTERISTICS OF THE SKULL

(1) Cephalic index	3
(2) Glabella	1
(3) Superciliary ridges	1
(4) Zygomatic trigone	2
(5) Phaenozygy	0
(6) Gabling of vault	3
(7) Slope of forehead	1
(8) Occipital torus	3
(9) Palate torus	1
(10) Rounded orbital border of malar	1
(11) Subnasal prognathism	2
(12) Anterior nasal spine	2
(13) Maximum supraorbital breadth	1
(14) Size of palate	2
(15) Width of naso-frontal articulation	3
(16) Median frontal ridge	3
(17) Parietal bosses	1
(18) External occipital protuberance	3
(19) Lower narial margins	1
(20) Post-orbital constriction	2
	36

SEX CHARACTERISTICS

(1) Glabella	1
(2) Superciliary ridges	1
(3) Zygomatic trigone	2
(4) Malar tuberosity	1
(5) Mastoid process	1
(6) Occipital markings	1
(7) Size of palate	2
	9

PLATE 2: Bones found at Coffs Harbour (7.1.72)

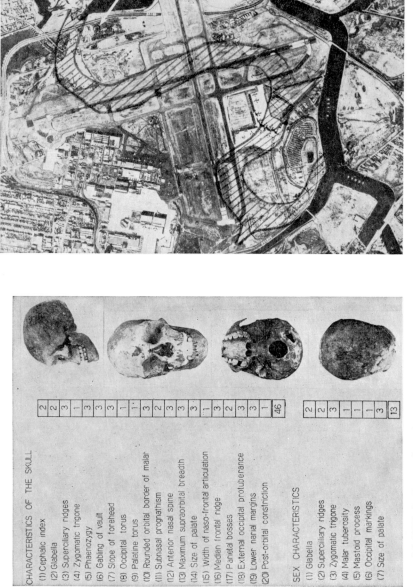

CHARACTERISTICS OF THE SKULL

(1) Cephalic index	2
(2) Glabella	2
(3) Superciliary ridges	3
(4) Zygomatic trigone	1
(5) Phaenozygy	3
(6) Gabling of vault	3
(7) Slope of forehead	3
(8) Occipital torus	1
(9) Palatine torus	1
(10) Rounded orbital border of malar	3
(11) Subnasal prognathism	2
(12) Anterior nasal spine	3
(13) Maximum supraorbital breadth	3
(14) Size of palate	3
(15) Width of naso-frontal articulation	1
(16) Median frontal ridge	3
(17) Parietal bosses	2
(18) External occipital protuberance	3
(19) Lower narial margins	3
(20) Post-orbital constriction	1
	46

SEX CHARACTERISTICS

(1) Glabella	2
(2) Superciliary ridges	2
(3) Zygomatic trigone	3
(4) Malar tuberosity	1
(5) Mastoid process	1
(6) Occipital markings	3
(7) Size of palate	3
	13

PLATE 3: Bones found at Mascot (11.10.71)

PLATE 4: Aerial photograph of Cook's River

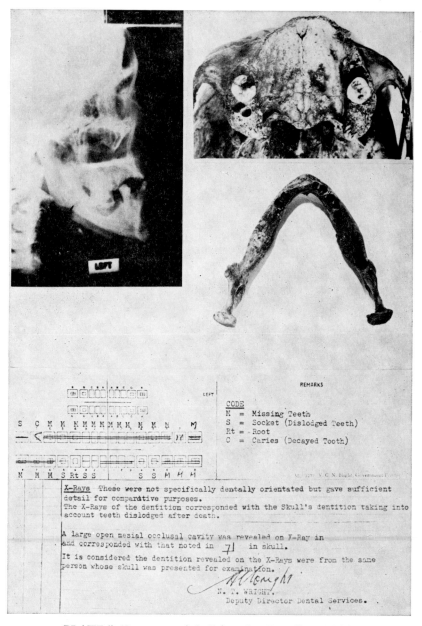

PLATE 5: Fragments of skull found at Engadine (8.4.72)

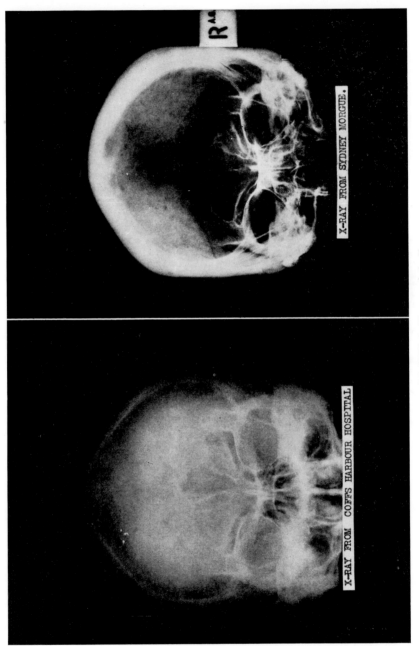

X-RAY FROM SYDNEY MORGUE.

X-RAY FROM COFFS HARBOUR HOSPITAL

PLATE 6: X-rays of skulls

with that found in the skull sent to Sydney. Beside the exact similarity of the dentition, a cavity shown in the routine X-ray is demonstrated in the skull (see Plate 2).

In addition, by taking an X-ray of the skull in the same plane as that taken at the Coffs Harbour Hospital and showing the frontal sinuses, that taken of the skull in Sydney was shown to be the same configuration (Achenson, 1965) as that of the woman in Coffs Harbour (Plate 3).

Case 2

In the second case a skeleton was found near the perimeter of Mascot airport by a bulldozer driver. In fact the skeleton was exposed by wind erosion.

The police had noticed during the excavation of the skeleton that there were in close association with the remains, items which were dated as being 1914-18 war buttons, a buckle and pieces of boot leather. The question was raised as to whether this represented the remains of an ex-soldier with all the associated implications.

However, the site was established to be that of the south bank of the Cooks river prior to the rechannelling of the river when the aerodrome was rebuilt in the thirties (see Plate 4). This site had been an Aboriginal camp and later a gypsy camp. A variety of relics of these functions were present all over the site.

The skeleton was incomplete. The bones were very fragile, and they showed an accretion of a woody material, which might be explained by the fact that much of the land to the west of the shoreline was marshy. From those parts of the skeleton available, it could be established that they belonged to an Aboriginal male (see Plate 5), height about 167 cm and age at death in the 3rd to 4th decades. Because the bones were very fragile, the time since the demise of the individual was felt to predate the European settlement and no inquest was held.

Case 3

The third case is that of a skull fragment found under a house in a southern Sydney suburb. Views of this fragment and the assessment are shown in Plate 6. Additional traits such as the sphenofrontal groove and crest were used to establish that this was the remains of an Aboriginal female adolescent, at the time of death aged about 13. The third molars had not erupted and the tooth development on X-ray was most consistent with the age mentioned. The sphenoid had not fused with the occiput—an occurrence of about the 25th year in the European. The teeth showed minimal wear. No frontal sinus development was found in X-rays taken of the fragment. Frontal sinuses develop slowly until puberty when their growth is much more rapid to about the 20th year. During this time the development is above the upper limits of the orbits. In the European agenesis occurs in about 4 per cent (Camps,

1969; Achenson, 1965). In a series of 69 Aboriginal skulls examined for this feature by Logan Turner, 30 per cent showed it to be absent (Cunningham, 1908).

The variety of skeletal remains that have been submitted to the Division of Forensic Medicine has persisted. They always present an additional facet to be examined and elucidated, and it would seem that there is an extensive opportunity to investigate a wide variety of Aboriginal anatomical characteristics apart from their craniology, where the parameters for Aborigines are not yet known. The paleopathology, too needs investigation and recording.

REFERENCES

ACHERSON, N., (1965) *Identification by Frontal Sinus Prints*, Lewis, London.

CAMPS, F. E. (ed.), *Recent Advances in Forensic Pathology*. Churchill, London, pp. 155-6.

CUNNINGHAM, D. J., (1908) 'The evolution of the eyebrow region of the forehead', *Trans. Roy. Soc. Edin.*, 46, 283.

DAWSON, W. R. (ed.), (1938) *Sir Grafton Elliot Smith*, Jonathan Cape, London, p. 178.

FENNER, F. J., (1939) : 'The Australian Aboriginal Skull. Its non-metrical morphological characters.' *Trans. Roy. Soc. South Aust.*, 63 (2), 248-306.

LARNACH, S. L. & FREEDMAN, L., (1964) 'Sex determination of Aboriginal crania from Coastal New South Wales, Australia', *Records of the Australian Museum*, 26 (11), 295-308.

LARNACH, S. L. & MACINTOSH, N. W. G. (1966) *The Craniology of the Aborigines of Coastal New South Wales*, The Oceania Monographs, No 13, Sydney, pp. 82-3.

MARTIN, R., (1928) *Lehrbuch deAnthropologue*, 2nd Ed., 3 vols, Jena.

List 1: 20 racially characteristic traits of the New South Wales coastal Aboriginal crania

(1) Cephalic index: 3 = below 75; 2 = 75 to 80; 1 = above 80. (87.8 per cent show an index below 75, and none above 78)

(2) Glabella: 1 = below Martin's grade 4; 2 = Martin's grade 4; 3 = above Martin's grade 4. (mean for the grades was 4.2)

(3) Superciliary ridges: 1, 2, 3 according to grades of size. (medium to large in 84.6 per cent)

(4) Zygomatic trigone: 1, 2, 3 according to grades of size. (medium to large in 89.1 per cent)

(5) Phaenozygy: 0 = absent; 1 = trace; 3 = distinct. (100 per cent in males)

(6) Gabling of vault: 0 = absent; 1 = trace; 3 = distinct. (present in 98.5 per cent)

(7) Slope of forehead (frontal curvature index): 1 = over 24.7; 2 = 23.5 to 24.7; 3 = under 23.5. (80.6 per cent show an index below 24.8)

(8) Occipital torus: 0 = absent; 1 = trace; 3 = distinct. (present in 100 per cent of males)

(9) Palatine torus: 0 = absent; 1 = trace; 3 = distinct. (present in 89.8 per cent)

(10) Rounded orbital border of malar: 0 = absent; 1 = trace; 3 = distinct. (present in 84.6 per cent)

(11) Subnasal prognathism: 1, 2, 3 according to prominence. (96.5 per cent of males show some degree)

(12) Anterior nasal spine: 3 = under Broca's grade 3; 2 = grade 3; 1 = over Broca's grade 3. (87.9 per cent show grade 3 or less)

(13) Maximum supraorbital breadth: 1 = under 104 mm; 2 = 104 to 108 mm; 3 = over 108 mm. (mean was 110.41 in the present series)

(14) Size of palate: 1 = module under 35; 2 = 35 to 39; 3 = module over 39. (98.4 per cent of cases showed a module of over 35)

(15) Width of naso-frontal articulation: 1 = under 10 mm; 2 = 10 to 12 mm; 3 = over 12 mm. (81.7 per cent were over 10 mm)

(16) Median frontal ridge: 0 = absent; 1 = trace; 3 = distinct. (present in 67.7 per cent)

(17) Parietal bosses: 1 = prominent; 2 = medium; 3 = slight. (69.7 per cent were slight and only 6.1 per cent were prominent)

(18) External occipital protuberance: 3 = absent; 1 = trace; 0 = distinct. (present in only 6.1 per cent)

(19) Lower narial margins: 0 = forma anthropina; 1 = ambiguous in form; 3 = distinctly non-anthropine. (90 per cent were distinctly non-anthropine and 10 per cent showed some resemblance to the forma anthropina)

(20) Post-orbital constriction: 1 = under 16 mm; 2 = 16 to 18 mm; 3 = over 18 mm. (77.1 per cent of cases over 18 mm—mean was 20 mm)

This is the difference between the maximum supraorbital breadth and the minimum post-orbital diameter (when the latter measurement is taken on the fronto-sphenoidal suture).

List 2: 7 characters used for sexing Australian Aboriginal crania from coastal New South Wales

Character:	Remarks:	Class 2 limits:
(1) Glabella	Prominence was assessed according to Martin's modification of Broca's scale (Martin, 1928).	Grade 4 (Martin)
(2) Superciliary ridges	These were graded according to their prominence. Their presence is judged independently of the size of the glabella and zygomatic trigone.	B. 171B 5
(3) Zygomatic trigone	The development of this feature (also known as the trigonum supraorbitale or external angular process) is similarly independent and should be assessed without reference to the above two.	= or 473 N.P.

(4) Malar tuberosity — Prominence of the tuberosity, which, as noted by Fenner (1939), may take the form of a ridge in the Australian Aboriginal. — 123 = or S. 744

(5) Mastoid process — Length x width x depth (nrst. mm) ÷ 100. — 55-80

(6) Occipital markings — General ruggedness, depth of fossae for rectus capitis posterior minor and semispinalis capitis mm, ruggedness of inion region, development of occipital crest and torus. — = or 512 = or 123

(7) Size of palate — Maximum alveolar length x breadth (nrst. mm) ÷ 100. — 35-39

9 EARLY MAN IN NEW GUINEA

J. Peter White

The ancestry and evolution of the humans who currently occupy New Guinea is still largely obscure. Apart from the celebrated Aitape cranial fragments (Hossfeld, 1965) and some fragmentary material from the Aibura site in the Eastern Central Highlands (Freedman, 1972), both dated to within the last 5,000 years and showing no significant differences from present populations, no fossil human material has been described. Recourse has therefore been had to the more refractory data of blood groups, stature, and aspects of culture such as language. The archaeological material derived from human activity in New Guinea and surrounding regions, however, is directly relevant to our view of the technological potential of early *Homo sapiens* in general.

This paper will argue that the prehistory of 'Indo-Pacific man', as Golson (1972) calls him, directly challenges the Eurocentric view of prehistory which is commonly held by people who have been educated within the European tradition. Such a view of the past is deep-rooted. We have been educated to look upon the technological development of our own civilization, the rise of our own race (to use that term in a very general way) and even perhaps the developmental adventures of *Homo sapiens* and Neanderthal man in Europe and Southwest Asia as *the* story of mankind. Such a view is reinforced by the plethora of prehistoric data from that area when compared with our scanty knowledge about other parts of the world.

Fifty years ago the situation was even more extreme. One might suggest, for instance, that there could be an emotional link between the success (and excesses) of diffusionist theories and the successes (and excesses) of European imperialism before World War I. European, especially British imperialism was, of course, the most superb example of the diffusion of culture. If it were seen as the latest and best model of a continuing historical process then this, in a very general way, would tend to validate the earlier examples.

Within the last twenty years however, the idea that it was only in one place and at one time that man ceased to be a hunter and gatherer and became a farmer and city dweller has been abandoned by many of us: the evidence from the Americas of the independent origin of agriculture over the last 7,000 years and the evolution of an indigenous form of city life based on this is just too overwhelming. But we are only just beginning to learn about the equally ancient and apparently equally independent developments of a similar kind in Southeast Asia and the western Pacific. Two examples of this will now be outlined.

(1) In most of the Old World the evidence for man's use of the sea and its resources at any time during the Pleistocene is so sparse that two commentators recently remarked:

> there is no evidence that the resources of river and sea were utilised until the late pre-agricultural period . . . it is likely that the basic problem in utilization of resources from the sea is that man cannot swim naturally (Washburn & Lancaster, 1968, p. 294).

This is a view which has gained some currency (e.g., Binford, 1968), although it is clearly inaccurate as far as the exploitation of riverine and littoral resources are concerned (e.g., McBurney, 1968, p. 59; Garrod et al., 1928, p. 109-12; Garrod, 1926). On the other hand, there is no evidence in European sites of deep sea fishing during the Palaeolithic (Chard, 1969, p. 152) and this must suggest the absence of adequate watercraft (see also Clark, 1952). Further, although crossings of the Straits of Gibraltar from Acheulean times onward are frequently claimed and some are a priori likely, many may indeed be unnecessary to our cultural constructs. For example, Smith's demonstration (1966) that the French Solutrean industries have an indigenous origin removes the need to postulate makers of Aterian tanged points voyaging across any part of the Mediterranean Sea.

The situation would appear to be somewhat different in the region to the west of New Guinea. The biogeographic realms of Australia and Southeast Asia have, of course, been separated by the sea barriers of Wallacea for millions of years, with the necessary implication that when man crossed this barrier he must have used water-craft of some kind. Bark-sheet canoes seem the most probable craft, given their widespread distribution within Australia in more recent times. Even during any period of maximum low sea level, such craft must have carried man over many kilometers of ocean. The Sunda route, through Timor, would require one voyage of around 100 km, while the more northerly Banda route required at least five crossings of between 10 and 80 km (N. W. G. Macintosh, personal communication). Craft capable of making these voyages were available at least 30,000 years ago. This age can be claimed with certainty on the basis of the radio-carbon dates for settlement in the Australian realm.

Within New Guinea, the earliest settlement so far discovered is dated to c.26,000 BP (White, Crook & Ruxton, 1970). Since this site is at an altitude of some 2,000 m. A.S.L. it may be inferred that occupation of the coastal regions occurred somewhat earlier. There is no evidence for believing, and I can see no particularly compelling reason to believe, that we have already discovered the earliest settlements in New Guinea —or Australia. There have been recent suggestions, indeed, of man's arrival within Wallacea during Pleistocene times (Glover & Glover, 1970), and even the occasional, suspect discovery in Australia.

However that may be, the point is rather that we need to think of man as adapting to a tropical environment within which familiarity with the sea and its resources was a normal, not an unusual part of his existence. Even if Washburn and Lancaster are right in saying man cannot swim naturally, do we have any real reason to suspect that the invention was made by *Homo sapiens* rather than by Neanderthal man or even earlier?

(2) The second example comes from much later in New Guinea's history. In 1966-7 pig bones were reported from two archaeological sites in the Highlands of Papua New Guinea, and they were dated to between 5,000 and 6,500 years ago (Bulmer, 1966; White, 1972). The number of specimens was too small for much morphological data to be determined, while modern ethnographies suggest that the traditional distinction between 'domestic' and 'wild' animals is unlikely to be very relevant in the New Guinea area. On the other hand, the presence of pigs in association with human occupation sites was suggestive. Pigs, of course, are not native to the Australian realm and while they might have arrived by accident—as Alfred Russell Wallace thought when he saw a pig swimming 'with great ease and swiftness' between Singapore and the Peninsula of Malacca (1869, ii, p. 141)—that this should have occurred at a time when, on theoretical grounds (Sauer, 1952), a more intensive symbiotic relationship between pigs and man could be expected to occur, seemed too happy a coincidence to be expected. Bulmer therefore suggested that these pigs indicated the presence of early agriculture and husbandry. Within the last two years this has been confirmed by palynological data which show forest clearance has been proceeding in the Highlands for at least the last 5,000 years (Powell, 1970).

The data from the New Guinea Highlands is, to date, the most comprehensive evidence of an independent agricultural development, the sources for which must be sought more generally in Southeast Asia (e.g., Solheim, 1972; Chang, 1970). While some domesticates, such as sugarcane, may well be indigenous cultigens, the majority of the plants and animals which have come under man's control belong to the Southeast Asian rather than the Australian realm. This in turn implies a development considerably earlier than 5,000 years ago. We know from both Southwest Asia (Flannery, 1969) and Central America (Byers, 1967) that early forms of agriculture develop for several thousand years within the natural environments of the plants and animals concerned; it is only after this that we find agriculturalists colonizing new and different environments. For the New Guinea Highlands, a cool montane marginal area within the tropics, to be successfully colonized, man must have had a comprehensive and adaptable understanding of his cultivated food resources.

These deductions in themselves imply that agriculture in Southeast Asia developed synchronously with that of Southwest Asia. That it was an independent development is implied on two grounds. The first is that there is to date no evidence whatever of external influences: neither the

Egyptians, Greeks nor even the Indian cultures left any traces at this stage in the Southeast Asian cultural record. The second ground is that the type of agricultural development which occurred was quite different to that in other parts of the world. The quality of this difference has been expounded elesewhere (e.g., Barrau, 1965), but I would point out that to place primary reliance on root and tree crops, on swidden agriculture and on pigs is a wholly different system to that which we know developed in southwest Asia and which is the basis for our own food producing system today.

It is certainly the case that the particular interpretations I am supporting here will prove to be as dependent upon the world-views of the current generation of archaeologists as were Grafton Elliot Smith's— and probably as mistaken as some of us now consider many of his to be (Daniel, 1962). This perhaps indicates the real value of this centenary celebration—not the parade of new knowledge or revised interpretations, but the opportunity to recognize that the challenge provided by older views of our history enlightens and illuminates our own researches.

REFERENCES

BARRAU, J., (1965) 'Gardens of Oceania', *Discovery*, 1, 12-19. (Peabody Museum, Yale University.)

BINFORD, L. R., (1968) 'Post Pleistocene Adaptations', in *New Perspectives in Archaeology*. Binford, S. R. & L. R. (eds), Aldine, pp. 313-42.

BULMER, S. E., (1966) 'Pig bone from two archaeological sites in the New Guinea Highlands', *J. Polynesian Soc.*, 75, 504-5.

BYERS, D. S., (1967) *The Prehistory of the Tehuacan Valley*, Vol. 1. Texas University Press.

CHANG, K-C., (1970) 'The beginnings of agriculture in the Far East', *Antiquity*, 44, 175-85.

CHARD, C. S., (1969) *Man in Prehistory*. McGraw Hill.

CLARK, J. G. D., (1952) *Prehistoric Europe, The Economic Basis*. Methuen.

DANIEL, G. E., (1962) *The Idea of Prehistory*. Watts.

FLANNERY, K. V., (1969) 'Origins and ecological effects of early domestication in Iran and the Near East', in *The Domestication and Exploitation of Plants and Animals*. Ucko, P. J. & Dimbleby, G. W. (eds), Aldine, pp. 73-100.

FREEDMAN, L., (1972) 'Human skeletal remains from Aibura Cave, New Guinea', in 'Ol Tumbuna'. White, J. P., *Terra Australis*, 2 pp. 153-9. (Dept of Prehistory, Australian National University).

GARROD, D. A. E., (1926) *The Upper Palaeolithic Age in Britain*. Cambridge University Press.

GARROD, D. A. E., *et. al.*, (1928) 'Excavation of a Mousterian rock shelter at Devil's Tower, Gibraltar', *J. Roy. Anthropological Inst.*, 58, 33-113.

GLOVER, I. C. & GLOVER, E. A., (1970) 'Pleistocene flaked stone tools from Timor and Flores', *Mankind*, 7, 188-90.

GOLSON, J., (1972) 'The remarkable history of Indo-Pacific man', *Search*, 3, 13-21.

HOSSFELD, P. S., (1965) 'Radiocarbon dating and palaeoecology of the Aitape Fossil human remains', *Proc. Roy. Soc. Vic.*, 78, 161-5.

MCBURNEY, C. B. M., (1968) *The Haua Fteah*. Cambridge University Press.

POWELL, J., (1970) 'The history of agriculture in the New Guinea Highlands', *Search*, 1, 199-200.

SAUER, C., (1952) [1969] *Agricultural Origins and Dispersals*. M.I.T. Press.

SMITH, P. E. L., (1966) 'Le Solutréen en France. *Publications de l'Institut de Préhistoire de l'Université de Bordeaux, Memoire 5*.

SOLHEIM, W. G. II, (1972) 'An earlier agricultural revolution', *Sci. Amer.*, 226 (4), 34-41.

WALLACE, A. R., (1869) *The Malay Archipelago*. Macmillan and Co.

WASHBURN, S. L. & LANCASTER, J. B., (1968) 'The Evolution of Hunting', in *Man the Hunter*, Lee, R. B. & De Vore, I. (eds), Aldine, pp. 293-303.

WHITE, J. P., (1972) 'Ol Tumbuna' *Terra Australis*, 2. (Dept of Prehistory. Australian National University).

WHITE, J. P., CROOK, K. A. W. & RUXTON, B. P., (1970) 'Kosipe: a late Pleistocene site in the Papuan Highlands', *Proc. Prehist. Soc.*, 36, 152-70

IO PERSPECTIVES ON SOME PROBLEMS OF EARLY MAN COMMON TO AMERICA AND AUSTRALIA

T. D. Stewart

Introduction

In the course of the last phase of man's spread over the face of the earth two geographical divisions have come to be recognized: an Old World and a New World. The Old World, consisting of the nearly continuous continental land masses of Eurasia and Africa, constituted, for all practical purposes, the whole of the documented world until 1492 when Columbus discovered lands across the Atlantic from Europe. He assumed that he had reached Marco Polo's Indies and Cathay but this identification turned out to be wishful thinking. Thereupon the astonishment with which Columbus' geographical misconception had been received gave way to greater astonishment that a New World could have remained so long unknown to enlightened Europeans; a discontinuous New World, moreover, that grew in expanse as explorations continued until by the mid-eighteenth century it rivalled that of the Old*.

To say that anyone *discovered* any part of the New World as recently as the fifteenth to eighteenth centuries is, of course, to indulge in an anachronism. By then virtually all of the habitable lands of the New World were already long occupied. As ultimately revealed, especially by Cook's voyages to the Pacific in 1765-79, there are only two widely-separated points, both on the eastern side of Asia, where the Old and New Worlds approach one another closely (Figure 10.1). One of these points is in the vicinity of the Arctic Circle where the 55-mile-wide Bering Strait separates Asia and North America; the other is just below the Equator where a succession of straits, none of great width, separates Asia from a series of islands, and ultimately one or more of the islands from the continent of Australia. In other words, the main continental areas of the New World are outliers of Asia, for which reason prehistoric Asians were the real discoverers of the New World.

* During the symposia I was chided for my provincialism in thinking that the expression 'New World' refers solely to America. As a result, the present Introduction reflects my newly-acquired point of view.

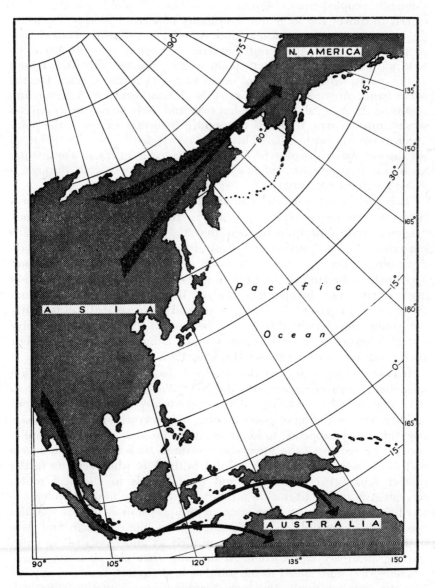

Figure 10.1 Map showing the only two points of near contact between the Old and New Worlds, and the main routes through them by which the New World was originally peopled.

A simple statement to the effect that America and Australia were originally peopled from different parts of Asia in prehistoric times fails utterly to convey the scale and significance of a tremendously important dual event in the history of mankind. America is a continuous land mass around 15 million square miles in area, extending some 10,000 miles southward from its far-northern point of near contact with Asia. Except at this point, broad expanses of ocean surround it on all sides. On the other hand, Australia is the largest land mass between America and southeastern Asia, albeit not elongated and only some three million square miles in area. It, too, is surrounded by oceans except at the point of near contact with Asia. This means that from the standpoint of prehistoric Asian discoverers and invaders each of these continental areas was a geographic *cul-de-sac*: A land mass accessible through a single restricted entrance.

This picture takes on an extra significance when it is realized that a *cul-de-sac* can be converted into a trap through closure of the lone entrance. It is now quite certain that the water level in the straits separating North America and Australia from Asia varied in depth, depending upon the amount of water taken up from the oceans and deposited on the land in the form of glaciers. At the peaks of glaciation many of the straits became land bridges. But in the interglacial periods the oceans transgressed the land bridges and again created straits. Without going into details, this process became in effect a one-way valve system allowing man (and at times other animals) to enter the New World, but rarely to return (cf. Hopkins, 1967, p. 476).

It is one thing to suggest that sea-level changes related to glaciation facilitated man's migration into the New World and quite another to show that he took advantage of the opportunity at one time and not another. Yet the timing of man's crossing over is crucial to reconstructing everything that happened to him thereafter. To some extent this applies also to the sedentes—the men who remained back in Asia. To better understand why this is so, it is helpful to think of what went on in the contact zone between the Old and New Worlds in chemical terms. Ancient Asia can be likened to a retort in which a solution (population) was being prepared. At some stage in the preparation of this solution two samples were siphoned off into test tubes (the American and Australian *cul-de-sacs*). These samples were then set aside (isolated) to finish reacting and reach equilibrium. At the same time new elements (genes, disease germs) were added to the solution in the retort, heat was applied (climatic amelioration), and new combinations (mutations) formed. Thought of in this way the contents of the test tubes now constitute a record of the nature of the solution in the retort at the time they were withdrawn. By analyzing the samples it should be possible to tell whether they lack some of the elements now in the retort. But this depends upon the rate of change in the samples during the process of reaching equilibrium; in other words, on how long they have been isolated.

The point to which all of the foregoing has been leading is that North America and Australia (the only parts of the New World that will concern us from here on) have in common numerous anthropological problems relating to their aboriginal populations owing to the latter's similar geographical setting, their obvious derivation from Asia, and the length of their isolation, whatever this may turn out to be.

Elliot Smith, the man in whose honor we are meeting, showed a general awareness of this situation when he wrote his book on 'Human History' (1929). This is best seen in his Figure 13, which has some features in common with my Figure 1. His figure is entitled, 'Map to suggest the directions of the wanderings of the various races . . . to reach the areas in which they ultimately found a home'. The directions are indicated by arrows, among which are two pointing toward Asia from the centre of the Mediterranean race in the Near East. One of the arrows passes through southern and southeastern Asia to terminate in Australia; the other passes northeastward to the centre of the Mongols in China and then sends off a branch toward the Bering Strait and North America off the map. In the accompanying text (p. 50) Elliot Smith added: 'But when [the penetration of these offshore lands] happened there is no evidence upon which to base any decision'.

I would like to think that Elliot Smith's acceptance of the invitation from the National Geological Survey of China to visit Peking in 1930 was motivated in part by his interest in the origins and characteristics of the New World populations. Although likely, I am unable to prove that it was indeed the case. The immediate purpose of the trip was to examine the newly discovered fossil remains of Sinanthropus *(Homo erectus)*, and the reports of his observations thereon (e.g., Smith, 1931) deal exclusively with evolutionary interpretations.

Incidentally, the only time I ever saw Elliot Smith was when he stopped over in Baltimore on his way back to London and lectured at the Johns Hopkins Medical School on his impressions of the Sinanthropus remains. My main recollection of the occasion, I regret to say, is visual: an image of a distinguished-looking gentleman, speaking extemporaneously with an air of authority. I was not so interested in ancient man at that time.

Since I am unable to connect Elliot Smith and my present subject more closely, I will proceed simply to consider some of the anthropological problems that stem from the original peopling of the New World and therefore are common to North America and Australia. In doing so I am better able, of course, to present and weigh the evidence from North America than that from Australia. But even with this handicap I regard the effort as worthwhile, especially on an occasion such as this when the examination of broad concepts is in order, because too often the problems in question are not viewed as related in the manner described.

Dating Aboriginal Man's Arrival in the New World

Since at least an approximation of the time of man's first crossing into the New World is crucial to studying the problems to which this event gave rise, it must be considered first. For reasons that will appear, the surest way of pin-pointing the time is by finding skeletal or cultural remains of the first invaders and dating them, directly if possible, by isotopic means. This is easier said than done, because the invasions probably began as a mere trickle and the search for the remaining evidence, either at the entrance to, or within, each *cul-de-sac* takes on the character of 'looking for a needle in a haystack'. Nevertheless, during the 20 years in which the C_{14} dating method has been available the reported ages for human bones and/or cultural remains found in circumstances suggesting antiquity have been extended further and further back in time both in North America and in Australia. Unfortunately, however, some of the reported dates are not widely accepted and for this reason only a general appraisal of the situation will be attempted here.

In North America numerous sites of the Clovis people—hunters of the Pleistocene megafauna who used distinctive stone spear points—have been dated rather consistently to the short period of time between 11,000 and 12,000 years ago (Haynes, 1969). The locations of these early sites in the central plains of the United States led to the idea that the Clovis people were the first true North Americans (in contrast to those who got no further than Alaska), since the only way that early man could have reached the interior of the continent at the close of the last ice age was through a north-south trending corridor in the waning continental ice sheet just east of the Canadian Rocky Mountains. Prior to the 12,000 year date, the argument goes, the corridor was closed for a long time and for this reason earlier-arriving men would have had time enough to leave much evidence of their presence. But this is not the case; evidence of earlier-man's presence either has not been found or its identification is disputed.

This argument has lost some of its weight in the last few years owing to the perfection of a method by Rainer Berger and associates (1964) for cleaning collagen (the organic constituent of bone) and thereby making possible the more-accurate dating of old bones. Previous attempts to date bones had failed because whole bones were used and no way had been found to free them from contaminants. Bone dating still suffers from the limitation that collagen tends to deteriorate with time and therefore yields minimal rather than maximal dates.

Following this technological break-through, the testing of putatively early, but previously undated bones, resulted in some being declared older than 12,000 years. The oldest so far is the Los Angeles skull with an age placed at $>23,600$ years (Berger, *et al.*, 1971). This is not a finite figure because the sample supplied did not fill the counting chamber. The fact that this early C_{14} date was obtained directly from the bones of a man is impressive, even though the recovered remains of this man consisted of an isolated skull lacking a cultural setting.

Age determinations have continued to be made, of course, on carbon from other putatively ancient sources, but the very old dates obtained in this way usually rest on assumptions as to man's relationship to the carbon sources. The earliest indirect date is still probably that of the Lewisville, Texas, site, said to be 38,000 years (Krieger, 1964). Aside from the charred vegetal matter used in the C_{14} test, nothing much else seems to have been recovered from this site to indicate man's presence there so far back in time. Indeed, the failure of the earliest dated sites to form a pattern connecting man with a distinctive culture is a strong argument for caution in accepting them.

The distinction that I have made between early man in the interior of North America and in Alaska is an important one, owing to the factor of glaciation. Geologists have found that the interior of Alaska and adjacent parts of Siberia, unlike Canada and the northern parts of the United States, were unglaciated in Pleistocene times (Hopkins, 1967). They have found also that at the peaks of glaciation the water level in the shallow parts of the Bering and Chukchi Seas separating Alaska and Siberia was lowered so much that a 1,000-mile-wide land-bridge was formed. The unglaciated areas, together with the land-bridge, have been designated 'Beringia'. The significance of Beringia for early man is that when it existed he could easily reach Alaska. But to pass southward into the interior of the continent he had to wait for the glaciers to wane and a corridor to open up. This means that the dating of early man remains in Alaska does not tell how long man has been in North America proper.*

In his studies of Beringia Hopkins (1967) has provided the following time periods for the existence of the Bering Land Bridge: (1) Between 10,000 and 14,000 years ago it was open twice briefly; (2) between 15,000 and 25,000 years ago it was open continuously; and (3) the time of the next earliest opening is not clearly indicated, but may have been around 50,000 years ago. Since, as already indicated, changes of sea level are a world-wide phenomenon, these dates have a bearing also on the other contact point between the Old and New Worlds—Southeast Asia-Australia—to which I will now turn.

It has long been evident from bathometric data that, just as in the case of the seas between Alaska and Siberia, those surrounding the island chain extending between Southeast Asia and Australia also are shallow. But they differ from their northern counterparts in not being continuously shallow. At least two of the inter-island straits are submarine trenches—Wallace's Deep and Weber's Deep—far too deep to have ever

---

* After this was written Irving and Harington (1973) reported a date of 27,000 $+$ 3,000 $-$ 2,000 years BP for a worked piece of caribou bone found in the northeastern part of Beringia.

been obliterated by changes in sea level within the period of human history. Therefore, the conclusion is inescapable that when glaciation caused the oceans to reach their lowest level between 18,000 and 20,000 years ago men could have travelled much of the way from Southeast Asia to Australia fairly directly by land, but still had to cross 60-mile-wide stretches of water at such points as those mentioned. According to Macintosh (1972), the latter circumstance implies that, if man really first made the trip at that time, he was in a cultural stage which enabled him at least to construct a sea-worthy raft—probably a not too great a feat in a tropical environment. By extension, it also implies that, if man's first arrival in Australia had already taken place prior to 20,000 years ago, some 50,000 years (according to the Bering-Sea findings cited above) must be allotted to his presence in Australia.

Proof as to which of these crossing-times was first utilized rests ultimately, as in North America, upon finding the oldest evidence of man's presence inside the continent. According to Macintosh (1972), the earliest reported Australian dates relate to finds at Lake Mungo in western New South Wales. Here, he says, 'proven dates of 32,000 years include cremated burial of human bones dated by charcoal at 25,000 BP from the same site' (p. 4). Leaving aside the likelihood that these earliest Australian dates relate to more substantial evidence of man's presence than is the case of the earliest dates cited above for North America, the interesting thing is that the same time range is represented in the two areas. Furthermore, this time range is beyond that for the last maximum lowering of the sea level. There is growing pressure on conservative-minded anthropologists, therefore, to admit that man started moving eastward out of Asia at the two available exits long before the last maximum lowering of sea level.

Physical Types of the First New World Men

If man was moving eastward out of Asia well before 20,000 years ago, what does this mean in terms of the kinds of men involved? So far as the evidence goes, the earliest people to reach North America were little, if any, different from modern Indians. They were predominantly Mongoloid in racial type and by Clovis times, around 12,000 years ago, had a culture traceable back through Siberia to Upper Paleolithic Europe (Müller-Beck, 1967). By contrast, the earliest people to reach Australia seem to have been unlike any of the present peoples of the Old World in that they had physical features best known to us in fossil forms. Also, their tools and weapons, which may have been simpler than those carried by the earliest Americans, underwent little elaboration in the new environment, so that by 10,000 to 12,000 years ago they were quite unlike those of the Clovis people in America.

But whether or not these physical and cultural differences reflect different departure dates from Asia is complicated by geographical and climatological considerations. The northeastern and southeastern tips of Asia are some 6,000 miles apart, the former at the Arctic Circle and the latter at the Equator. In between is the world's greatest mountain massif, which has served to keep the Asian populations separated, except to the east and west. Owing to these circumstances, the people who went northeastward had to develop a type of culture, along with physical adaptations, that would enable them to survive in an extremely cold environment. On the other hand, those who went southeastward did not leave the climatic range wherein most of human evolution is believed to have taken place and for which very little cultural change and physical adaptation were required.

Unfortunately, records from the field of human paleontology for the whole of Asia are scanty. Perhaps the most important fact to note here is that some half a million years ago man (*Homo erectus*) was already living in caves near Peking (40° N. latitude) and in the open on the island of Java (7° S. latitude). No immediate successors of *Homo erectus* have been found in China, but in central Java a series of skulls from the Solo River region indicates the presence there, probably sometime in the last glacial period, of a type of man only a little less primitive than *Homo erectus*. Some would class Solo man with the Neanderthals, but the skull form seems too primitive for that. Besides, the use of the term 'Neanderthal' in this case does violence to the concept of the latter being the bearer of the Mousterian culture. So far as known, the Mousterian cultural complex does not extend eastward beyond the peninsula of India.

The putative earliest evidence in Asia of the modern form of man (*Homo sapiens*), although having a distribution comparable to that of the oldest finds, leaves much to be desired in the matter of accurate dating. For example, Woo (1958) characterized a find at Tzeyang, Szechuan Province, as the 'earliest representative of modern man in China', even though he could estimate its age only in general terms of Pleistocene faunal associations. On the other hand, Oakley (1964) gives a C_{14} date of 39,600 ± 1,000 years BP for a skull from the Niah Cave in Sarawak (Borneo), but qualifies this with a footnote reading 'Assuming contemporaneity [with associated Upper Paleolithic cultural objects].' The appearance of the Niah skull is nowhere near as primitive-looking as most Australian Aboriginal skulls. For this reason the Niah skill could well be sacrificed to get a collagen date which would clear up the uncertainty of its age. Hopefully, radiometric dates will be forthcoming in the near future from China.

Besides the two foregoing finds, there is another from China that has pertinence here, not so much from the standpoint of its antiquity as from the standpoint of the anthropological attention it has attracted. I am referring to the recovery of three nearly complete adult skulls from an Upper Cave at the site of Choukoutien near Peking which also yielded the *Homo erectus* finds. Cultural evidence suggests an age for these skulls of perhaps 30,000 years. In describing them, Weidenreich (1939) characterized one (an old male) as looking 'like some of the European skulls of the Upper Palaeolithic' (p. 163). He characterized one of the remaining two (both females) as Melanesian, and the other as Eskimo. Racial impressions of skulls are highly subjective, as is indicated by the re-interpretations of these same skulls by Birdsell (1951) and Neumann (1956). Both of these anthropologists were considering the Upper Cave skulls from the standpoint of the peopling of America, but Birdsell had in mind also the peopling of Australia. Both rejected the idea that a very high and long skull could only be Melanesian. To Birdsell's way of thinking, therefore, the Upper Cave

> population may be considered to consist of two discrete racial elements: (1) An archaic Caucasoid type related to and presumably ancestral to both the Ainu and the Murrayians [Birdsell's name for the type of Australian aborigines found in purest Murrayian form in the Murray River drainage system and the nearby coastal regions], and (2) A long, narrow-headed and high-vaulted form of Mongoloid. (p. 19)

Birdsell went on to explain that the latter element 'seems to have been submerged by other brachycephalic Mongoloids in Asia, but can be detected among some of the marginal populations of the Americas'. Neumann put it more simply: 'All of the traits in question appear repeatedly in various early American Indian populations and should be regarded as expressive of the natural variability of the groups.'

In addition to the several mentioned efforts to connect the Upper Cave and New World skull types, there has been a notable effort by Macintosh and Larnach (1972) to relate the non-metrical cranial-vault traits of the Australian and *Homo erectus* populations. This is possible because Weidenreich (1943) provided clear descriptions of a series of such traits distinguishing *Homo sapiens* from *Homo erectus pekinensis*. Macintosh and Larnach selected a total of seventeen traits for comparison and weighted each of them on a scale of three, depending on whether the trait's presence or absence was considered of most significance (with ambiguous states assigned the value of one). This rating scheme yielded mean scores of 51 for *Homo erectus pekinensis*, 7.7 (range 0-20) for 202 Australian skulls, and 4.7 (range 0-16) for 75 New Guinea skulls. Although the scores of the two modern groups are widely different from that of *Homo erectus pekinensis*, very likely no other modern group ranks as high (for example, the score for 21 Mongoloid skulls was 3.33; that for 10 European skulls 2.6).

Although American populations do not figure in this comparison, in my opinion they would rate close to Macintosh's and Larnach's Mongoloid sample; in other words, American crania have a much less primitive appearance than do Australian crania. Moreover, the primitive appearance of Australian crania increases when the face is also taken into consideration. I can illustrate this with two observations made by Hrdlicka when he visited Australia in 1925 and measured nearly 1,000 crania: (1) He found the inferior border of the nasal aperture so indistinctly defined that he was forced to measure nasal height differently from the way he was accustomed in American crania (Hrdlicka, 1928, p. 2); and (2) he saw more evidence of receding chins than he had ever seen before in modern man and acquired through exchanges some fine examples for the Smithsonian museum.

All of this suggests that in late Pleistocene times at least two *Homo sapiens* populations were present in Asia, one in the north represented by the Upper Cave people and the Mongoloids that peopled North America, the other in the south represented by the Australian Aboriginals. If this was the case, and if the differences in appearance between the northern-moving and southern-moving populations implies a chronological difference, then it may turn out that the peopling of Australia preceded that of North America. Movement in the former direction also might have been easier, as I have noted, because of the far more endurable climate.

Changes in the New World Aboriginal Populations

Although the paleontological evidence as to the dates of the first peopling of North America and Australia is inconclusive, evidence of a different sort remains to be examined. I am referring to the relative amounts of differentiation that the two New World populations underwent between the times when they entered their *cul-de-sacs* and the times when they were discovered by Europeans. It is generally assumed that this differentiation should be proportional to the duration of the isolation. When I looked at the situation in North America from this standpoint in 1960 I concluded that it was consistent with a relatively short period of time; i.e., somewhere around 20,000 years at most (a figure which at that time I regarded as liberal). Here I will limit attention to three population characteristics: (1) anthropometric variability; (2) blood group pattern; and (3) disease susceptibility.

1. Anthropometric variability

The concept of race most often used by physical anthropologists is the traditional one of zoology based in the living on external characters —colour of skin, eyes and hair, hair form, stature, body and limb proportions, etc.—and in the skeleton on metrical and non-metrical traits. When physical anthropology became an organized science around the middle of the nineteenth century it was far easier for anthropologists to go to museums and study collected skeletal remains than to go to distant lands to study the living native peoples. It is understandable, therefore, that in the case of the American Indians and Australian Aborigines craniological studies preceded studies on the living. Actually, no extensive anthropometric studies on living North American Indians were made until 400 years after Columbus' first voyage (Boas, 1895). As for the Australian Aborigines, Howells (1937) implied another, albeit shorter, delay when he said of Lloyd Warner's measurements of inhabitants of northern Australia made in 1927:

> The scientific importance of the Australian aborigines is an anthropological axiom. That Warner's data comprise a valuable accretion to existing knowledge becomes obvious when it is realized how small is the amount of detailed investigation that has been carried out on the physical characteristics of the race. (p. vii). For detailed comparative purposes there are only two other series of adequate size [those of Burston (1913) and Campbell and Hackett (1927)]. (p. 19)

I mention all this because in trying by means of anthropometry to get at the relative amounts of physical differentiation that took place in the two New World populations the lengths of the intervals between the times when they were discovered by Europeans and the times when they were studied scientifically were great enough for considerable racial intermixture to have taken place. That this certainly was true in North America by the end of the nineteenth century is indicated by the following statement by Boas regarding his pioneer anthropometric study:

> the great frequency of half-breeds among all these tribes made an investigation on these races very interesting. I decided, therefore, to pay particular attention to the question regarding the anthropology of the half-breeds. In fact, this has proved to be one of the most fruitful fields of the investigation. (1894, p. 38)

The relative accuracy of measurements on the living and on skeletal remains also has a bearing on this problem. When anthropologists measure native peoples under field conditions they seldom remeasure the same individuals. I recall that when I repeated some measurements on Indians while working in Guatemala in 1947 and 1949 I was shocked by the amount of difference in the two sets of figures. The desirability of repeating measurements had been strongly impressed upon me when I reported (1939) large variations between the results of different anthropologists measuring the same subjects in Labrador. Errors of this sort are due mainly to four factors: (1) The subject's lack of co-operation (or understanding) in positioning his body so as to yield maximum diameters; (2) the anthropologist's failure to locate correctly some of the landmarks between which the measurements are taken; (3) the anthropologist's inability to provide a smooth floor surface for the subject and anthropometer to stand upon and his further inability often to hold the anthropometer vertical; and (4) the anthropologist's failure occasionally to read the measuring scale correctly and/or to record the measurement correctly. Obviously, faulty measurements cannot be rechecked after the field trip has ended.

Unlike measurements on the living, which can vary from the true values by a half centimeter or more, those on skeletal remains tend to vary within much smaller limits—usually 2 to 3 mm (cf. Stewart, 1942). However, a greater source of error here is in sexing. As Larnach and Macintosh (1970) have shown, the most experienced physical anthropologists can differ in their sexing of aboriginal Australian skulls in over

15 per cent of cases. No doubt the same holds true for American Indian skulls.

In view of the many ways in which observational errors can creep into anthropometric records, it is unfortunate that there is no better gauge of the physical differentiation of the aboriginal American and Australian populations. The records tell different stories depending upon the basis being the living or the skeletal remains. In America gross body size, particularly stature, varied with climate in accordance with Bergmann's rule, the tallest Indians having been in the temporate zones and the shortest in the tropics (Newman, 1953). Otherwise, it is clear only that the living varied in head shape, which mostly reflects variations in cradling practices.

In Australia the situation as regards the living is simpler on account of the smaller range of climatic variation and the absence of head deformation. Yet the observers are divided into two camps: (1) those who claim their samples to be homogeneous (Howells, 1937, 1970, for example); and (2) those who claim their samples to be heterogeneous (Birdsell, 1951, 1967, for example). Howells' opinion (1937, p. 40) is stated in a way to make it especially pertinent in the present connection:

> The one remarkable phenomenon is that an entire continent should be so homogeneous, while New Guinea, close on the north, teems with physically contrasting peoples. Next to Australia, North America probably has the simplest racial complexion, and it is instructive to contemplate the variety of types which might be found in any equal area of the latter. Even the Eskimos, taken by themselves, can hardly be compared with the Australians.

By contrast, Birdsell (1967, p. 153) says that his data 'demonstrate the existence among the Aborigines of marked regional differences culminating in three polar types of populations'.

Turning now to the study of the skeletal remains, Dixon's (1923) study of skull types provides an evaluation of population variability in the two areas under consideration that has the merit of having been done by one person using a uniform method (what one thinks of the method is not important here). For North America Dixon used four maps to show the distributions of the eight types he found present: Proto-Australoid and Proto-Negroid, Caspian and Mediterranean, Palae-Alpine and Mongoloid, and Alpine and Ural. He said:

> In broad lines the distribution of types in North America leads to the conclusion that . . . we can discern, beginning in earliest times, a series of drifts or waves of differing physical types, which have on the whole arranged themselves in such fashion that the dolichocephalic and presumably older peoples are found distributed mainly along the margins of the continent, whereas the brachycephalic, younger peoples occupy in a solid, unbroken mass the whole interior. (p. 404)

Dixon found a very different situation in Australia. He used only two maps to show the two types that he found predominant there: Proto-Australoid and Proto-Negroid. He said:

The Australian population thus appears to be made up almost entirely of two types, the Proto-Negroid and Proto-Australoid, of which the former is concentrated in the north and northeast, the latter in the south and southeast. This gradual decline in importance of the Proto-Negroid and increase of the Proto-Australoid is, in a measure, carried a step farther in Tasmania. (p. 374)

The foregoing selected studies serve very well to bring out some of the most notable conclusions based primarily on metrical characters and the indices of shape derived therefrom. Additionally, in Australia the degree of population differentiation has been assessed primarily also through non-metrical cranial characters. This has resulted in much the same difference of opinion as in the case of the studies on the living. Fenner (1939), the first to make such a study, found two subtypes (B and C) occurring respectively in the coastal Northern Territory and the Queensland areas, and a third subtype (A) occurring over the greater part of southern and southeastern Australia. By contrast, the more recent studies of Larnach and Macintosh (1966, 1970) on the crania of Queensland and coastal New South Wales have stressed population homogeneity. They say,

> Not only do these results fail to support Birdsell's theory of the trihybrid origin of Australian Aborigines, but they show that there is no basis for any theory that alien racial groups other than intrusive Papuans and possibly Indonesians occur in Queensland. Apart from the influence of the latter groups, it seems clear that any differences in Queensland groups of Aborigines can be accounted for by local selection, including random processes. The Queensland Aborigines, in the main, are closely allied to the New South Wales coastal Aborigines. (1970, p. 69)

In this limited review of a very complex subject all that I have endeavoured to do is to point up the difficulty of judging the amount of physical differentiation which took place in each area before European contact. It is impossible to compare the measurements on the living for the two areas because in North America population decimation and racial admixture were already far advanced by the time the first measurements were taken. Whatever one may think of Dixon's cranial-type approach, it alone of the studies mentioned measures the physical variation in the two areas against a single objective scale. Even though better measures of variability and many more prehistoric skeletons are now available, I doubt that further studies along this line will yield a significantly different picture. I agree with Dixon that the American population is more variable than the Australian. However, as I have indicated, the first peoples to enter the two *cul-de-sacs* must already have been different, culturally as well as physically, and certainly were subjected to contrasting ranges of environment during their periods of isolation. Under these circumstances the available measures of physical variation by themselves can hardly be expected to give reliable estimates of how long the American and Australian populations have been isolated.

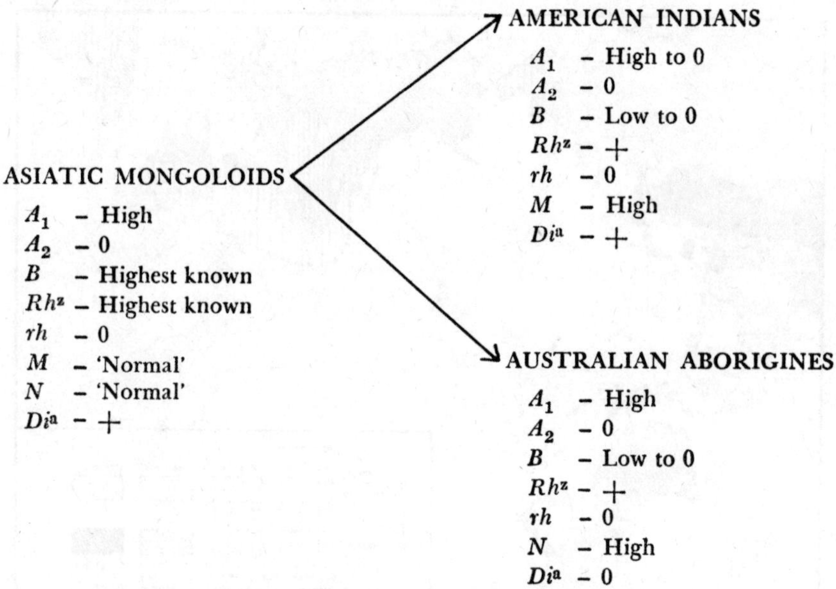

AMERICAN INDIANS

A_1 – High to 0
A_2 – 0
B – Low to 0
Rh^z – $+$
rh – 0
M – High
Di^a – $+$

ASIATIC MONGOLOIDS

A_1 – High
A_2 – 0
B – Highest known
Rh^z – Highest known
rh – 0
M – 'Normal'
N – 'Normal'
Di^a – $+$

AUSTRALIAN ABORIGINES

A_1 – High
A_2 – 0
B – Low to 0
Rh^z – $+$
rh – 0
N – High
Di^a – 0

Figure 10.2 Boyd's (1950) definitions of three genotypic races schematized for easy comparison. (Data on Di^a added from Simmons, 1957.)

2. Blood-group pattern

With the rapid rise of the science of genetics in this century a new concept of race was added to the traditional one employed by the zoologists and anthropologists. The new concept is based upon single-gene traits, especially blood groups. This kind of race is called genotypic to distinguish it from the traditional type now also called phenotypic to indicate its multiple-gene basis. When William C. Boyd (1950) reviewed the frequencies of blood groups on a world-wide basis he arrived at a series of five genotypic races corresponding in general to the continental areas (Europe, Asia, Africa, America and Australia) and to the previously-recognized racial stocks (white, yellow, black, 'red' and brown). His definitions of the present genotypic races of Asia, America and Australia, along with data on the Diego blood group (Simmons, 1957), provide the comparison shown in Figure 10.2. Although there are now more single-gene traits that might be added to these definitions, it is sufficient for the present purpose to note that the American Indians differ from the Asiatic Mongoloids in having low frequencies of genes A_1, B and Rh^z, but a higher frequency of gene M. The Australian Aborigines also have low frequencies of B and Rh^z, but differ from the American Indians in having a high frequency of N and no Di^a.

Actually, the blood-group picture is not as simple as this. When the A-B-O frequencies for Asia, America and Australia are plotted on a map (Figure 10.3), they grade fairly regularly from Asia through the

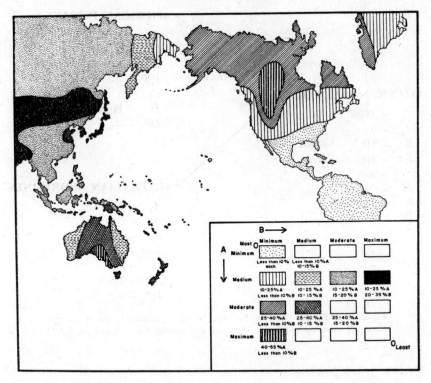

Figure 10.3 Percentage frequencies of blood-group genes A and B in the aboriginal populations of Asia and the New World. (From Mourant, 1954, maps 4 and 5 combined.)

points of entrance into America and Australia and southward. This is especially evident in America where group B is limited to northwestern North America, group A disappears a little farther southward, and group O alone is present in the remainder of the hemisphere. One could not wish for a better indicator of the entrance into the hemisphere. The indicator of the entrance into Australia is nearly as good, for group B is limited to an area in the north and from there on southward group A increases in frequency to a maximum in the south-central part (cf. Birdsell and Boyd, 1940, map 2; Kirk, 1971, pp. 329-30).

The restriction of blood-group B to areas just within the entrances to the *cul-de-sacs* suggests that gene *B* was introduced by later migrations. Candela (1942) pointed out that this gene arrived late in Europe also. He interpreted this to mean that *B* arose in Asia by mutation after the first peopling of America (he probably was not aware of the situation in Australia). Beyond this, no one has satisfactorily explained the excessively high frequency of group O in America, the different frequencies of M and N in America and Australia, and the irregular distribution of the Diego group (it is highest in northern South America). Furthermore, as regards attempting to estimate the length of time required to achieve such a degree of diversity as represented by the genotypic races, I agree with Kirk (1971, p. 339) that this will always be inaccurate because the assumptions involving events in the past are too numerous and uncertain.

3. Disease susceptibility

When the Spanish began their conquest of the high civilizations of the Americas early in the sixteenth century they unknowingly had powerful confederates in the form of three contagious diseases: smallpox, typhus and measles. Had it not been for the ravages of these diseases, the Spanish probably would not have reached their goal so quickly. As it was, the Indians succumbed to these diseases in great numbers and the succeeding famines and cultural disruptions continued the rapid population decline for many years.

I have attributed the American Indian's lack of immunity to Old World diseases to their long isolation and to the germ filter in the Far North through which their ancestors had to pass (Stewart, 1960). From this viewpoint these ancestors literally walked away from whatever acute diseases existed in the Old World in ancient times. Also, the lack of wholly different diseases among their descendants lends support to the idea that the latter have not been in the Americas long enough to have developed diseases of their own.

Chronic diseases are another matter. Opinions have shifted back and forth as regards the existence of syphilis and tuberculosis in America in pre-Columbian times. I will take up these diseases after looking at the situation in Australia.

In contrast to the well-documented American disease picture, there seems to be surprisingly little assembled evidence of a comparable set of circumstances for the post-contact period in Australia. For instance, Barwick (1971) cites only hearsay records for the Aboriginal population of Victoria prior to the 1840s. After mentioning that smallpox disappeared from Victoria soon after 1860, she states that

> A number of early settlers saw many adult Aborigines marked by the disease before 1841 and were told that it had spread, many years earlier, among the tribes of every region but Gippsland [the highlands of southeastern Victoria]. (p. 307)

She expresses the opinion also that the few recorded deaths from infectious diseases (measles, mumps and scarlatina) among the adult Aborigines after 1876 may be due to the fact 'that many had achieved immunity as survivors of the disastrous known epidemics before 1876' (pp. 306-7). Among these epidemics may have been the one that she mentions as having occurred at Coranderrk Aboriginal Station in 1875 during which 'thirty-one of approximately 150 . . . residents died of measles or subsequent pleuro-pneumonia' (p. 308).

Since I have not been able to pursue this matter further in the time available to me, I am going to assume that, if fuller evidence from other parts of Australia exists, it supports Barwick's meager indication of a susceptibility on the part of the Aborigines to the acute diseases of the Old World. Although I would prefer not to have to proceed on the basis of an assumption, I feel that this course is reasonable owing to the additional fact, that, just as in the case of the American Indians, the Aboriginal Australians did not have distinctive diseases of their own. For these reasons there is the possibility that the original Australians also 'walked away' from the acute diseases of the Old World and thus missed the opportunity to develop immunities thereto. If this was the case, a germ filter in the form of intense cold does not seem to be an essential intermediate stage in the process. On the other hand, if cold is not the essential element in this process that I have assumed, another explanation might be that the diseases in question had not yet come into existence at the time the American and Australian populations became isolated in their *cul-de-sacs*, and hence there was nothing of the sort for the migrants to 'walk away' from.

Unlike the introduced acute diseases, the two chronic diseases already mentioned—syphilis and tuberculosis—figure prominently in the recent health records of the Aboriginal Australians (Barwick, 1971; Hackett, 1936). Essentially the same thing is true in North America, although here tuberculosis has received a larger share of attention than has syphilis (Hrdlicka, 1909). The greater attention accorded the chronic diseases is accounted for in part by the success of the indirect immunization methods in keeping the acute diseases in check, and in part to the sedentary way of life on the reservations or stations—a 'benefit' which favors germ transmission. Yet now that effective methods are available for treating syphilis and tuberculosis, these two chronic diseases are also coming under control.

Also unlike the acute diseases, syphilis and tuberculosis tend to involve the skeleton. For this reason, collections of pathological bones, if properly dated and accurately interpreted, offer opportunities for determining the distribution and antiquity of these diseases. The qualifications are necessitated by two facts; (1) most of the earlier human skeletal collections are poorly documented; and (2) the science of paleopathology has not yet developed sure means of identifying the skeletal lesions of syphilis and tuberculosis. In spite of such handicaps the advances made in the anthropological study of each of these diseases is worth reviewing here.

Syphilis. The sudden appearance of this disease in Europe following the discovery of America gave it the appearance of having originated in America. The cause of syphilis was not discovered, of course, until after the disease had spread all over the world. Then came the further discovery that the same causative organism, the treponema, was responsible for three or four closely-related diseases: yaws, endemic syphilis, venereal syphilis, and pinta (?). Together they are often referred to as the treponematoses.

Hudson (1958) believes that this disease complex represents different responses of the causative organism to variations in climate (temperature and humidity) and man's way of life (nomadic and urban). Yaws was first encountered in human groups living essentially a nomadic life in *humid*, warm areas. Endemic syphilis, on the other hand, was first encountered in human groups living essentially a nomadic life in *dry*, warm areas. Both of these forms are transmitted in infancy and childhood by non-venereal routes and produce some immunity. Venereal syphilis, which, as the name implies, is transmitted by the venereal route, is not affected by climate and is assumed to have appeared first in urban centres. Pinta, reported mainly from America, does not seem to fit into this scheme and is believed by some to be simply a phase of yaws.

Hackett (1963) has theorized that pinta is the original treponemal disease that was endemic in animals and ultimately disappeared everywhere except in America; that it was succeeded in the ancient Old World by yaws and endemic syphilis, depending on the climate; and that venereal syphilis arose in turn from the non-venereal forms in European urban centres about the time of the discovery of America. According to Hackett's world map (1963, Figure 8), before 1492 America had pinta alone, whereas Australia had endemic syphilis in the interior and yaws on the northern coast. Arrows indicating lines of transmission after 1492 show America and Australia receiving venereal syphilis from Europe, and America also receiving yaws from Africa.

My cursory search of the Australian literature has not turned up satisfactory evidence for or against Hackett's historical reconstruction. If the evidence is indeed lacking, I suspect it is due to the two limiting circumstances mentioned above. Certainly as late as 1938 MacKay was not clear as to the nature of the pathological changes present in the bone collection at the Australian Institute of Anatomy in Canberra. His pictures indicate pathological changes not unlike those found in many American Indian bones, but in the absence of dates there is no way of telling whether or not they represent pre-contact disease(s).

I have studied evidence bearing on this problem from North America (Stewart, 1940; Stewart & Quade, 1969) and from the island of Saipan in Micronesia (Stewart & Spoehr, 1952). Two things about this evidence strike me as probably significant: (1) in North America the frequency of bone lesions most likely to have been caused by syphilis rapidly decreases as one reviews successively older collections beginning with the early historic period; and (2) crater-like lesions of the frontal bone, such as I described for cases of putative yaws from Australia and Saipan, do not appear to exist in American Indian skulls. If one could prove that the pathological bones from America of undoubted pre-Columbian date are indeed the result of syphilis, Hackett's historical reconstruction would require modification. Could it be that endemic syphilis reached both North America and Australia during the period of original peopling?

Or alternatively, is it possible that pinta evolved independently in America, reaching a highly virulent form just before the Spaniards arrived on the scene?

Tuberculosis. General awareness of the existence of this disease did not come with dramatic suddenness late in the historic period, as was the case with syphilis. Evidence of its presence in the Old World as far back as 1,000 BC was preserved to recent times due to the successful practice of embalming in Egypt (Smith, 1908). The ancient Greek physicians called it 'phthisis', a name which has continued in use (often in translation as 'consumption') until recent times. However, the discovery of the causative organism, the tubercle bacillus, dates only to the late nineteenth century. This discovery also led to the union of a number of different forms of the disease which had been described as separate entities. Among these entities is one—Pott's disease—which is of particular interest here because it involves the bony spine and manifests itself as a backwards curvature or 'hunchback'.

Numerous descriptions of putatively pre-Columbian hunchback spines have appeared in the North American anthropologico-medical literature (e.g., Lichtor & Lichtor, 1957). If there are similar records for Australia, my short search has not led me to them. I have not been able to determine, therefore, what the attitude is among Australian anthropologists about the possibility of tuberculosis being a pre-contact disease among their Aborigines. As for North American anthropologists, it is my impression that prior to 1961 they were willing to accept the pronouncements of the clinicians who had looked at the prehistoric American kyphotic spines and judged them to have been caused most likely by tuberculosis. In 1961, however, a tuberculosis specialist, Dan Morse, cast doubt on this opinion after reviewing the evidence and pointing out that at least 13 other diseases can cause kyphosis (cf. also Morse, 1967).

I cannot leave the subject at this point without noting that an American pathologist who has been studying Peruvian mummies has identified tubercle bacilli in histological preparations from a specimen which he believes to be pre-Columbian (personal communication). Since writing this, the results of the research have been published. Allison, M. J. *et al.*, 1973.

So far as I can determine, therefore, tuberculosis reached America, but may not have reached Australia, before European contact. If this ultimately proves to have been the case, the determining factor may have been climate. The climate of the Arctic through which the ancestors of the American Indians had to pass forces people to seek shelter for considerable periods of time in closed quarters. As I remarked earlier, this is a situation which tends to perpetuate the tubercle bacillus and to facilitate its transmission from individual to individual. The climate of the tropics in which the ancestors of the Australian Aborigines were living, on the other hand, forces people to avoid closed quarters and the resulting close contact.

Concluding comment

Time after time in this all-too-sketchy review of the peopling of the New World, I have had to admit that the correct interpretation of what appears to have happened to the aborigines within the American and Australian *cul-de-sacs* depends upon the duration of their isolation. The recent advances in dating procedures have largely removed guess work in this matter. What is needed now, therefore, is further early evidence of man's presence and a more concerted effort to get all such evidence dated.

Aside from this basic need, I was impressed while making this study by the haphazard nature of the anthropological attack on problems common to such a large part of the world. Most of the references I have cited are the work of a relatively few individuals who have gone out of their way to examine problems of unusual scope. Organized efforts along this same line involving large numbers of individuals and institutions are uncommon. Partly for this reason, perhaps, I had difficulty in finding summarized anthropological information on Australia and ended up relying on the bibliographies of individual scholars. It is certainly time for a *Handbook of Australian Aborigines* comparable to the series of American Indian *Handbooks* (Hodge (ed.), 1907-10; Steward (ed.), 1946-59; Wauchope (ed.), 1946—; Sturtevant (ed.), 1976?—). Hopefully such a *Handbook* would go beyond its predecessors in America in recognizing the common anthropological problems of the whole New World.

REFERENCES

ALLISON, M J., MENDOZA, D. and PEZZIA, A., (1973) 'Documentation of a case of tuberculosis in pre-Columbian America', *American Review of Respiratory Diseases*, 107, 985-91.

BARWICK, D. E., (1971) 'Changes in the Aboriginal Population of Victoria, 1863-1966', in *Aboriginal Man and Environment in Australia*. Mulvaney, D. V. and Golson, J. (eds), Canberra, pp. 288-315.

BERGER, R., HORNEY, A. G. & LIBBY, W. F., (1964) 'Radiocarbon dating of bone and shell from their organic components', *Science*, 144, 999-1001.

BERGER, R., PROTSCH, R., REYNOLDS, R., ROZAIRE, C. & SACKETT, J. R., (1971) 'New Radiocarbon Dates Based on Bone Collagen of California Paleoindians'. *Contributions of the University of California Archaeological Research Facility* (Berkeley), 12, 43-9.

BIRDSELL, J. B., (1951) 'The Problem of the Early Peopling of the Americas as Viewed from Asia', in *Physical Anthropology of the American Indian*. Laughlin, W. S. (ed.), The Viking Fund, Inc. New York. pp. 1-68. Laughlin, W. S. (ed.).

——, (1967) 'Preliminary data on the trihybrid origin of the Australian Aborigines', *Archaeology and Physical Anthropology in Oceania*, 2, 100-55.

BIRDSELL, J. B. & BOYD, W. C., (1940) 'Blood groups in the Australian Aborigines', *American Journal of Physical Anthropology*, 27, 69-90.

BOAS, F., (1894) 'The Anthropology of the North American Indian', *Memoirs of the International Congress of Anthropology* (Chicago, 1893), pp. 37-49.

——, (1895) 'Zur Anthropologie der nordamerikanischen Indianer', *Zeitschrift für Ethnologie*, 27, 366-411.

BOYD, W. C., (1950) *Genetics and the Races of Man*. Boston.

BURSTON, R., (1913) 'Records of the anthropometric measurements of 102 Australian Aboriginals', *Bulletin of the Northern Territory of Australia*, 7.

CAMPBELL, T. D. & HACKETT, C. J., (1927) 'Adelaide University Field Anthropology: Central Australia. I. Introduction: descriptive and anthropometric observations'. *Transactions and Proceedings of the Royal Society of South Australia*, 51, 65-75.

CANDELA, P. B., (1942) 'The introduction of blood-group B into Europe', *Human Biology*, 14, 413-43.

DIXON, R. B., (1923) *The Racial History of Man*. New York.

FENNER, F. J., (1939) 'The Australian Aboriginal skull: Its non-metrical morphological characters', *Transactions of the Royal Society of South Australia*, 62, 248-306.

HACKETT, C. J., (1936) 'Critical survey of some references to syphilis and yaws among Australian Aborigines', *Medical Journal of Australia*, 1, 731-45.

——, (1963) 'The human treponematoses', *Bulletin of the World Health Organization*, 29, 7-41.

HAYNES, C. V., JR, (1969) 'The earliest Americans', *Science*, 166, 709-15.

HODGE, F. W. (ed.), (1907-10) 'Handbook of American Indians north of Mexico', *Bulletin of the Bureau of American Ethnology*, 30, 2 vols.

HOPKINS, D. M., (1967) *The Bering Land Bridge*. Stanford, California.

HOWELLS, W. W., (1937) 'Anthropometry of the natives of Arnhem Land and the Australian race problem', *Papers of the Peabody Museum of American Archaeology and Ethnology, Harvard University*, 16 (1), 97 pp.

——, (1970) 'Anthropometric grouping analysis of Pacific peoples', *Archaeology and Physical Anthropology in Oceania*, 5, 192-217.

HRDLICKA, A., (1909) 'Tuberculosis Among Certain Indian Tribes of the United States', *Bulletin of the Bureau of American Ethnology*, 42, 48 pp.

——, (1928) 'Catalogue of Human Crania in the United States National Museum Collections: Australians, Tasmanians, South African Bushmen, Hottentots, and Negro', *Proceedings of the United States National Museum*, 71 (24), 140 pp.

HUDSON, E. H., (1958) *Non-Venereal Syphilis*. Edinburgh.

IRVING, W. N. & HARINGTON, C. R., (1973) 'Upper Pleistocene radiocarbon-dated artefacts from the Northern Yukon', *Science*, 179, 335-40.

KIRK, R. L., (1971) 'Genetic Evidence and the Implications for Aboriginal Prehistory', in *Aboriginal Man and Environment in Australia*, Mulvaney, D. J. and Golson, J., (eds), Canberra. pp. 326-43.

KRIEGER, A. D., (1964) 'Early Man in the New World', in *Prehistoric Man in the New World*. Jennings, J. D. and Norbeck, E. (eds), Chicago, pp. 23-81.

LARNACH, S. L. & MACINTOSH, N. W. G., (1966) *'The Craniology of the Aborigines of Coastal New South Wales'*, The Oceania Monographs, 13, 94 pp.

——, (1970) *'The Craniology of the Aborigines of Queensland'*, The Oceania Monographs, 15, 71 pp.

LICHTOR, J. & LICHTOR, A., (1957) 'Paleopathological evidence suggesting pre-Columbian tuberculosis of the spine', *Journal of Bone and Joint Surgery*, 39A, 1398-9.

MACINTOSH, N. W. G., (1972) 'Radiocarbon Dating as a Pointer in Time to the Arrival and History of Man in Australia and Islands to the Northwest', *Public Lecture, 8th International Radiocarbon Dating Conference, Lower Hutt, New Zealand* (mimeographed).

MACINTOSH, N. W. G. & LARNACH, S. L., (1972) 'Persistence of *Homo erectus* traits in Australian Aboriginal crania', *Archaeology and Physical Anthropology in Oceania*, 7, 1-7.

MacKay, C. V., (1938) 'Some pathological changes in Australian Aboriginal bones', *Medical Journal of Australia*, 2, 537-55.

Morse, D., (1961) *'Prehistoric tuberculosis in America'*, *American Review of Respiratory Diseases*, 83, 489-504.

——, (1967) 'Tuberculosis', in *Diseases in Antiquity*, Brothwell, D. and Sandison, A. T. (eds), Springfield, Illinois, pp. 249-71.

Mourant, A. E. (1954) *The Distribution of the Human Blood Groups*. Springfield, Illinois.

Müller-Beck, H., (1967) 'On Migrations of Hunters Across the Bering Land Bridge in the Upper Pleistocene', in *The Bering Land Bridge*, Hopkins, D. M. (ed.), Stanford, California, pp. 373-408.

Neumann, G. K., (1956) 'The upper cave skulls from Choukoutien in the light of Paleo-Amerind material', *American Journal of Physical Anthropology*, 14, 380 (abstract).

Newman, M. T., (1953) 'The application of ecological rules to the racial anthropology of the aboriginal new world', *American Anthropologist*, 55, 311-27

Oakley, K., (1964) *Frameworks for Dating Fossil Man*. Chicago.

Simmons, R. T., (1957) 'The Diego (Di^a) blood group: tests in some Pacific peoples', *Nature*, 179, 970-1.

Smith, G. E., (1908) 'Anatomical report', *Bulletin of the Archaeological Survey of Nubia*, 1, 25-35.

——, (1929) *Human History*. New York.

——, (1931) 'The discovery of primitive man in China', *Antiquity*, 5, 21-36 (reprinted with slight changes in the *Smithsonian Report for 1931*, pp. 531-47).

Steward, J. H. (ed.), (1946-59) 'Handbook of South American Indians', *Bulletin of the Bureau of American Ethnology*, 143, 7 vols.

Stewart, T. D., (1939) 'Anthropometric observations on the Eskimos and Indians of Labrador', *Anthropological Series of the Field Museum of Natural History*, 31 (1), 163 pp.

——, (1940) 'Some historical implications of physical anthropology in North America', *Smithsonian Miscellaneous Collections*, 100, 15-50.

——, (1942) 'Variations in the technique of measuring skulls', *Anthropological Briefs*, 2, 1-6.

——, (1960) 'A physical anthropologist's view of the peopling of the New World', *Southwestern Journal of Anthropology*, 16, 259-73.

Stewart, T. D. & Quade, L. G., (1969) 'Lesions of the frontal bone in American Indians', *American Journal of Physical Anthropology*, 30, 89-110.

Stewart, T. D. & Spoehr, A., (1952) 'Evidence on the paleopathology of yaws', *Bulletin of the History of Medicine*, 26, 538-53.

Sturtevant, W. C. (ed.), (1976) 'Handbook of North American Indians' (18 projected volumes in preparation).

Wauchope, R. (ed.), (1964—) *Handbook of Middle American Indians*. 13+ vols. Austin, Texas.

Weidenreich, F., (1939) 'On the earliest representatives of modern mankind recovered on the soil of East Asia'. *Peking Natural History Bulletin*, 13 (3), 161-74.

——, (1943) 'The skull of *Sinanthropus pekinensis*. A comparative study of a primitive hominid skull', *Palaeontologia Sinica* (N.S.), D, 10, 298 pp.

Woo, Ju-K., (1958) 'Tzeyang paleolithic man—earliest representative of modern man in China', *American Journal of Physical Anthropology*, 16, 459-71.

PART III
DIFFUSION OF CULTURE

II ELLIOT SMITH AND THE DIFFUSION OF CULTURE

A. P. Elkin

The Context

To appreciate the role played by Grafton Elliot Smith in ethnology, we must keep in mind the ethnological context of the first three decades of this century; the geographical context in which he worked in its first decade; and the historical context which he evoked. He was Professor of Anatomy in Cairo from 1901-9. This was a period of much archaeological activity in Upper Egypt, including the Valley of the Tombs near Thebes, and after 1907, in the 'cemeteries' in Nubia, which were destined to be flooded by an increase in height of the Aswan Dam.

As anatomist, and in the circumstances, perforce anthropologist, Elliot Smith examined many thousands of human bodies (skeletons and mummies) many of which had been preserved for up to six millenia by the hot dry sands of the region and some through the highly technical procedure of mummification. These remains came from both Early and Late Pre-Dynastic periods as well as from Dynastic periods. He became familiar with the physical constitution and even the appearance of the Proto-Egyptians and aware of the later presence in the population of what he called the 'Giza' or Armenoid traits.

More relevant, however, to this paper, was his observation firstly of the corpse, and secondly of the articles placed with it in the grave or tomb, and thirdly of the varied types of tomb ranging from a simple structure of wood or stone protecting the body and its paraphernalia from the sand, to the mastaba and on to pyramids and associated temples. These customs and practices revealed the development of technical equipment and skill; especially in the procedure of mummification, in the crafts of the carpenter and stone mason following the discovery of copper and its use for tool-making, and in the arts of sculpture, painting and architecture. They also indicated variations in the economic and social position of the population, and finally they expressed Egyptian religious doctrines in general as well as beliefs regarding the fate of the dead.

In Elliot Smith's view it was more than a coincidence that in Egypt, where the hot dry sands preserved the corpse as though the deceased were asleep, people came to regard the preservation of the body, its appearance and tissues, as essential for a continuous existence after death. But when the mourners sought to ensure this happy state by providing coffins, and tombs and funerary equipment, including the luxuries of life, the result was the opposite of what they intended. The basic conviction, however, did not change, nor did the practice of protecting the corpse from the sands of inhumation. Therefore the priests and 'undertakers' began about 3400 BC to develop methods for preserving the tissues and features of the deceased by artificial means. But because the embalmers failed for centuries to retain the distinctive features, the sculptor the sa'nkh, 'he who causes to live', was called in to make a portrait statue of wood or stone. This was set up above or before the tomb in its own forecourt or temple, and was made a 'living image' by appropriate ritual, including libations and incense. And even when in the Twenty-first Dynasty the mummy was made at last, for those who could afford the cost, a living simulacrum of the dead, it was hidden in an underground chamber, away from the robbers who sought the precious metals and valuable furniture entombed with it.[1]

To obtain copper and gold and shells, aromatic materials, 'life-giving' woods (such as cedars from Lebanon), to be used mainly in the service of the dead, expeditions by land and sea went from quite early times to nearby and then more distant countries. Boat designing and building for sea voyaging was involved. And behind all this activity as well as in the erection of tombs and pyramids, temples and great statuary, was the organization of workers and managers, tradesmen and artists, and their provisioning and housing. Contemplating years later this complex of beliefs, needs and activities, Elliot Smith coined one of his many intriguing, and often challenging, summary statements: 'The cemeteries of Egypt were truly the birthplace of the arts and crafts of civilization.'[2]

This, however, was only part of the story of the growth of civilization in Egypt. The other, and indeed, fundamental part was connected with the Nile and the provision of food for an increasing population. The annual cycle in a practically rainless climate of the great river flooding the plain at the end of the hot season, the seeds of wild barley and millet sprouting up as the waters receded, and the natural crop being ready for gathering by the start of the next summer, was indeed a prelude to irrigation and agriculture. Eventually a thoughtful food-gatherer, realizing the life-giving power of water, lengthened a natural channel or scooped out a fresh one to extend the range of flood water from the river, and then later blocking such a channel, took the first steps towards 'basin irrigation'. Thus, the whole complex of irrigation was begun: from tools for digging channels, to an instrument for measuring the height of the river, and a calendar to correlate the movements of the river in relation to the moon, and later to the sun, and a calendar to mark the times for the various agricultural tasks.

This important advance implied social and administrative organization. It was also accompanied by the development of religious doctrines and ritual, and by endowing the Ruler with power over the waters on which the life of man and nature depended and indeed, by ascribing to him the status of a deity. This status continued after his death, especially as in the ritual of mummification he was made 'alive' and his presence retained. As Elliot Smith wrote: 'It is no mere coincidence that the first "god" should have been a dead king, nor that he controlled the waters of irrigation and was specially interested in agriculture'. This dead king was said to have been the culture hero, and later cult-hero, Osiris. Summing up this apotheosis, Elliot Smith throws out another of his challenging epigrams: 'the creation of the first deities was not primarily an expression of religious belief, but rather an application of science to national affairs.'[3] The Ancient Egyptians were a very practical people.

Historical Emphasis

Elliot Smith's unfailing question when confronted with an unfamiliar phenomenon or feature, whether in brain or skeleton or anything else, was 'what is the significance of this?'—in other words, what is its function, and how did it come to be as it is and to have that function? Therefore, when he was confronted by the new data revealed in the archaeological and anthropological research in Egypt during 1901-9, he asked the same question and for an answer sought to educe the history of the Egyptians, for meaning comes in and through history. It is an aspect of continuity.

The point of the brief and inadequate sketch with which I have begun this paper, is that in the context of his work in Egypt Elliot Smith was concerned with the *history* of Egyptian civilization as a way of understanding the significance of those striking cultural elements with which he was conversant, especially, the making of rock-cut tombs and megalithic structures, elaborate burial rituals and mummification, and the ascription of divinity to the chief ruler, the Son of the Sun. As he saw and interpreted that history, dependence on the Nile and belief that continuation of life after death could be assured were two of its dominant themes. In addition, the discovery of copper in Upper Egypt in the middle Pre-dynastic period and its use for tools and weapons 'quickened the pace of invention and stimulated the advancement of the arts and crafts' as well as widening 'the scope of human endeavour'.[4] His first book, as distinct from his constant output of articles, reports and monographs year by year, was an historical study of the Ancient Egyptians as a race, of their culture and of their relations with neighbouring peoples. Published in 1911, its keynote was 'the Coming of Copper' and the title: *The Ancient Egyptians and their Influence upon the Civilization of Europe*. The wider aspects of Egypt's history arose from his conviction that 'the essential facts of Egyptian anthropology would be seen in truer perspective if one tried to correlate events in the Nile Valley with what was happening contemporaneously in the rest of the ancient world'.

Diffusion

This wide historical approach, however, led Elliot Smith to realize that the influence of one culture on another was an inevitable effect of the direct or indirect contact of peoples, unless such contact was very transitory. In particular, anthropological evidence showed that groups of mixed Egyptian-Armenoid descent from Lower Egypt migrated along the North African littoral. There too, the many megaliths tell of the influence of Egypt, just as the wide range of stone monuments (dolmens, menhirs and so on) do along the coast of Spain and Western Europe, as well as in southern Italy and the islands in between. Moreover, the use of copper followed this same route and also the route of megaliths north through Palestine and Syria to Asia Minor and the Black Sea. And thence over a long period, waves of people from this southwest corner of Asia, relying on the advantages of metals for weapons and tools, migrated to Western Europe, and contributed to the development of culture there; this was also influenced by the wave of megalithic culture from North Africa.[5]

Having expounded this hypothesis, Elliot Smith sounded a note from which he never wavered. Diffusion of culture was *not transplantation* of culture traits. Ideas, customs and practices spread, but were worked over or 'conventionalized' (to use W. H. R. Rivers' term) by every recipient people, before being passed on further. So although Western Europe and Britain were influenced by Egyptian culture, although 'they assimilated the wisdom of Egypt and Asia' and adopted arts and crafts from those sources, yet 'they used the new knowledge to develop their own culture and raise it to a higher plane'.[6]

The full title of the book to which I have been referring, *The Ancient Egyptians*, includes the words: *and their Influence upon the Civilization of Europe*. But when the second edition came out in 1923, the title was *The Ancient Egyptians and the Origin of Civilization*. The author had flung his cultural net over a wider range by land and by sea, to the far east as well as to the west. In the meantime he had searched the literature, written many papers and given many lectures on the influence of Egyptian civilization on the development of the culture of many peoples, and he had met much opposition. He was impelled to try to understand the causes of, and basic reasons for, this opposition and to make clear what he meant by the concept of diffusion.

An important stage in the working out of his ideas was reached during his visit to Australia in 1914 for the meeting of the British Association for the Advancement of Science. In Sydney and in Brisbane he saw three Torres Strait Islanders' mummified bodies and examined two of them. This was for him an exciting experience. He was convinced from his knowledge of the technical details of mummification in Ancient Egypt, that in spite of these mummies being smoke-dried and not prepared by steeping the bodies in a solution of natron as in Egypt, they supplied 'the most positive demonstration of the Egyptian origin of the methods employed'. Moreover, 'they revealed a series of curious procedures such as were not invented in Egypt until the New Empire and some not until the XXIst Dynasty'; therefore the knowledge of the procedure could not have come from Egypt directly or indirectly before the ninth century BC. Elliot Smith was most interested in the Islanders' adoption of the technically difficult procedure of removing the brain through a hole in the occiput, a method not adopted in Egypt until the XVIIIth Dynasty. The other details on which he commented are given in his Manchester Memoir, 1915, pp. 21-5, and in the communication by Professor D. M. S. Watson in *Sir Grafton Elliot Smith* (W. R. Dawson (ed.), 1938), pp. 62-6.[7]

Elliot Smith was so impressed by his observations and also by the records of the other funerary practices and beliefs associated with mummification in the Torres Strait Islands, that he hastened to call the attention of the Anthropological Section of the Congress at its Melbourne session to the facts and to his interpretation of them. To his utter amazement he was met with the criticism that the attempt to preserve the dead, and in doing so to remove the putrescible parts through the flank and so on, was a natural thing to do. The suggestion seemed preposterous to him that the lengthy procedure which took the embalmers of Egypt centuries to work out under favourable conditions should have been invented by the Torres Strait Islanders in the hot, damp atmosphere of their region. The effect, however, of this reaction to his diffusionist interpretation, was to send him to the literature and then to write a memoir 'On the Significance of the Geographical Distribution of the Practice of Mummification—A Study of the Migration of Peoples and the Spread of certain Customs and Beliefs'. This was read to the Manchester Literary and Philosophical Society in February 1915, only six months after the Congress in Australia. As published on 6 April 1915, it is a sustained argument of 135 pages, which he hoped would convince his critics.

In this memoir, however, he not only maintained firstly, that mummification and its ritual, the building of megaliths, and other elements of a culture complex of customs and beliefs had been slowly built up over millenia in Ancient Egypt, and secondly that this complex had influenced, and in its turn had been modified by, east Mediterranean, east African and Mesopotamian cultures; he also argued that it had then spread east to south India, Ceylon, Southeast Asia and Indonesia, and at length even to the Americas, where 'like a potent ferment it gradually began to leaven the vast and widespread aboriginal culture of' that region. As for the more sumptuous edifices in the Central Americas, 'the *primary stimulus* of Egyptian ideas, profoundly modified by Babylonian, and to a lesser extent by Indian and Eastern Asiatic, influences is indubitable'.[8] Further, he emphasized that the historical source of these culture traits in the Americas is revealed not merely in mummification practices and in the designs of buildings, but also in the art, symbolism and nature of cults such as those of the sun and the serpent.

In view of criticisms which followed the publication of this Memoir and Elliot Smith's later expositions of his interpretation of the distribution of certain culture traits, I emphasize the wording of the title of the Memoir. This indicated that he proposed to deal with the *significance* of the geographical distribution of mummification, and with the spread of *certain* customs and beliefs. At no time did Elliot Smith suggest that the culture of early Egypt was adopted in its entirety in any country influenced by that culture, nor that all worthwhile American achievements were derived from the Old World (Spinden). Neither did his collaborator for twenty years and more, W. J. Perry, make any such claims. The latter plotted and interpreted the distribution of the traits of a culture complex, which he named, possibly somewhat unfortunately, the 'archaic civilization'. At the same time he plotted the distribution of certain objects of value, particularly precious metals and pearls, which from early millenia in the ancient East, men have sought because of their practical or ritual use. The significance of this complementary distribution was clear. It revealed the motive which impelled men to sail the seas and oceans to foreign coasts and islands and to push inland in strange countries—namely, to obtain materials which were highly valued.

Men, millenia ago, as now, given adequate motive, will venture far, and in difficult and dangerous circumstances if need be, to get what they want.

> The maps of distribution shown by Mr. Perry reveal with a clearness which has few, if any parallels in the history of Ethnology that the carriers of Egyptian culture (or persons imbued with that culture) were impelled by the same motives as those which lead people of our own time.

Those were the words of W. H. R. Rivers, probably the most influential social scientist, field-ethnographer and ethnologist of the first two decades of this century, and a convert to Elliot Smith's concept of diffusion.[9]

As I have pointed out, Elliot Smith in his 1915 Memoir had definitely brought America into the range of the influence of the 'heliolithic' culture complex, and referred incidentally to China and Japan. During the years of World War I he continued his researches into the eastern influence of that complex, possibly as relief from War Hospital work and from struggling on with his Manchester Department of Anatomy with depleted staff. He published several relevant notes and abstracts as well as longer communications on the topic. Their theme was 'The Influence of Ancient Egyptian civilization in the East and in America', the title of a John Rylands Library Bulletin (1916). Three other contributions in the Bulletins of this Library (1917 and 1919), were reprinted as *The Evolution of the Dragon*, 1919. *Elephants and Ethnologists* which did not appear until 1924, was foreshadowed by notes in *Nature* in 1915 on 'Pre-Columbian representations of the Elephant in America', and by short contributions to *Science* N.Y., 1916 and 1917, on 'The Origin of the pre-Columbian Civilisation of America'. Thus the stage was set for debate on the American implication of his theory of diffusion. The influence on the pre-Columbian 'high civilizations' of the 'heliolithic' culture complex, with its Indian, Cambodian, Indonesian and Chinese modifications and elements was regarded by Elliot Smith as the crucial test of the hypothesis. He therefore set himself to understand doubts and criticisms.

Criticism of Diffusion

To read again after forty or fifty years, Elliot Smith's exposition of his thesis, the attitudes of his critics and the substance of their criticisms, throws interesting light on anthropologists and ethnologists. Just as we are today, so most of them were, creatures of their period, of their geographical and historical context, and of prevailing theoretical doctrines and cherished ideas.

In the nineteenth century and early part of the twentieth, the approach to the development of civilizations was 'evolutionary': a developing civilization passes through similar phases in similar circumstances, though whether circumstances are ever similar is a doubtful proposition which the holders of the doctrine were inclined to ignore. Akin to this prevailing evolutionist approach, were the doctrine of the similarity of the working of the human mind, or the psychic unity of mankind, and also Adolph Bastian's doctrine of 'elementary thoughts' or 'ideas' common to mankind, which found expression in 'folk-ideas'. These ideas arising independently in many places, gave rise to similar cultural features.

This concept of independent evolution of historically distinct and separated cultures, together with the associated ideas of parallel and convergent development of culture traits, became fashionable. Moreover, it could be useful, if regarded as providing analogies drawn from the biological field;[10] but put forward as doctrine or as dogma, it revealed in Elliot Smith's opinion, a 'misunderstanding of what the biologist means by evolution—derivation from a common origin and the diffusion in space and time from the centre of origin'.[11] This, however, implied the opposite meaning the stalwarts of independent cultural evolution (that is, evolutions) intended to convey.

In the climate of evolutionism and psychic unity still prevailing in Great Britain in the second decade of this century, Elliot Smith, not unexpectedly, met strong criticism on 'the floor of the house', as it were, when he expounded his theories at meetings of the British Association for the Advancement of Science. The intellectual conflict was earnest, but did not last long. World War I involved British people in another conflict of thought and of action, and after that War, the attention of social and cultural anthropologists became oriented towards 'present-day' problems of contact, diffusion and administration. Field-work amongst pre-literate and colonial populations was called for. A functional approach to, and interpretation of, culture was emphasized. In 1924, Malinowski, immersed in writing up his experience and observations among the Trobriand Islanders, considered (*Nature*, pp. 300-1) that Elliot Smith's teachings and W. J. Perry's *Children of the Sun* (1923) would by 'their positive claims . . . force the old school to revise its evolutionary position'. In 1927, however, after echoing the truism that 'extreme diffusionism' is as futile 'as the belief that every culture follows an independent course of evolution', urged that anthropology should be based on observation 'of real fact', and made to 'bear upon the practical and vital issues of today'.[12] This synchronic functionalist approach avoided the difficult problems of culture-history which became labelled conjectural-history by him and Radcliffe-Brown, meaning 'sheer speculation'. However, those who sought the origin and development of man's behaviour, of his customs, cultures and civilizations, considered they were proceeding not by unfounded conjecture, but by legitimate inference from observed data—archaeological, prehistoric and historical, and also current 'primitive'.[13] And they went on their way, as also did the British functionalists. The latter, according to Evans Pritchard, one of them, 'regarded the fight between evolutionists and diffusionists as a family quarrel between ethnologists and none of their affair'.[14]

American anthropologists, however, were interested in the Diffusion-Independent Evolution problem. They could look back to the work of their country's distinguished historian, W. H. Prescott. Noting the close resemblances of aspects of these amazing civilizations of Mexico and Peru to those of the Old World and of Eastern Asia, some of the features being 'arbitrary peculiarities', W. H. Prescott suggested in his *The Conquest of Mexico*, 1843 (Vol. II, p. 484), that 'some primitive communication with (the) great brotherhood of nations on the old continent seemed reasonable'. In his later work, however, *The Conquest of Peru*, 1847 (Vol. I, p. 103), he regarded such striking resemblances as analogies, 'adduced not as evidence of common origin, but as showing the coincidences which might naturally spring up among different nations under the same phase of civilization'. The implied concept of 'psychic unity' together with Prescott's classification of the resemblances in pre-Columbian civilizations to elements of Old World cultures as analogies, and not homologues, became a feature of American criticisms of Diffusion.

Seventy-four years later Goldenweiser generalized that we find 'an universal or nearly universal distribution of such cultural features as flow directly from man's psychic nature and his relation to his physical and social environment'.[15] And Spinden in his criticism of the diffusion theory as a means of explaining similarities in culture traits between the Western and Eastern hemispheres, wrote that they were all 'susceptible to convergences'. He finds the explanation in the theory that men are 'approximately equal in the matter of mental and bodily machine and started off approximately equal on the Neolithic plane of culture'.[16]

Kroeber, however, who for years was the doyen of American anthropologists, summed up this approach succinctly in the Huxley Memorial Lecture, 1946: '19th Century anthropologists could still fall back on a sort of spontaneous generation to explain cultural likenesses remote in space and time . . . Today we hesitate to invoke autogenesis.' This latter was the doctrine which Elliot Smith ever combated, and to the decline of which he contributed. But it is not yet quite dead. A very important, recent book, *Man across the Sea*, 1971, recording the papers presented at a symposium, 1968, shows that the transfer of culture traits across the seas to America, especially to the middle Americas in pre-Columbian times, is a plausible theory worthy of further research. The editors, however, wondered why anti-diffusionists seemed reluctant to take part in the symposium (p. 446). Hitherto, the anti-diffusionists challenged diffusionists to produce actual and irrefutable proofs of the transfer of culture from or through Asia and Indonesia to middle America, or at least to produce material evidence of the boats of the culture carriers, or of objects they brought with them. *Now,* the challenge also goes out to the erstwhile challengers to show that the Mayan, Mexican and Peruvian 'high civilizations' were indigenous. This means much archaeological work to uncover sites where the evidence might be, and to prepare an overall account of the stages preceding what has been claimed to be the sudden and almost spontaneous rise of those civilizations about the time the Elliot Smith theory suggested. Some such research undertaken in middle America, was described by Alfonso Caso in 1953. He outlined seven horizons, of which the *Archaic*, the *Formative*, the *Classic* and the *Toltec* possibly fall within the period in which, according to Elliot Smith's theory, Asiatic influences were reaching the Americas. The theory, however is neither proved nor disproved,[17] but more of this sort of research in the Mexican, Middle American and Peruvian regions will surely provide a decision.[18]

The Critics, Isolationism, and the Oceans

The writings of the period on diffusion give the impression that the contemporary critics had not examined thoroughly the theory as Elliot Smith developed and presented it in his books and articles from 1911 to 1933, or as W. J. Perry presented it in *The Children of the Sun*, 1923, and W. H. R. Rivers in *The History of Melanesian Society*, Vol. II, 1914, and in his articles in Part III of *Psychology and Ethnology*, 1926. Did the critics see the proposition in its complexity and entirety? Or, when coming to, or lighting at random on, a statement, a suggestion, or an inference which ran counter to their long accepted opinions and theories, did they, as I suspect, reject the concept 'lock, stock and barrel'? They probably read no more, at least not with the 'seeing eye'. This is a 'natural' reaction to the uncongenial, to that which disturbs. In this case it was expressed partly in making debating points, though not always successfully; e.g., (i) that pyramids in South America were built of adobe bricks, not of stone as in Egypt (Dixon); or (ii) that American indigo dye was obtained from a species of Murex which differed from the Mediterranean and Indian species of Murex (Spinden). Substitution of material does not necessarily disprove spread of a concept or a practice. On the contrary, it often proves this.[19]

Criticisms, however, often seemed to be attempts to protect an inherited or traditional position, though more was involved than the so-called natural conservatism of man and society. This is suggested by the vehemence of some criticisms; e.g., Elliot Smith's methods are uncontrolled flights of imagination and his theory 'a reckless use of diffusion to interpret widespread similarities';[20] it is an 'extravagant hypothesis long since relegated to the rubbish pile of scientific discards';[21] and the 'notorious Heliolithic Theory of Smith and Perry' uses points which are 'mostly curiosae without really important relations to the matters of social life'; indeed, its influence is 'occult'.[22]

A somewhat different debating point charges diffusionists with mentioning traits of supposed western Pacific origin which were found in pre-Columbian South America, while being 'silent about characteristic traits of Indonesian and Melanesian culture not found in South America'.[23] Actually, however, Elliot Smith was not silent about this sort of situation.[24] Migrants, traders or adventurers are not culture-missionaries, only culture-carriers. They do not expect or try to implant all the characteristic traits of their home cultures, nor would the local populations adopt them all—even if that were the newcomer's aim. Culture adoption and adaptation are selective, and possibly also stimulatory.

Behind these various types of criticism was, at least in some degree, the American Monroe doctrine of international political isolationism. It had become a general attitude of mind, and was applied, probably unconsciously, to the cultural field and backwards in time to the pre-Columbian period of American history. Even A. L. Kroeber, a 'judicial' critic, admitted as late as 1950 to being 90 per cent 'Chauvinist in Americanism'.[25] Such an attitude took for granted that good things in America, including the High Civilizations of that period, were as indigenous as the Indians. Therefore, Elliot Smith's hypothesis was disturbing. To criticize it hard and often became the 'in-thing', the ethnological fashion. This meant finding arguments for so doing.

For example: cultural diffusion to America from the Old World, from the east or the west was said to be out of the question. The Americans were isolated effectively by two oceans. Elliot Smith's series of arrows on maps of the Pacific to indicate routes of diffusion or of migratory bands proved nothing.[26] The critics, however, omitted to note that before drawing such maps, Elliot Smith had studied and drawn attention to the relevant literature which witnessed to the sea-worthiness of the large canoes and sailing rafts used in the Pacific region, and to the practice of Polynesians and others making long voyages in them. The same literature included records of individuals and small groups blown off course, surviving for long periods.

Because of the foregoing facts, Elliot Smith had no doubt that many groups of emigrants looking for islands on which to settle, and of traders seeking places in which to obtain desired substances (precious metals, pearls, incense-wood and so on), landed on the Pacific coast of

America. He only cites one specific case, that of a Mangarevan style wooden sailing craft which was found on the coast of the Inca Empire. But the chances of finding the remains of such wooden craft after many hundreds of years are few; moreover, some of the travellers may have sailed away to the west again. His point is that if culture traits or complexes in the High Civilizations of the Americas are to be explained by diffusion from the Old World, the Pacific Ocean was not an insuperable barrier. Nor were the boats unequal to the journeying.

R. B. Dixon (*The Building of Cultures*, 1929, p. 190) regards as preposterous the idea that 'a handful of strange wanderers sea-worn after their unbroken journey in frail canoes across 5,000 miles of open sea', could then go about their business on land. However, new research referred to in *Man across the Sea* (1971) supports Elliot Smith's approach: 'drift voyages between Asia and America not only are clearly possible, but actually have occurred repeatedly in historic time', and 'there appears to be no question that rafts could have crossed the Pacific repeatedly and in appreciable numbers' in pre-Columbian times. Indeed, the sailing rafts of the Old World and the New World may be considered as one widely distributed tradition of great antiquity.[27]

In addition, the possible diffusion from the Old World of cultural elements and stimulus ideas is no longer left only to the trans-Pacific routes. As R. A. Kennedy points out, transatlantic immigrants had the craft, and there were 'probably many landings over a long period giving rise to several source cultures'. Moreover, these would have been linked through North Africa and also the Mediterranean area, particularly Spain, with the 'industrial and craft knowledge' of Ancient Egypt in the period from 3000 to 15000 BC, but more recently in Western Meso America. And this was 'one of the greatest periods for group mobility or voyaging in man's history'.[28]

Arguments that the Oceans are highways for, not barriers against, migration and diffusion, do not prove that the latter have actually occurred. But, as a result of research, the list of culture traits which imply such contact, is growing impressively long, and will grow longer; but even then we will still have to show 'how the spark of societal change' was ignited which lead to civilization.[29]

At least, present day students have demolished the transoceanic barriers—barriers which existed in the mind of Elliot Smith's generation, thalassophobia it has been called, and regarded as 'one of the most critical deterrents to rational evaluation of common traits on opposite sides of the Pacific'. Graebner called this attitude *Raumfurcht* (timidity with regard to space), which Frobenius had sought to overcome by attempting to explain 'similarities between cultures thousands of miles apart and separated by an ocean without recurring to the easy expedient of ascribing them to the "psychic unity of mankind" '.[30]

Thalassophobia or Raumfurcht is really an aspect, a hidden defence, of isolationism, and the latter in its turn must justify itself by a doctrine of the psychic unity of mankind, or of common 'elementary ideas', so as to explain the development of similar cultural complexes in populations isolated from each other for a long period, probably from the Old Stone Age.

The Epistemological Background of Criticism

Isolationism was an understandable reaction of ethnologists to Diffusion in the American context of the first few decades around the turn of the century.[31] It was not an explanation of the similarity of culture traits and complexes in regions long and distantly separated; but it did imply that such similarities were developed independently within each region. Elliot Smith's hypothesis of Diffusion was deemed to be devoid of 'any real method', and even the culture-historical method devised by such European scholars as Ratzel and Frobenius, Graebner and Wilhelm Schmidt, and involving geographical distribution, migrations and culture diffusion, was not acceptable. In vain did Schmidt write that there was no obstacle to establishing by this method relations in the past between such cultures 'over great distances and in the cases of discontinuous diffusion'.[32]

Apart from method, hypotheses of Diffusion, except within a specific and limited region, were superfluous in view of the widely and generally accepted theory of 'independent evolution' along with the doctrine of psychic unity. This theory had the prestigious backing of E. B. Tylor and James G. Frazer. The latter refers in the abridged edition of *The Golden Bough*, 1922, p. 2, to 'the essential similarity with which, under many superficial differences, the human mind has elaborated its first crude philosophy'. Tylor in his early writings attributed an essential role to diffusion in certain circumstances, but by 1910 he had changed his view: The old theory 'that a similarity of customs and superstitions, of arts and crafts, justifies the assumption of a remote relationship . . . between races' must be abandoned. It is certain now that there has ever been an inherent tendency in man, allowing for the difference of climate and material surroundings, to develop culture by the same stages and in the same way. Therefore 'American man need not necessarily owe the minutest portion' of his cultural development 'to remote contact with Asia or Europe, though he were proved to possess identical usages'.[33]

In Elliot Smith's view, however, the implied assumption of Tylor and the evolutionist 'school' generally that 'all human beings everywhere have within themselves the possibilities of originating the basic elements of civilization'[34] did not explain the historical phenomena in question. The food-gathering age lasted for an enormous span of time. The 'Neolithic Revolution' which included tilling the soil and growing crops, and forming settled communities, began not more than eight or ten thousand years ago and then probably only in one region (the Middle East) where geographical conditions 'invited' agriculture and where percipient individuals recognized those conditions and so made the forward move possible. This step might be shown to have occurred independently elsewhere, e.g., in Southeast Asia and in Central America, though Elliot Smith at the time doubted it. But the point is still clear: the origin of civilization arose in historical circumstances, and not because of some evolutionary or innate impulse, or of some 'elementary' ideas common to all men, as Bastian had proposed.

Elliot Smith, therefore, looked for the source of the theory, or dogma as it seemed to him, of independent evolutionism and associated concepts. In an article in 1927 on 'The Philosophical Background of Ethnological Theory' (*Journal of Philosophical Studies*, Vol. 2, No. 6), and later in his *Human History* (Chapter I), 1930, in Chapter 2 of *In the Beginning*, 1932, and in *Diffusion of Culture*, 1933, he traced it back to Fontenelle, the popularizer of Cartesian philosophy, and so to Descartes. The latter initiated a 'modern' phase of philosophy by his effort to reduce the principles of knowledge, epistemology, to 'clear and distinct ideas'—to fundamental axioms the soundness of which required no demonstration. They are 'innate ideas', the potentials of which are born with man, and while 'called' into consciousness by happenings of experience, are not derived from experience. Through man's faculty of thinking, by means of this innate endowment, he arrives at *a priori* principles in which our experience is subsumed.[35]

Here, indeed, was epistemological background to the prevailing ethnological theory of the early decades of this century, which confronted Elliot Smith.

In a recent profound exposition of Levy Bruhl's philosophical ethnology, Dr Rodney Needham writes (1972) that in the latter's view, Tylor and Frazer tried to explain the relation between 'savage' and 'civilized' thought, not by examination of the facts, but by postulating a 'human mind' that was logically the same in all periods and in all places. Their approach was *a priori*. Dr Needham adds that the British anthropologists' intellectualist arguments assumed certain premises regarding 'the association of ideas and the inevitable chains of causality', from which 'they could retrace the mental routes by which primitives had been led 'naturally' to certain beliefs and practices', whereas in societies of different structures mental operations might differ. At least, said Levy Bruhl, we must give up the *a priori* reduction of mental operations to one single type.[36]

Descartes, a mathematician, accepted 'mathematics as the fundamental instrument of scientific theory', but as 'mathematical propositions were timeless and unchanging' the flow of historical events, of change and development, lost all fundamental significance; they merely provided illustrations of unchanging geometrical laws.[37] For geometrical laws read 'natural laws' and we have the Cartesian doctrine as promulgated by Bernard de Fontenelle in the late seventeenth century and by Charles Montesquieu in the mid-eighteenth century. The concept of invariability, or of mathematical 'authority', of laws of nature, was to be applied in the study of man, society and culture. Man's nature or innate constitution was postulated to remain stable throughout the ages. Therefore, the varied achievements of different ages and societies were the result of external factors—of 'general causes' as Montesquieu termed them.[38]

In the mid-nineteenth century, too, the influence of Cartesianism was still strong in a very erudite work which challenged Elliot Smith in his epistemological phase. H. T. Buckle in his *History of Civilization in England,* 1857-61, while emphasizing the essential role of observation and the inductive method of historical work, held that the importance of a country's history depended 'upon the degree to which its actions are due to causes springing out of itself', for 'every foreign or external influence which is brought to bear upon a nation is an interference with its natural development'. Holding this Cartesian doctrine, he sought to study a people who had worked out their civilization entirely by themselves because such a history would 'present a condition of normal and inherent development, and would show the laws of progress acting in a state of isolation.[39]

Thus, by stripping away historical interferences or accidents, the Cartesian 'law of nature', of inherent development and 'progress', of 'independent evolution' is revealed. Elliot Smith, on the other hand, held that the diffusion and modification of culture through migration and settlement, even of small groups, to exploit natural resources, and the stimuli provided by such contact, were fundamental in the development of distinct cultures. Cultures elaborate, and have elaborated, their own complex structures through interpenetration which is the only rational clue to their development.[40] Even Egypt which played so vital a part in the beginning and development of civilization, was not isolated. It was not only part of northeastern Africa. Lower Egypt was neighbour to the Near East. In addition, as Elliot Smith pointed out in *The Ancient Egyptians,* Egypt had already in the pre-dynastic period received an infusion of Armenoid immigrants. And Flinders Petrie in his *Revolutions of Civilization* (1911, 1922, Ch. 6) drew attention to the migrations and mixture of different peoples in giving an impetus to culture change and progress in Egypt, the Near East and elsewhere.

Elliot Smith's basic criticism of the Cartesian concept of 'natural law' in its application to history was that it ignored 'the distinctive qualities of man' whose thoughts and actions are profoundly influenced by his personal experience and cannot be forced into conformity with any system of so-called 'laws of nature'.[41]

In what I have called Elliot Smith's epistemological phase, he drew a good deal on F. J. Teggart, 'The Humanistic Study of Change in Time' (1926),[42] who emphasized the continuing influence in all phases of the study of man and of society, of the distinction Greek philosophers made between 'natural' change and 'accidental' or 'historical' change, the latter being the result of external circumstances. Moreover, scientific inquiry, being concerned with determining the natural cause of change in abstraction from all 'accidental' happenings, as defined by the Cartesians and by Buckle, is 'inapplicable in the study of change in time'.

Elliot Smith, however, was concerned with historical change and circumstances, external influences and all. In this he was surely echoing John Stuart Mill's Chapter in *A System of Logic*, 'Of the inverse deductive, or historical method', first published in 1843, the year in which Prescott's *History of Mexico* went to press, but thirteen years before the publication of Buckle's masterpiece.[43] Mill wrote that

> the order of succession which we may be able to trace among the different states of society and civilization which history presents to us, could never amount to a law of nature. It can only be an empirical law . . . It is not possible setting out from the principles of human nature and from the general circumstances of the position of our species, to determine *à priori* the order in which human development must take place and to predict the general facts of history up to the present. The influence over each generation by the generations which preceded it becomes more preponderant over all other influences.

What we do is determined in a very small degree by the universal circumstances of the human race, but mainly by the whole previous history of humanity.[44]

Oikoumene

Thus, after discussing for years factual data of migrations and of the diffusion of culture, Elliot Smith found himself in the final decade of his life, embarking on epistemological inquiry and philosophy of history. This was a logical development of his prevailing interest. Diffusion was not an abstract concept, but like migration with which it was associated, was an historical process as he realized in 1911 when he wrote *The Ancient Egyptians and Their Influence*. This was an historical study of a people in relation to its own 'localized' past, and also 'to events in the rest of the Ancient World'. Later he saw that this influence had extended from centre to centre in a wider world, and was to some degree reciprocal.

R. H. Lowie in a review of Elliot Smith's *In the Beginning* and W. J. Perry's *Gods and Men*,[45] wrote that they attempted to see culture as one connected whole and to trace connections over the entire globe. Professor Kroeber agreed that this was the ultimate, natural unit for ethnology, and adopted for it the classical concept of Oikoumene as 'an Historic Culture Aggregate'. He defines this as 'a great web of culture growth', extensive and rich in content, within which 'inventions or new cultural materials have tended to be transmitted . . . from end to end'. In addition, primitive peoples in or adjoining to the Oikoumene are fully intelligible only in terms of 'Oecumenical' civilization. Elliot Smith would have accepted this concept, though he would have extended its range to cover the New World as well as the Old World of Eurasia and Africa, to which Kroeber limited it.[46] It is this large concept and vision for which Elliot Smith stood. Whether some important culture trait was developed here or there, before or after some other event, was not necessarily significant. He saw the whole civilized world as one

Oikoumene, of which diffusion, or the interpenetration of culture traits and complexes, was the means of ensuring continuity in space and time.

I conclude in the words of a modern specialist in the History and Philosophy of Science:

> The image is no longer that of a static state but of restless design, transmission and change over the millenia since the New Stone Age. It could hardly be otherwise, if we want to account for the variety which has given us China and Babylon, Greece, Mexico, Egypt and India.[47]

And for their part in this revival of historical perspective in ethnological theory, the author, Professor de Santillana, pays tribute to the British School of Diffusionists to whose achievements 'justice will be done eventually'.

Of them, the genius was Grafton Elliot Smith.

Postscript

My aim in this paper has not been to evaluate Elliot Smith's hypothesis in the light of historical, archaeological and ethnological research during the past forty years, but to underline what he said about, and meant by, Diffusion or Migrations of Culture, and what in his opinion was the fallacy in the current doctrines of culture-evolutionism and psychic unity.

To gain perspective, I re-read after several decades almost everything Elliot Smith wrote on ethnology from about 1911-34. During this period, his thinking passed through three overlapping phases, each marked by a different emphasis: (1) a Manchester or historical phase from 1911-17, in which he was concerned with the origin of civilization and with the distribution of certain culture traits; (2) a Manchester-London (a) phase from about 1918-26, in which his preoccupation was with the origin, significance and spread of symbolism; and a London (b) phase (1927-34) in which he developed a strong interest in the philosophical aspects of Diffusion and of criticisms of it.

Moreover, throughout these years we see a deepening and a 'liberalizing' or widening of the concept of Diffusion. Whether the origin of significant culture traits and complexes, around which civilization developed as 'a complexly inter-related system', was in Egypt, or alternatively, or also, in Sumer, India or elsewhere, he came to see diffusion or migrations of culture as the growth of foci or centres of culture stimuli— a kind of 'chain reaction'.

In the course of millennia many populations north and south, west and east of the Old World 'heartland', Egypt and the Middle East, were involved in the historical process of cultural diffusion. Each local population, influenced by immigrant traders, exploiters of natural resources, and other settlers, adopted some of the newcomers' customs and institutions, but the cultural capital thus borrowed was developed in a distinctive way. Consequently, modifications of, and accretions to, the culture traits or complexes they adopted appeared from region to region. Some were lost and new ones developed out of the blend of old and new.[49]

In this process inventions occurred, though rarely, if ever, of an institution, custom or belief which had arisen in a *different* cultural and historical tradition. This was improbable 'because of the complexity of the circumstances and the many fortuitous factors involved in any invention of which we have adequate history'.[50]

Finally, Elliot Smith emphasized that

> the invention of civilization was due not so much to persons endowed with intellectual pre-eminence or exceptional initiative, as to the existence of a particular set of circumstances that forced upon men's attention the possibility of embarking upon a certain course of action and the immediate benefit of doing so. [For] No one claims that the Egyptian and Sumerian pioneers—both members of the so-called Mediterranean Race—were endowed with a mental equipment which was superior to that of all the other members of their own race, or of the Nordic, Alpine and Mongolian races.

Whether or not Negroes and Australian Aborigines would have seized the same opportunities which the Egyptians seized, Elliot Smith said (in 1932) 'we have not the evidence to decide'.[51]

I have referred briefly to these few aspects of Elliot Smith's hypothesis, because of certain pejorative aspersions cast on him by some critics in the past and also more recently: namely, that he was a 'cultural hyper-diffusionist'; in particular, a 'pan-Egyptian hyper-diffusionist' and that he regarded the ancient Egyptians as a 'megalithic master race' or a 'master civilizing people'.[52] I suggest that a dispassionate reading of his books and articles from 1911 onwards shows that such aspersions are not well grounded. In particular, the idea of a 'master race' was anathema to him, and moreover, he specifically refuted the views that Egyptian civilization was transplanted to other peoples and regions, and that it was carried by groups of Egyptians establishing colonies. Scholars interested in the historical development and spread of culture would do well to read objectively what Elliot Smith wrote during his 'Diffusion years', 1911-34.

Needless to say, his hypothesis, which he emphasized was just that, was always open to criticism in total and in details, and is more so today with the advance of research in prehistory and in symbolism. If he were with us now, he would re-examine his hypothesis and attempt a wider synthesis.

NOTES AND REFERENCES

1 Smith, G. E., (1923) *Tutankhamen and the Discovery of his Tomb*, especially pp. 15-19 (for an indication of the wealth hidden in the tombs). Smith, G. E. and Dawson, W. R., (1924) *Egyptian Mummies*, especially the Introduction and Chs II ('The Death and Burial of an Egyptian') and IX ('The Accessories of the Mummy'). Smith, G. E., (1919) *The Evolution of the Dragon*, Ch. I, especially pp. 10-23. Smith, G. E., (1911) *The Ancient Egyptians*, 1st edn, pp. 47-8 (for Pre-dynastic burials), pp. 112-13 (for preservation of the body and continuous

life and portrait statues). And for the development of tombs, Smith, G. E., (1913) 'The Evolution of the Rock-cut Tomb and the Dolmen', in *Essays and Studies presented to William Ridgeway*, pp. 493-546.

2 Smith, G. E., (1932) (rev. edn) *In the Beginning*, p. 38. First published 1928, but all references in this paper are to the 1932 edn.

3 Smith, G. E., (1919) *Evolution of the Dragon*, pp. 29-31.

4 Elliot Smith relied in 1911 for the period in which copper was discovered, on Reisner, G. A., (1908) *The Early Dynastic Cemeteries of Naga-ed-der*, and still did so in 1932 in his *In the Beginning* (1932, new edn; 1st edn, 1927).

5 See also G. E. Smith, (1913) 'The Evolution of the Rock-cut Tomb and the Dolmen', in *Essays and Studies presented to William Ridgeway*, pp. 493-546.

6 G. E. Smith, (1911) *The Ancient Egyptians*, pp. 182-3.

7 Pretty, G., (1969) 'The Macleay Museum Mummy from Torres Straits: A Postscript to Elliot Smith and the Diffusion Controversy', *Man*, 4 (1), 24-43, considers that for the Torres Straits Islanders, who were familiar with preserving meats and fish by drying, smoking and salting, 'the method would have held no undue significance'. Elliot Smith, however, had pointed out in 1915 that the essential processes of mummification—(1) salting, (2) evisceration, (3) drying, and (4) smoking (or even cooking)—are identical with those for the preservation of meat (*On the Significance* . . ., p. 53). These procedures, however, were only part of mummification ritual. Incidentally, Mr Pretty does not note that his two quotations (p. 39) from Elliot Smith, *On the Significance* . . ., do not refer to the introduction of mummification as such, but (1) to the difficult operation of extracting the brain through a hole in the occiput, and (2) to the Islanders' practice of removing 'the skin-thimbles and nails'.

8 *On the Significance* . . ., p. 119.

9 W. H. R. Rivers' comments were made at the 1915 meeting of the British Association for the Advancement of Science and reprinted in his *Psychology and Ethnology*, 1926, pp. 165-6. Cf. p. 118 for the same opinion. See W. J. Perry, 'The Relationship between the Geographical Distribution of Megalithic Monuments and Ancient Mines', *Mem. and Proc. Manchester Lit. and Phil. Soc.*, 1915; and particularly, maps in his *Children of the Sun*, 1923.

10 Kroeber, A. L., (1931) 'Historical Reconstruction of Culture Growths and Organic Evolution', reprinted in *The Nature of Culture*, 1952, pp. 57-62.

11 Smith, G. E., (1932) *In the Beginning*, p. 18.

12 Published in *Culture: a Symposium* (Smith, G. E., (ed.)) 1928, pp. 30-1.

13 Cf. White, L. A., (1959) *The Evolution of Culture*, pp. 70-2.

14 Evans-Pritchard, E. E., (1951) *Social Anthropology*, p. 47. This was true of the rising generation of anthropologists in the 1920s and 1930s. Apart from a few passing references, I heard nothing of the 'quarrel' during 1925-7 when I was at London University. Certainly, W. J. Perry did not criticize Functionalism. He was trying to work out a way of handling and interpreting the vast amount of data, which might throw light on the development of human institutions. In *Children of the Sun* he had, he thought, made some contribution, and he was at the time working on material for *The Primordial Ocean*, 1935.

Incidentally, Radcliffe-Brown was supported in his application for the new Chair of Anthropology, University of Sydney, 1925, by the 'Diffusionists', Elliot Smith and Perry.

15 Goldenweiser, A., (1921) *Early Civilization*, p. 307.

16 Spinden, in *Culture: a Symposium*, 1928 by G. Elliot Smith, et al., p. 60.

17 Caso, A. 'New World Culture History: Middle America', in *Anthropology Today*. Prepared under the Chairmanship of A. L. Kroeber. 1953, pp. 226-37.

18 Glyn Daniel (*The Idea of Prehistory*, 1962; Pelican edn, 1971, p. 105) writes: 'almost every cultural element in the New World can be explained as of purely local growth'. The early agricultural communities there 'developed into the Urban Civilizations of Central America' apparently 'without any contact of a serious nature from abroad. It was in fact a tale of independent cultural evolution'. In fact, however, we need evidence to substantiate this return to Spinden and Prescott. The work of the symposium (1968) recorded in *Man Across the Sea* (1971) throws doubt on Daniel's assertion. Prehistoric Archaeology has still much to do in pre-Columbian America.

19 A recent prehistorian, Glyn Daniel of Cambridge, England (*The Idea of Prehistory*, Pelican edn, 1971, pp. 99-100) makes another point: the pyramids of Egypt and of Central America are 'superficially identical', that is, in form. In Egypt, however, they were tombs, whereas in Central America they were temple platforms on which rites were performed. That is, they differ in function. Therefore, in Daniel's view, they should not be compared, nor should an attempt be made to derive one from the other.

Difference of function, however, of an identical or similar culture trait in two regions does not necessarily prove absence of historical connection. Similar or identical structures, the idea or pattern of which is from a common source, can be used for different purposes in different cultural contexts. In this particular case, we should note that temples for rites were associated with Egyptian pyramids.

20 Goldenweiser, A., (1921) *Early Civilization*, p. 311.

21 Morley, S. G., '*The Inscriptions at Copan*', 1920, p. 224. He was referring particularly to the hypothesis of a possible Asiatic origin of Maya civilization, and, indeed, to any attempt to establish direct cultural connection between the Maya and any old-world civilization, Egyptian or Mongolian.

22 Spinden, H. J., (1928) in *Culture, the Diffusion Controversy*, p. 60; and p. 83 'the ancient Americas achieved by far the greater portion of their culture without occult help from the dominant civilizations of the Old World'.

23 Dixon, R. B., (1929) *The Building of Cultures*, p. 208.

24 Smith, G. E., (1917) 'Ancient Mariners', *J. Manchester Geog. Soc.*, Vol. XXXIII; *Ships as Evidence of the Migrations of Early Culture*, 1917; *Elephants and Ethnologists*, 1924, pp. 99-100, 121; *Diffusion of Culture*, 1933, pp. 224-5, 231-2.

25 In *An Appraisal of Anthropology Today*, 1953, p. 47. (Report of a Symposium, 1952, Sol Tax, *et al.* (eds)). During the same discussion (p.47), A. V. Kidder said 'it is awfully hard to get over one's prejudices . . . I think I still remain 100 per cent American in the matter of Eurasian influence on the development of New World civilizations'.

26 Smith, G. E., (1915) 'On the Significance of the Geographical Distribution of the Practice of Mummification', *Mem. and Proc. Manchester Lit. and Phil. Soc.*, p. 14. 'Ancient Mariners', *J. Manchester Geog. Soc.*, Vol. XXXIII, 1917. *Human History*, 1930, p. 385. *In the Beginning*, 1932, p. 108.

27 Doran, E. Jr, (1971) 'The Sailing Raft as a Great Tradition', in *Man Across the Sea*, pp. 135-6.

28 Kennedy, R. A., (1971) 'A Transatlantic Stimulus Hypothesis for Meso America and the Caribbean, *c.* 3500 to 2000 B.C.' in *Man Across the Sea*, pp. 266-74, especially pp. 272-4.

29 Edwards, C. R., (1971) 'Commentary B' in *Man Across the Sea*, pp. 296-7.

30 Heine-Geldern, R., (1964) 'One Hundred Years of Ethnological Theory in the German-Speaking Countries: Some Milestones' in *Current Anthropology*, 5 (5), p. 411.

31 Professor Wang Gungwu suggests in his chapter in this symposium that in a certain phase of Chinese history, Chinese scholars expressed a similar attitude to Diffusion.

32 Schmidt, W., (1939) *The Culture Historical Method of Ethnology*, Ch. I. Haddon, A. C., (1934) *History of Anthropology* (Thinker's Library), pp. 113-15, 123. Penniman, T. K., (1935) *A Hundred Years of Anthropology*, pp. 324-9, for a brief exposition and criticism of Graebner and Schmidt.

33 Tylor, E. B., (1910) 'Anthropology' in *Encyclopaedia Britannica*, 11th edn, Vol. 2, p. 119. Summaries of Tylor's views are given by Marschall, W., (1972) *Transpazifische Kulturbeziehungen*, pp. 28-34, and by Penniman, T. K., (1935) *A Hundred Years of Anthropology*, pp. 174-85. But the latter does not refer to Tylor's change of view. A. C. Haddon does in his *History of Anthropology* (Thinker's Library), 1934, p. 119.

34 As summed up by T. K. Penniman, *A Hundred Years . . .*, p. 307, who suggests that the evolutionists were right.

35 Descartes, R., *A Discourse on Method*; *Meditations*, and *The Principles of Philosophy* (first published, 1837-41-44). Everyman's Library Series reprint with Introduction (1912) and Notes by A. D. Lindsay. Pp. 98, 250-2. 'The discoveries of reason are not made by deducing the particular from the universal, but from perceiving the universal in the individual instance.' (Lindsay's Introduction, p. xiv.) According to Lindsay (p. xix) the Cartesian philosophy which flowed from Descartes' epistemology had 'a fatal influence on modern theories of knowledge'.

36 Needham, R., (1972) *Belief, Language and Experience*, Ch. 10, especially pp. 177-82.

37 Toulmin, S. & Goodfield, J., *The Discovery of Time* (1965; Pelican 1967), pp. 94 ff. especially 95-7. A very helpful exposition of some of Descartes' ideas.

38 Toulmin, S. & Goodfield, J., *The Discovery of Time*, p. 324. 'The concept "laws of nature" acquired a central position in European natural philosophy only in the 17th Century'. See pp. 140-4, for a discussion of Fontenelle and Montesquieu.

39 Buckle chose England as the country in which these conditions had been most nearly followed, at least for a few centuries. Buckle, H. T., (1857-61) *History of Civilization in England*. Elliot Smith used the 1902 edn. My references are to the 1867 edn, viz. Vol. I, pp. 157-9, 231-2. On p. 230 he emphasizes the necessity to observe the facts first and then find their laws. In Vol. II, pp. 77-92, Buckle summarizes Descartes' contributions, and also pays him a high tribute: 'he effected a revolution more decisive than has ever been brought about by any other single mind'.

40 Smith, G. E., (1927) 'The Philosophical Background of Ethnological Theory', *Journal of Philosophical Studies*, 2 (6), p. 182. Smith, G. E., *In the Beginning*, Ch. VIII, especially pp. 95-7.

41 Smith, G. E., (1930) *Human History*, pp. 35-41, 55-7. Smith, G. E., (1932) *In the Beginning*, pp. 17-20.

42 Teggart, F. J., *The Journal of Philosophy*, Vol. XXIII, pp. 309-14.

43 In the 5th edn, 1862, however, in a new chapter, 'Additional Elucidations of the Science of History', Mill refers to Buckle's *History of Civilization in England*, especially to the verification à *posteriori* of the law of causation in its application to human conduct. Mill, Vol. II, pp. 525-6.

44 Mill, J. S., (1862) *System of Logic*. I quote from the 5th edn, pp. 505-6.

45 Perry, W. J., (1930) *The American Anthropologist*, Vol. 32, pp. 165-8.

[46] Kroeber, A. L., 'The Ancient Oikoumene as an Historic Culture Aggregate', being the Huxley Memorial Lecture for 1945. Reprinted in *The Nature of Culture*, 1952, pp. 379-95; see especially pp. 392-5.

[47] De Santillana, G., (1961) *The Origins of Scientific Thought*, p. 10.

[48] Smith, G. E., 'Nordic Race Claims', address at International Congress of Anthropology and Ethnology, London, 1934. Reprinted in *Sir Grafton Elliot Smith*, W. R. Dawson (ed.), p. 259.

[49] Smith, G. E., (1930) in *The Making of Man*, V. F. Calverton (ed.), pp. 393 ff. Smith, G. E., (1933) *Diffusion of Culture*, pp. 224-32. Smith, G. E., (1932) *In the Beginning*, Ch. VIII, especially pp. 95-6, 101 ff. For Elliot Smith's earlier statements, *The Ancient Egyptians*, 1911, pp. 182-3; and 'The Evolution of the Rock-cut Tomb and the Dolmen', in *Essays and Studies presented to William Ridgeway*, 1913, pp. 493 ff.

[50] Smith, G. E., (1933) *Diffusion of Culture*, p. 218.

[51] Smith, G. E., (1932) *In the Beginning*, pp. 25-6, and compare his paper to the International Congress of Anthropology and Ethnology, London, 1934, on 'Nordic Race Claims' in *Sir Grafton Elliot Smith*, W. R. Dawson (ed.), 1937, p. 259.

[52] E.g., Daniel, G. in *The Idea of Prehistory* (Pelican Books 1964; 1st edn, 1962), Ch. Five (and elsewhere, e.g., pp. 86-7, 117) provides what appears to be a tirade against Elliot Smith, not a scholarly criticism of his work.

Pretty, G., (1969) 'The Macleay Museum Mummy from Torres Straits', *Man*, 4 (1), pp. 26-7, says that Elliot Smith provided a racial application for a cultural movement which brought several cultural traits to America; and that the migrating bands which transmitted the cultural traits had 'racial affiliations to ancient Egyptians'. What 'racial application' means is not clear, but if the second statement means that the migrating bands who reached America were Egyptian, it should not be attributed to Elliot Smith.

12 CULTURAL DIFFUSION FROM, IN AND TO AFRICA

Raymond A. Dart

Introduction

A centenary commemoration such as we are now celebrating, inevitably causes antique specimens such as myself to cast retrospective glances over those deeds, or misdeeds of our lives, that we can attribute to stimuli awakened in some special field more or less directly by the influence of the particular person being commemorated.

My mother was the first person to put into my hands a book dealing with Egypt. It was Adolf Erman's *Life in Ancient Egypt* (trans. 1894). So it would be misleading to blame Sir Grafton Elliot Smith for that interest; he had fertile soil to work upon. But it surprised me on reviewing those of my papers dealing more or less directly with influences impinging upon South Africa foreign to Bush, Hottentot or Bantu culture, to find that over fifty had dealt directly or indirectly with such recent cultural matters as foreign influences in mural art and in rock paintings, polished stone ornaments, bored stones and their ritual use, burial customs, ancient mining of metallic ores, not only for gold and iron, but also for copper and tin and the making of bronze.

Hence, during the half-century that has elapsed since England was relieved from my brief residence there (1919-22) excluding the one year (1920-1) spent in America, archaeologists and cultural anthropologists —who under D. Randall-MacIver's early guidance, had relegated Zimbabwe along with all it represented, to the then ignominious status of a 'mediaeval kaffer kraal'—were considerably irritated by some of these repetitive sallies into this archaeologically-unoccupied ancient mining territory as listed at the end of this article and written by a thitherto unknown product of the amateur diffusionist school of Elliot Smith and W. J. Perry.

Mapungubwe and Bambandyanalo, or pre-European Cultural Diffusion

Miss G. Caton-Thompson's subsequent excavational work in 1929 carried the story of Zimbabwe back to an undeterminable stage, but possibly through beads to 800 AD. Then from 1932 on, the discovery of gold ornaments from graves at Mapungubwe on the south, or right, or Transvaal side of the Limpopo River about 40 miles west of Messina, afforded the late Dr Alexander Galloway the opportunity of examining critically at the outset, some eleven individuals from the actual hill burials! He found they were not Negro, but 'a Bush-Boskop people showing sporadically a few Negro features . . . Mapungubwe represents a homogeneous Boskop-Bush population physically akin to the post-Boskop inhabitants of the coastal caves' (Galloway, 1937).

Subsequently a raised area on a less elevated hill on the opposite, or western side of the narrow valley separating it from the Mapungubwe gold-burial hill site was trenched. So many astonishing remains of beast burials were found that work was continued there for three years; and 74 human skeletons of all ages and sexes were unearthed.

Of these 74 skeletons disinterred up to 1936, 37 were studied by the late Dr Alexander Galloway (who subsequently became Professor of Anatomy and first Dean of the Makerere Medical School in Uganda) in the period of 1935-7. His study was accepted for the DSc degree of the University of the Witwatersrand and was published in full as *The Skeletal Remains of Bambandyanalo* (P. V. Tobias (ed.), 1959), for which I wrote the Foreword. In this Foreword I drew attention firstly to the report by the experienced excavator, the late Captain G. A. Gardner that:

> These burials, six of which were uncovered, consisted of bones, portions of skulls and teeth of cattle and were buried ceremoniously under a pile of sherds from the deliberately broken pots. There was a small chamber or focal point which contained one bone and sometimes sea-shells, copper bracelets and other objects. Curiously enough, in every case except one, a broken-spouted pot was part of the funerary furniture; no spouted bowls were ever found among the human interments. I cannot go into detail here, but these bovine burials are unquestionably relics of an old Hamitic cult, and may be compared with the beast burials of the Badarian culture of Upper Egypt, but there the funerary pots are lacking (Dart in Galloway, pp. xvi-xvii quoting Gardner).

On the basis of this cultural information I concluded firstly that,

> Culturally, as well as in their burial customs, these Bambandyanalo people differed from the Bantu. They were experts in pottery making but, instead of being agriculturalists, were like the Hottentots found by the first European settlers at the Cape, pastoral in habit, dependent upon their cattle and sheep but having no hoe-culture. No bones of other domesticated animals have been discovered; their implements were chiefly made from bone; iron is conspicuously absent and copper was used only for adornment (Dart in Galloway, p. xvii).

Secondly, I quoted Dr A. Galloway's remarks after his painstaking analysis of these Bambandyanalo, or K2 people:

> I state deliberately and with full comprehension of its significance that there is not a single specifically negro feature in any of the skulls hitherto recovered at K2. The K2 are thus true representatives of a pre-negro indigenous people, with which the Bantu-speaking peoples had never hybridized (Dart in Galloway, p. xvii).

Thirdly, I drew attention to the fact that in 1952 from a series of 21 samples excavated from Bambandyanalo and Mapungubwe Dr E. S. Deevey, Director of the Geochronometric Laboratory, had only been able through the many calls upon his laboratory at Yale University, to test the date of the Beast Burial no. 6 which was '900 ± 65 years or approximately 1055 AD.' (Dart in Galloway quoting Deevey, p. xviii).

Before the actual publication of Galloway's physical anthropological study Professor P. V. Tobias received further information from Dr E. S. Deevey and also from Mr Roger Summers about radio-carbon datings at Zimbabwe as determined by Dr W. F. Libby himself. So he was able to amplify the comparison between Mapungubwe and Zimbabwe in a note as follows:

AD	AD
Zimbabwe 591 ± 120 years	Bambandyanalo 1055 ± 65 years
702 ± 92 years	1370 ± 60 years
714 ± 80 years	1410 ± 80 years

(Tobias in Galloway, p. xi)

According to Mr Summers' own article on Zimbabwe in the 1969 edition of the *Encyclopaedia Britannica*

Radio-carbon dates show that Zimbabwe Hill was first occupied in the 3rd century A.D. by some of the earliest Iron Age people in Rhodesia. Thereafter the site seems to have been abandoned, not to be re-occupied until about the 9th (or 10th) century.

In my Foreword my commentary on the Bambandyanalo and Zimbabwe radio-carbon datings was:

These beast burials were therefore being practised on the Limpopo when England was still Saxon and before the Battle of Hastings. According to Libby's estimates, the age of the piece of tamboetie or *ubane wood* extracted from the Inner Wall of the Parallel Passage in the Elliptical Building of the Zimbabwe Ruins ranged between 1011 and 1575 years, the average of all estimations being 1361 ± 120 years. This wall was therefore built at the same time which could have been as early as A.D. 377, or late as A.D. 941, a range of possibility provided also by Beck on the evidence of beads found by Miss Caton-Thompson. The mid-point between these two extreme dates is A.D. 504: i.e. when the Huns had invaded India and broken the Gupta Empire or about a century after the Western Roman Empire. (Dart in Galloway, p. xviii)

In the same Foreword (pp. xviii-xix), I wrote:

Sofala, from which much gold was brought . . . according to Masudi, was inhabited by a tribe of Abyssinians who had emigrated recently, and whose king, called the Waklimi, had his capital near there . . . So historical literary evidence shows that in the tenth century A.D. not only was Portuguese East Africa inhabited by a Bush-Hottentot people called Wak-Wak, but the king of Sofala was called the Waklimi and his occupation force was composed of Abyssinians. The fact that the Axumite kingdom flourished in

Abyssinia from the first to the seventh century corroborates the inference that Abyssinian trading influence was dominant in the Red Sea to Rhodesia between the third and seventh centuries, i.e. for the half-millennium during any part of which the Inner Wall of the Parallel Passage at Zimbabwe could have been erected. (Dart in Galloway, quoting Miss K. M. Kenyon)

Twenty-two years earlier I had summarized in the first chapter on 'Racial Origins' in *The Bantu-speaking Tribes of South Africa* (I. Schapera (ed.), 1937) the historical background of the East African coast prior to Da Gama's circumnavigation of the coast in 1498, through its Moslemic occupation from the fifteenth to the eighth centuries and its previous Abyssinian dominance of the seventh back to the fourth century, when it had replaced that of the Sabaean Himyaritic Arabians. Not only Cosmas Indicopleustes (*c.* AD 547) but the Greek author of the *Periplus of the Erythraean Sea* (*c.* AD 60) also had provided historical evidence which demonstrated the continuity of foreign trading influence with the pre-Bantu, as well as the Bantu-speaking population of South Africa throughout the present or recent Christian era.

Repeated Far East Influence upon Africa

The Empire Exhibition held in Johannesburg in 1936 afforded me the opportunity of studying the /?Auni≠Khomani tribe of Southern Bushmen. There in the most southern part of Bushman land I paid particular attention to their facial appearance by making a mathematical estimate of the foreign racial features they presented. I was not surprised to find that 23.4 per cent of their faces had Brown, or Mediterranean features and 15.6 per cent exhibited Armenoid traits; but I was astonished to find that the greatest percentage of facial features foreign to South Africa, i.e., 24.7 per cent were Mongolian.

Hence I was deeply impressed to find in 'The /?Auni≠Khomani Bushmen' (*Bantu Stud.*, 11, 175-246) not on South Africa's east coast but in its western Kalahari desert area in 1936 not only the wide extent of past hybridization but also in particular, the admixture of mongoloid features preponderant. Then in addition, I encountered a few years later in Southern Rhodesia over 2,000 miles away to the northeast, the fact that a Bantu tribe in Hondi Gorge had used on the wall of a school the Chinese symbol for the word 'Tien', a Chinese family-name; and that this had been recognized spontaneously by Mr C. H. Tien on his previous visit to St Augustine's Mission (see Dart, 1939).

So it was patent that the impact of mongolian influence upon Africa was not superficial, nor restricted geographically to Indonesia but had been recent enough to include a Bantu phase and even Chinese writing; and yet that far eastern influence had also been sufficiently ancient to affect physically a quarter of the still extant and most southern group of Kalahari Bushmen. So it had probably operated upon the South African population at two very different but relatively recent historical stages: firstly a Khoisan population—hybridizing stage, and a later more recent writing-introducing phase after the Bantu had replaced the Bush-Hottentot population in Southern Rhodesia and the northern part of Portuguese East Africa.

Repetitive European Influence upon Africa

The concurrent studies leading to my chapter (1937) on 'Racial Origins' had shown that the Negro population itself on the east side of Africa exhibited more brachycephalic hypsicephals the further northward one proceeded towards Asia while on the west side one encountered more dolichocephalic hypsicephals the nearer one approximated Europe. So I examined all the then available data on the crania of Egyptian people from Early Pre-dynastic to modern times; and found that Egypt had experienced no less than four population-changing intrusions not from Asia alone as Elliot Smith had surmised, but essentially from eastern and western Europe. Hypsicephals, both dolichocephalic and brachy-cephalic had overrun Egypt four times at approximately 1,500 years distance from one another during the past 7,000 years.

That paper was published in 1939, two years after Elliot Smith's death, in the *Proceedings of the Royal Society of South Africa*, shortly before World War II. After the war ceased physical and anthropological interest in Africa had become more intently fastened upon the australo-pithecine phase of man's prehistory than upon the hybridization of mankind, that has been inseparable from commerce and cultural diffusion.

Colin Renfrew (1971) however, has been showing recently in 'Carbon 14 and the prehistory of Europe' *(Scientific American, 225, 63-75)* that the radio-carbon dating laboratories of Arizona, Pennsylvania and California (at San Diego) in conjunction with Dr C. W. Ferguson of the University of Arizona have made the critical discovery that the divergence between carbon 14 and tree-ring dates becomes progressively greater the farther they are traced back. This has resulted from Dr Ferguson's success in building up 'a continuous absolute chronology reaching back nearly 8,200 years' with the aid of bristlecone pine trees.

The divergence between tree-ring and radio-carbon dating methods was so small that at first people thought the differences were due to faults in the radio-carbon method. Then Eric H. Willis, Henrik Tauber and Karl O. Munnik analysed samples of a giant sequoia and found, as Renfrew points out (1971, p. 68) that

> Although the carbon-14 dates and the tree-ring dates agree to within 100 years all the way back to A.D. 650 (i.e. 1300 years) some minor but real fluctuations were observed. This suggested that there had been definite small changes in the rate of carbon-14 production in the past.
> At San Diego Hans E. Suess has analysed more than 300 such (bristlecone pine tree-ring and radio-carbon dating) samples and has built up an im-pressively clear and coherent picture of these discrepancies.
> While divergence between the carbon-14 and the tree-ring dates is not

serious after 1500 B.C. Before that time (c. 4450 years ago or about the middle of the fifth millennium before the present) the difference becomes progressively larger and amounts to as much as 700 years by 2500 B.C. The carbon-14 dates are all too young, but Suess's analysis can be used to correct them.

The divergences exhibit both large first-order, and smaller second-order fluctuation or 'kinks', the Czechoslovakian geophysicist V. Bucha has shown that there is a striking correlation between the divergence in dates and past changes in the strength of the earth's magnetic field. The first-order variation is probably due to the fact that as the strength of the earth's field changed, it deflected more or fewer cosmic rays before they could enter the atmosphere. There are strong indications that the second-order fluctuations are correlated with the level of solar activity. Both the low-energy particles of the solar wind 'and the high-energy particles that are the solar component of the cosmic radiation may affect the cosmic ray flux in the vicinity of the earth. Climatic changes may also have influenced the concentration of carbon-14 in the atmosphere'. (Renfrew, 1971, p. 68.)

Renfrew as an archaeologist was more deeply concerned with such facts as firstly that 'a carbon-14 date of about 2350 B.C. for the walls and tombs at Los Millares in Spain must now be set around 2900 B.C. This makes the (Spanish) structures older than their supposed prototypes in the Aegean'. Secondly that 'The (Stonehenge) monument is now seen to be several centuries older (than 1500 B.C.) and Mycenean influence is clearly out of the question'. He finds that 'when we compare areas that have calibrated carbon-14 dates with areas that are dated by historical means' a greater hiatus occurs between prehistoric Europe and the Aegean and eastern Mediterranean.

Now it is clear that megalithic chamber tombs were being built in Brittany earlier than 4000 B.C., a millennium before monumental funerary architecture first appears in the eastern Mediterranean and 1,500 years before the raising of the pyramids. The origins of these European burial customs and monuments have to be sought not in the Near East but in Europe itself. (p. 69)

The part of Renfrew's paper I found surprising is not these facts revealed by radio-carbon dating, but his inferences therefrom: firstly, that 'Diffusion has been overplayed' (p. 70) and secondly, that these European dates are 'turning the tables on the old diffusionists' by suggesting that the early measurements and innovations in Europe inspired the pyramids of Egypt or other achievements in the Near East. That (he states) 'would merely be to reverse the arrows on the diffusionist map, and to miss the real lesson of the new dating' (p. 72).

What a source of fascinated astonishment it would have been to Elliot Smith if he had lived to read about the discoveries made by Gerald S. Hawkins concerning Stonehenge during the 1960s; and to learn through his preface to *Stonehenge Decoded* (1965) that 'Many facts, for example the 56 year eclipse cycle, were not known to me and other astronomers, but were discovered (or rather rediscovered) from the decoding of Stonehenge'. How greatly he would have savoured the fact that it was C. A. Newham's interest in Diodorus's story about Apollo's repetitive visits to the Celtic island temple every nineteen years and R. S. Newall's kindness in drawing G. S. Hawkin's attention thereto, which led to the latter's discovery of the computer potentiality of Stonehenge and led him 'into fields of the humanities as well as fields of science' as he has stated (p. 72).

The Vast Antiquity and World Wide Impacts of Cultural Diffusion

It has become patent not only from these far earlier European radio-carbon datings from Europe but also from the studies made by Alexander Marschack since 1964 that lunar, seasonal and even annual recordings by means of notchings on bones and implements go back to Aurignacian times. Serial markings with pointed tools of different types on the surfaces of bone and stone (see also his *The Roots of Civilisation*, McGraw Hill, N.Y. 1972, 413 pp., illus) are showing that mathematical recordings of the passage of time and of the recurrence of seasons in terms of lunar cycles were very ancient and persistent European pursuits. Thus systematic celestial observation originated and diffusing widespread, apparently underwent its evolution in Central and Western Europe from Czechoslovakia through Germany and France to Spain between Aurignacian times, probably some 25,000 years ago and onwards into the Mesolithic and Neolithic eras.

As these late palaeolithic discoveries made by Marschack are so recent and fragmentary it is impossible as yet to trace their directional inter-relations in detail any more than we can define at present the actual source of their development in Europe. But it is patent from the mural art of Europe itself that great advances in communication were in progress there during the late palaeolithic era, which could not have happened without the discovery of language, reckoning and planning (see Dart, 1959). It is common cause that burial rituals had become widespread from Western Europe to Afghanistan from one or more centres even in Mousterian times.

During the Internationl Quaternary Congress (INQUA) in Paris in 1969, Miss E. Schmid of Basle, Switzerland, described a presumably Mousterian silex (flint) mine in the Swiss Jura. In discussion I pointed out that at the Ngwenya Iron Mine in Swaziland radio-carbon dating of prehistoric mining had been carried out; and that the Lion Cavern site, showed that haematite in the forms of red ochre (or bloodstone) and specularite (or black micaceous 'looking glass' ore) had been mined from the forty-third millennium BP onwards, and had persisted at that site for over 30,000 years (see J. Vogel, *Radiocarbon*, 12, 162, 444, 1970).

Two presumptions were therefore justified from this discovery: firstly that bloodstone was the earliest material so far proven to have been mined; and secondly that this mining could only have been for its symbolical significance (see Dart, 1968a 'The birth of symbology', *Afr. Stud.*, 27, 15-27). We know that the use of haematite in burial ritual goes back to Mousterian times in Western Europe as at La Chapelle and La Ferrassie (see J. Maringer, *The Gods of Prehistoric Man*, 1960). Fortunately, too there is little room for disagreement about the assumption that haematite, i.e., bloodstone, received its name in both the Greek and the English languages for the same reason as Elliot Smith stated in *The Evolution of the Dragon* (1919, p. 114),

> In course of time the practice of human sacrifice was abandoned and substitutes were adopted in the place of the blood of mankind. Either the blood of cattle, who by means of appropriate ceremonies could be transformed into human beings (for the Great Mother herself was the Divine Cow and her offspring cattle), was employed in its stead; or red ochre was used to colour a liquid which was used ritually to replace the blood of sacrifice. When this phase of culture was reached the goddess provided for the king the elixir of life consisting of beer stained red by means of red ochre, so as to simulate human blood.

Or, as Elliot Smith had also put it in 'The idea of the supernatural in Human Development' (Ch. 10 in *Universal History of the World*, J. A. Hammerton (ed.), 1927, 249-364, 356),

> The earliest members of our species whose remains had been recovered in the Grottes des Enfants at Mentone, at Predmost in Moravia, in the Dordogne Valley and elsewhere in France, and in Paviland Cave in South Wales, had red ochre and shells placed in the grave with their bodies. There are reasons for believing that the red ochre was put there as a substitute for blood, which was regarded as the life-stuff, and the shells as a symbol of birth, or life-giving. Both red ochre and shells were amulets believed to be capable of adding to the deceased's vitality—in other words, of increasing his chance of prolonging existence.

Thus Elliot Smith realized the vast antiquity of red ochre rituals.

It will be obvious to present-day diffusionists that these Mousterian dates for red ochre mining put an entirely different complexion upon the whole question of its world wide diffusion. This I took up two years ago in several articles, one of which was about 'Bloodstone and its iron revolutions' (Dart, 1970). Diffusion has been active not just for the last four millennia but for over forty millennia.

Is Persistence of Past Antagonisms Useful?

In the *Megalith Builders of Western Europe*, Glyn Daniel (1962, pp. 24-5) made the misleading observation that 'Sir Grafton Elliot Smith and his pupil W. J. Perry spent a lifetime in advocating that civilization was due to the spread of a master-race from Egypt'; and sought thereby to justify 'Archaeologists and anthropologists (who) have not unnaturally reacted against the monocentric-diffusionism of the Elliot Smith-Perry school'. Yet when faced in his concluding chapter with the enigma of their existence and spread he was unable to find any better explanation of megalithic tomb building activities in Europe (pp. 136-7) than the diffusional one of trading for metals by a people with a strong religious faith of east Mediterranean origin and complicated funerary practices that Elliot Smith and Perry had advanced.

Only through reading such comment as the fifth chapter on 'Diffusion and Distraction' in Daniel's *The Idea of Prehistory* (1962) however, can one assess the bitterness of the antagonism evoked amongst some English and American prehistorians by the writings of these two men, who in fact had attributed world wide diffusion not to the propagational activities of the Egyptians themselves, but to the persistent influence of the undying cultural practices within Egypt upon those of other countries both near and remote. In any event it is astonishing and somewhat sad to find the memory of gifted scientists, whose contributions predated World War II and the vast advances in precisional knowledge since their death, being minimized a generation or more after nuclear physicists have been flood-lighting prehistory for a decade with objective dating.

Elliot Smith expected all his assistants, such as myself, to go beyond, or should I rather say to extend by confirmation or by modification, the sort of work that he himself had initiated or left incomplete. Whereas he had illustrated in *The Ancient Egyptians* the brachycephalic Armenoid populational intrusion into Egypt, I had no hesitation about showing in 'Population fluctuation over 7,000 years in Egypt' (Dart, 1939) how such Armenoids had been accompanied in Late Dynastic and had been preceded in Early Dynastic times, by long-headed ellipsoid Nordic intruders into Egypt. His previous work had led the way to such understanding on my part, but he died before my paper was published.

So it was thrilling to a hyper-diffusionist such as myself to be instructed today by these longest-living bristlecone pines, that Dr Colin Rendrew (1971) finds 'the revision of carbon-14 dates for prehistoric Europe has a disastrous effect upon the traditional diffusionist chronology'; and that

> megalith chamber tombs were being built in Brittany earlier than 4000 B.C., a millennium before monumental funerary architecture first appears in the eastern Mediterranean and 1500 years before the raising of the pyramids. The origins of these burial customs and monuments have to be sought not in the Near East but in Europe itself.

Such a radical reversal of direction from prehistoric Europe to prehistoric Egypt would have thrilled Elliot Smith equally, I believe.

There is nothing inconsistent between these recent data and those published thirty-three years ago in my 1939 paper. On the contrary they provide independent corroboration of the trans-Mediterranean invasions from Europe I postulated then. Unfortunately Sir Grafton had passed away two years earlier, but I cannot imagine that his reaction thereto would have differed from my own to aquatic migrations by sea from Europe into Egypt. He would never stoop to twist facts to prove a hypothesis, however cherished. Nobody could have believed less than he in an Egyptian 'master race', nor opposed that idea more earnestly than he who had also upheld the 'natural goodness and kindliness of human beings'. Strangely enough too the moderate type of diffusion that Glyn Daniel so greatly preferred and attributed to Gordon Childe, probably owed its evocative stimulus and development to the insight that his senior, fellow-Sydney graduate Elliot Smith had rendered inescapable.

At any rate it is beyond the capacity of those who knew him personally to comprehend such statements as 'Elliot Smith rejected the idea of archaeological prehistory as unsatisfactory'; or to assume with Daniel and Lowie that this Australian neurologist, who laboured for years with Maspero and Reisner in Egypt, displayed either 'crass, or unfathomable ignorance in ethnography'. That dissent does not signify that Elliot Smith's conclusions were always right or final; it means that he expected and accepted that anybody travelling the same or a parallel road could, and having the privilege of living longer and seeing more, probably would go further toward the goal of truth than he had been permitted to travel himself.

At his own instigation as was typical of his procedure, I had followed the same road he had travelled with the fossil Archaeoceti (or Zeuglodonts) from the Egyptian Fäyum, and went further. That met with his complete approbation. So too did my work on his own territory of the corpus striatum and the dual structure of the cerebral cortex. In his recognition of the potential significance of *Australopithecus* deeply as that was prejudiced by Piltdown's fraudulence, he went at the outset beyond my own observations and inferences.

Yet I imagine nobody could have appreciated better than he too, how Joseph Shellshear's and my rejection of Wilhelm His's doctrine affected current neurological inference; and how much further confrontation could be deferred or avoided in post-World-War-I Europe, by settling Joseph Shellshear in Hong Kong and myself temporarily in Johannesburg. Divergent as the outcome may have been from his, or our own expectations in 1922, his strategy from the strictly anatomical and medical angles that interested most profoundly the Rockefeller Foundation that had done so much both for world medicine and for ourselves, at that juncture fifty years ago, was faultless. The Foundation's business was 'the well-being of mankind'.

Other historians like Jacquetta Hawkes (1963, 1, p. 99) of *The World of The Past* (2 vols) minimize Elliot Smith's memory by terming him and Perry 'fanatical' and by coupling them in the following fashion with those who failed earlier and for far less reason to believe in the absolute separateness of human culture in America; but

> looked to Atlantis, to the Egyptians, the Phoenicians and to Africa, or have postulated large-scale immigration from Asia within historical times. Fanatical diffusionists such as W. J. Perry and Eliot (sic) Smith were naturally particularly attracted to such ideas and the latter's fancy that he could recognise elephants on some Maya sculpture at Palenque and elsewhere led

to a well-known controversy. It can be pursued by those fascinated with such oddities in Eliot (sic) Smith's *Elephants and Ethnologists*.

By quoting 'Tomb robbers and mummies' in extenso from Elliot Smith's *Tutankhamen* (1923) in the same work (1, 586-90) however, she at least indicated the calibre of the man whose birth we are honouring and the value to archaeology of whose anatomical and other observations for our understanding of Egyptian history and culture and their dispersal we are commemorating.

Glyn Daniel (1970, pp. 163-6) preferred the reverse tactic of recognizing his brilliance but finding him rather alien, 'an Australian', who

> had a 'kink': when he studied mammals in Egypt and found the technique of mummification very highly complicated—although, in fact it is the standard procedure for dealing with any dead animals—he believed it was a technique that could not have been independently invented elsewhere. This naturally led Elliot Smith to study mummification in other parts of the world, and there, or so he thought, he found the same techniques and ritual as existed in Ancient Egypt. It all must have started in Egypt: so he and his disciple, W. J. Perry, had Egyptians spreading a Heliolithic Civilization all over the world. By the way, Ancient Egypt in America is still a popular cult although there is no basis for it whatsoever.

By inserting this misrepresentation of Elliot Smith's factual mummification studies between his previous comments on 'The Lost Tribes of Israel hypothesis and *The Book of Mormon*' and his later discussion of the 'Calendar of lunacies' and 'crackpots' Daniel cleverly contrived to place Elliot Smith and W. J. Perry in the midst of 'the lunatic fringes of archaeology', which he hoped and thought, not in vain 'will narrow, if not disappear, as precise archaeological dates provided by C 14 dating reduce the area in which speculation is possible'.

Neither orthodoxy nor misrepresentation separate human knowledge from the facts that science ultimately reveals. The frequent alterations that orthodoxies have had to undergo, should however preserve us from hanging on to past beliefs so firmly, as to misrepresent those whose discoveries lead to alternative hypotheses, that have stimulated further scientific investigation.

Cultural Diffusion and Discriminant Dating

It is not my purpose nor that of this centenary commemoration to rectify, much less to eliminate such writing. Least of all has it been a review of cultural diffusion in Africa, or of Elliot Smith's, or of my own contributions to the immensity and diversity of that vast subject. But I have appended to this article a list of references to such articles as I have written for the convenience of such Australian writers as may happen to be interested in the cultural diffusion that created the human population of their own continent and the potential parts played therein not only by the Egyptian but also by other populational elements from other parts of the continent of Africa in their movements across the Indian Ocean, which was possibly the earliest of all oceans to be skirted around extensively and finally to be crossed not only to Australia itself but also to and from Africa.

Further it is fundamental for both those who stay in Europe and for those at the other ends of the world to realize that revolutionary discoveries about the directions of cultural spread across the world have been, and are likely to continue being made peripherally outside and not centrally inside Europe. It was Elliot Smith's realization of Egypt's cultural meaning to mankind through the persistence there of the practice of mummification and of pyramids and everything that went with that practice irrespective of their ancestral centre, that made his contribution to palaeolithic as well as protohistoric archaeology in terms of diffusion across the globe distinctive and inescapable. What radio-carbon dating, tree-ring dating and potassium-argon dating have already done is to free the world outside Europe from the trammels of ceramics and trade goods that limited the viewpoints of Elliot Smith's contemporaries.

The source of greatest frustration at the present juncture has been the lack of dating techniques capable of bridging discriminatively the vast time gap between tree-ring and radio-carbon dating that carry our temporal perspectives back to the fortieth millennium on the recent side, and that of potassium argon, which deals with millions of years but leaves us in suspense at about half a million, on the distant side of human cultural time.

If Jeffrey L. Bada's recent hopeful announcement about 'The dating of fossil bones using the racemization of isoleucine' (*Earth and Planetary Science Letters*, 15, 223-31, 1972) proves correct, this chemo-physical method should render a great service in helping to fill that present vacant void in our ability to compare happenings in different parts of the globe temporally during that vast time lapse.

Personal communications from Dr Bada (dated Sept. 27, 1972) have already indicated to Mr Peter Beaumont and to myself that bone from the upper part of the Middle Stone Age deposit in the Border Cave has given an age in the region of 55,000 years (based on a cave temperature of 18°C). This is so early a stage in the exploration of the technique in general and of this cavern in particular that I report it here provisionally for its potential interest. The Middle Stone Age deposit in this cave is about two metres in depth and presents two phases of its later development there. If this antiquity, which is beyond the capacity of radio-carbon to assess discriminatively, characterizes its upper portion it would not be surprising if Bada should find by means of the racemization of isoleucine that the lower part of the deposit is twice that age, or more.

At any rate Dr Bada's letter states that 'The amino acid method is more applicable in the region 50,000 to 500,000 years' and that 'The Border Cave samples which Reiner Protch, who visited South Africa last year, received from Mr. Peter Beaumont are extremely interesting'.

So probably we will hear more about them and others as well as the racemization technique's usefulness during the next few years.

Meanwhile, as the use of haematite extends into the base of this deposit it is apparent that the antiquity of the fascination exercised by the redness of bloodstone and the glitter of specularite upon humanity is certainly far greater than the 43rd millennium date determined for its mining at the Lion Cavern site. It may be of the order of the hundred, rather than that of the two or three score of millennia ago.

Indeed J. Pfeiffer in *The Emergence of Man* (1971) reported that red ochre and tools for its grinding had been found by Henri de Lumley's team of excavators at the Terra Amata site on the raised beach at Nice. An Acheulean age comparable with that of the Spanish mammoth-hunting sites of Torralba and Ambrona, i.e., 300,000 years has been attributed to Terra Amata. An age of 200,000 years has been assigned since then to the Arago skull from Tantavel, near Perpignan, northeast of the Pyreneés. Patently ideas about the antiquity of human rituals and the place of red ochre in them and about where their source is, and what the directions of spread of its mining and commerce were, will not be fully resolved for some time to come.

APPENDIX

PUBLICATIONS BY R. A. DART REFERRING TO 'CULTURAL DIFFUSION FROM, IN AND TO AFRICA'

DART, R. A., (1923) 'Boskop remains from South-east African coast', *Nature*, 112, 623-5.

——, (1924) 'The Rooiberg cranium', *S. Afr. J. Sci.*, 21, 556-68.

——, (1924) 'Nickel in ancient bronzes', *Nature*, 113, 888.

——, (1924) 'Ancient mining industry of Southern Africa', *S. Afr. Geog. J.*, 7, 7-13.

——, (1925) 'Historical succession of cultural impacts upon South Africa', *Nature*, 115, 425-9.

——, (1925) 'Present position of anthropology in South Africa', *S. Afr. J. Sci.*, 22, 73-80.

——, (1925) 'Round stone culture of South Africa', *S. Afr. J. Sci.*, 22, 437-40.

——, (1925) 'South African antiquities', *S. Afr. Rlys Herb. Mag.*, 1925 (Dec.) , 1172-83.

——, (1926) 'Natives of South Africa: an ethnographic review', *Union of South Africa. Official Yearbook*, No. 7, 8 pp.

——, (1929) 'Bronze age in Southern Africa', *Nature*, 123, 495-6.

——, (1929) 'Phallic objects in Southern Africa', *S. Afr. J. Sci.*, 25, 553-62.

——, (1931) 'Rock engravings in Southern Africa and some clues to their significance and age', *S. Afr. J. Sci.*, 28, 475-86.

——, (1931) 'Ancient iron-smelting cavern at Mumbwa', *Trans. Roy. Soc. S. Afr.*, 19, 379-427.

——, (1932) 'Rock engravings in Southern Africa', *Rhod. Min. J.*, 6, 195-7.

——, (1933) 'Studies in native animal husbandry. The domesticated animals of pre-European South Africa', *J. S. Afr. Vet. Ass.*, 4, 61-70.

——, (1934) 'Discovery of a stone age manganese mine at Chowa, Northern Rhodesia', *Trans. Roy. Soc. S. Afr.*, 22, 55-70.

——, (1937) 'Racial Origins'. In Ch. 1 *Bantu-Speaking Tribes of South Africa*, I. Schapera (ed.), Routledge, London, pp. 1-31.

——, (1937) 'The hut distribution, genealogy and homogeneity of the /?Auni≠ Khomani bushmen', *Bantu Stud.*, 11, 161-74.

——, (1937) 'The physical characters of the /?Auni≠Khomani bushmen'. Repr. in *Bushmen of the Southern Kalahari*, J. D. Rheinalt Jones (ed.), Jhb. Witwatersrand University Press.

——, (1938) 'Fundamental human facial types in Africa', *S. Afr. J. Sci.*, 35, 341-8.

——, (1939) 'A Chinese character as a wall motive in Rhodesia', *S. Afr. J. Sci.*, 36, 474-6.

——, (1939) 'Population fluctuation over 7,000 years in Egypt', *Trans. Roy. Soc. S. Afr.*, 27, 95-145.

——, (1948) 'Water cattle', *S. Afr. Sci.*, 2, 81-3.

——, (1939) 'Ritual employment of bored stones by Transvaal Bantu Tribes', *S. Afr. Archaeol. Bull.*, 3, 61-6.

——, (1949) 'A polished stone pendant from Makapansgat', *S. Afr. Archaeol. Bull.*, 4, 83-6.

——, (1951) 'African serological patterns and human migrations', Presidential Address, S. Afr. Archaeol Soc. 1950, *S. Afr. Archaeol. Bull.*, 6, 1-xxxiv.

——, (1952) 'The Garamantes of Central Sahara', *Afr. Stud.*, 11, 29-34.

——, (1952) 'A Hottentot from Hong Kong: pre-Bantu population exchanges between Africa and Asia', *S. Afr. J. Med. Sci.*, 17, 117-42.

——, (1953) 'The southern aspect of pulsating humanity', *S. Afr. J. Sci.*, 50, 37-49.

——, (1953) 'Rhodesian engravers, painters and pigment miners of the fifth millennium B.C.', *S. Afr. Archaeol. Bull.*, 8, 91-6.

——, (1954) 'The oriental horizons of Africa'; a series of 8 talks. Johannesburg, S. Afr. Broadcasting Corp. and the author, 24 pp.

——, (1955) 'Foreign influences of the Zimbabwe and pre-Zimbabwe eras', *NADA*, 32, 19-30.

——, (1955) 'Three Strandloopers from Kaokoveld coast', *S. Afr. J. Sci.*, 51, 175-9.

——, (1957) The earlier stages of Indian transoceanic traffic, *NADA*, 34, 95-115.

——, (1959) 'Human figurines from Southern Africa', *Tran. Soc. portug. Anthrop. Etnol. Fac. Cienc. Porto*, 17, 457-73.

——, (1959) 'An australopithecine scoop from Herefordshire', *Nature*, 183, 844.

——, (1959) 'Osteodontokeratic ripping tools and pulp scoops for teething and edentulous australopithecines', *J. dent. Ass. S. Afr.*, 14, 164-78.

——, (1959) 'The ape-men tool-makers of a million years ago: South African *Australopithecus*—his life, habits and skills', *Illus. Lond. News.*, 234, 798-801, 9 May.

——, (1959) Foreword to *The Skeletal Remains of Bambandyanalo*, Alexander Galloway. Johannesburg, Witwatersrand Univ. Press, pp. xiii-xxii.

——, (1959) *Adventures with the Missing Link*, with Dennis Craig. Repr. 1967 Philadelphia, Institute for the Achievement of Human Potential.

——, (1959) 'On the evolution of language and articulate speech', *Homo*, 10, 154-65.

——, (1960) 'The persistence of some tools and utensils found first in the Makapansgat grey breccia', *S. Afr. J. Sci.*, 56, 71-4.

——, (1960) 'Africa's place in the emergence of civilisation', Johannesburg, S. Afr. Broadcasting Corp., 95 pp., illustrations.

——, (1960) 'The recency of man's aquatic past', *New Scientist*, 7, 1668-70.

——, (1961) 'Further information about how *Australopithecus* made bone tools and utensils, *S. Afr. J. Sci.*, 57, 127-34.

173

——, (1961) 'An australopithecine scoop made from a right australopithecine upper arm bone', *Nature*, 191, 372-3.

——, (1962) 'From cannon-bone scoops to skull bowls at Makapansgat', *Amer. J. Phys. Anthrop.*, n.s. 20, 287-95.

——, (1962) 'Death ships in South West Africa and South-East Asia', *S. Afr. Archaeol. Bull.*, 17, 231-4.

——, (1963) 'Paintings that link South with North Africa', *S. Afr. Archaeol. Bull.*, 18, 29-30.

——, (1965) 'Fish as symbols of life and luck', *Sci. S. Afr.*, 1, 507-10.

——, (1965) 'Australopithecine cordage and thongs', in *Homenaje a Juan Comes*, II. Editorial libros de Mexico, 1965, 43-61.

DART, R. A. & BEAUMONT, P., (1967) 'Amazing antiquity of mining in the Southern Africa'. *Nature*, 216 (5113), 407-8.

DART, R. A., (1968) 'The multimillenial prehistory of ochre mining', *NADA*, 9 (5), 7-13.

——, (1968) 'The birth of symbology', *Afr. Stud.*, 27, 15-27.

——, (1968) 'Ratification & retrocession of earlier Swaziland iron ore mining datings', *S. Afr. J. Sci.*, 64, 241-6.

——, (1969) 'Evidence of iron ore mining in Southern Africa in the Middle Stone Age', *Curr. Anthrop.*, 10, 127-8.

——, 'The bloodstone source of metallurgy', *Trab. Soc. Portug. Anthrop. Etnol. Fac. Cienc. Porto.*, 21, 119-29.

——, 'Indian trans-oceanic navigation; its primary place', *Bull. Indian Geol. Ass.*, 2 (3/4), 75-85.

——, (1970) 'Bloodstone and its iron evolutions', AGO (England), 1, 7-11, Pt 1.

——, (1970) 'Bloodstone and its iron evolutions', AGO (England), 2, 8-11, Pt 2.

——, 'Foreword' in *Ndedema Gorge*, by Harald Pager, Graz, Akademische Druck-u. Verlagsanstalt, pp. viii-xi.

13   CULTURAL DIFFUSION IN THE MIDDLE EAST DURING THE SECOND MILLENNIUM BC

E. C. B. MacLaurin

The late Sir Grafton Elliot Smith was one of those rare individuals who can excel in several different fields of scholarship[1]. His contributions to the problems of cultural diffusion were, when they were made, remarkable, and the only factor which has invalidated his conclusions is the tremendous volume of new discovery in this field. His reasoning is sound, the premises on which he based his reasoning—the work of other scholars—are now outdated. During his lifetime two main schools of thought struggled for acceptance—those who believed that the cradle of civilization was to be found in Mesopotamia (another great Australian Dr G. W. Thatcher, at that time one of the world's leading Semitic scholars, had championed this cause from his Oxford post) and the Egyptian school supported by Sir Grafton. Little was known of the great and ancient civilization on the Indus Valley, of the empire of Dilmun and the culture of Makan—still barely discerned or guessed at—of the unexpected wealth of Canaanite culture so recently become available to scholars at Ugarit which is throwing light on dark places in Old Testament and Homeric learning.

The Land of Canaan is a land-bridge joining the continents of Eurasia and Africa, bounded on the west by a sea of water and on the east by a sea of sand. Population pressures have always been exerted southward down this land-bridge, possession of which has for five millennia been an essential element in the defence of Egypt. Not only armies but also cultures have reached the Nile Valley by this dual route[2] following either the coastal road which led to the Delta or else the Kings Highway east of the Jordan which reached the sea at the port of Aqaba. As early as 2900 BC Egyptian ships of the 1st Dynasty came to this port to load with copper, worked probably by the ancestors of the Midianites at the mines operated by Solomon nearly 2000 years later[3]. It was the key material which made the cutting of the huge stones for the Pyramids possible, but its history in Palestine began two millennia before Cheops began his eternal monument.

E. C. B. MACLAURIN

The Legendary Period

Egyptian legend indicated a tradition of Palestinian priority; Plutarch[4] preserves a belief that the Osiris legend contains certain non-Egyptian elements and one attractive theory holds that the story conflates the life of a prehistoric hero or king with that of the dying and rising god of the Levant[5]. Rameses IV believed that the nature of Osiris was greater than that of any god. The home-town of Osiris was Busiris in the North Delta, yet he was not the ancient local deity of the place. This local deity was Anedjity whom Osiris later absorbed. Osiris was both god of fertility and god of the dead and the dual concept was neatly expressed by the ritual of seed sown in a box full of damp earth as a symbol of resurrection. The antiquity of this concept of resurrection is hardly yet recognized by the Old Testament scholars[6], although the archaeologists have evidence of it as early as 7000 BC at Neolithic Jericho and even earlier elsewhere. But this concept of rebirth, resurrection, from the womb of the earth was quite out of harmony with the ancient Egyptian belief that the earth was a male being[7]; Osiris represented life after death in the netherworld whereas indigenous Egyptian belief connected life after death with the sun-god Ra triumphantly crossing the heavens. Whereas Ra symbolizde the post-mortem life of the king alone, Osiris became a symbol of eternal existence for all men, and some modern scholars find in him the original figure from which Hebrew YHWH was evolved[8]. Worship of Osiris became dominant during Vth (2560-2420 BC) and VIth (2420-2270 BC) Dynasties whose Pyramid texts provide the oldest information about him.

Osiris the king is said to have come from the neighbourhood of Byblos, and to have introduced the arts of agriculture into Egypt. It is certainly true that the crops of ancient Egypt—as of our modern Western civilization—are mostly derived from primitive stocks which still are to be found growing wild in the hill-country north of Jericho[9], and the fact that civilization in this area had reached a high standard is attested by contemporary archaeological evidence from such places as Tell el-Farah whose substantial walls commanded the Wadi Farach, the only wide pass leading from the Jordan Valley into the heart of Palestine, and Beth Shan where the exquisite Khirbet Kerak ware was now in use and which the Egyptians were later to make their chief Palestinian stronghold.

The wide spread of culture before this date is shown by the discovery of Jemdet Nasr type seals, ascribed to the end of IVth Mill BC, in a pre-dynastic grave at Naga-ed-der in Upper Egypt and, inscribed with archaic heiroglyphs, under the pavement of a later sanctuary at Byblos, whilst Jemdet Nasr type pottery was found at Jebel Hafit at Buraimi in the Sheikdom of Abu Dhabi on the Persian Gulf[10]. There is clear evidence that such cultural diffusion was not solely dependent on land-routes, for at the beginning of IV Millennium BC boats made of reeds—a pattern which has survived in the Persian Gulf until recently[11]

—on the Egyptian style were used at Bahrain and presumably travelled, as documents 1,500 years later indicate, to Ur Kasdim where Abraham was to be born to Amorite stock well over 2,000 years ahead. Not only the smooth waters of the Persian Gulf were thus traversed by sailor-traders, but also the tempestuous Mediterranean where, in Neolithic times the Great Mother Goddess, in the first expansion of a Universal Middle Eastern religion[12], had reached Malta as part of her conquest of Europe. The domestic cat spread from Egypt in Neolithic times to Crete which also received the olive from its original home on Mt Carmel and in Upper Galilee, and obsidian, the hardest cutting material known to Stone Age man from Melos[13]. It is hardly to be wondered that the Ugaritic poet—whose works survive in a late recession from XIIIth century BC, speaking of the craftsman-god Hiyan (Koter w Hasis) said

> Crete is the throne on which he sits
> Egypt is the land of his inheritance (Baal V vi 15)[14]

Some evidence of the spread of this legend is given in another passage in the Ugaritic epic (Baal VI iii 19) where El (the Supreme God of the Semites, Amorites, Canaanites, Hebrews and Arabians alike) summoned Hiyan to the twin mountains of the north and Hiyan agreed to

> leave Crete for the most distant of Gods
> Egypt for the most distant of ghosts,—
> two layers beneath the springs of the earth
> three spans under the rocks—

This place is at the confluence of the rivers (cf. Gen. 2:8 ff.) where the sweet waters of the abyss (Heb. tehom Gen. 1:2, 6 ff.) mingled with the salt waters of the sea, at the place where the fruit (flower) of immortality was to be found. The Babylonian legend of Gilgamesh identifies this with Dilmun where, at Bahrain, strong fresh water springs still emerge from the bed of the ocean[15]. So there was a contact between Egypt, Crete, Mesopotamia and the little-known states of the Persian Gulf possibly as early as Neolithic times. Such speculations are enormously interesting and are mentioned in introduction but lack of space compels the writer to restrict his comments to a brief period, from the early part of IIIrd Millennium to the latter part of the IInd Millennium BC.

Egypt is the Throne of His Heritage (Ugaritic Epic)

As already remarked the Egyptians of Ist Dynasty imported copper, probably by sea, from Aqaba. They learnt how to harden it, by prolonged hammering and this was no doubt a major factor in their rapid advance during 28th and 27th centuries BC. The technical secret was strictly kept within her guilds of draftsmen so that, 1,900 years later, the Hebrews were still unable to work metal[17]. The key figure in this cultural progress was a man whose multi-sided capacities are not unlike those of the man we honour at this Commemoration. Imhotep was a most distinguished physician, statesman, artist and architect whose most lasting memorials are the Pyramids of Zakkara which he built for King Soser. He learnt how to carve a fluted column—perhaps copying in solid material the columns made of bundles of reeds by the early Sumerians of the Euphrates delta and still produced by the Marsh Arabs of today in the same area—to represent the trunk and foliage of a tree out of the material of a wall. Twenty centuries before Greek sculpture attained its skills he 'perfected the basic forms of architecture, columns with astrygal bases and flowered capitals, wall-niches and projections, portals, ornamental friezes and pillared halls'. His original genius must be given due respect when evaluating the debt of Greece to Egypt and the Levant[18].

Yet originality was not all Egypt's perquisite; Egyptian texts of IInd Dynasty refer to 'ships of Byblos', and a stone vessel bearing the name of a IInd Dynasty Pharoah was found on the site of a temple of Byblos; alabaster jars made during the IIIrd Dynasty were deposited at Ai about 2800 BC and the Egyptians took, almost as if in exchange, Canaanite loan-words and pottery. About 2650 BC a cylinder seal of Cheops, inscribed 'beloved of Hathor' was deposited at Byblos, and some scholars have concluded that the goddess of Byblos and Egyptian Hathor were already identified; a little later a timber-worker, cutting cedar of Lebanon near Beirut, lost a bronze axehead bearing the cartouche of Cheops who was using this timber in the construction of the Great Pyramid. This timber was brought to the Nile by ship; the Annals of Inefru (2615 BC) says that large sea-going ships were built of cedar. They seem to have belonged both to the Egyptians and to the Canaanite rulers. Prior to this time the Egyptian texts had referred to Canaan as 'a land flowing with milk and honey'—a phrase preserved by the Hebrews over a millennium later[19]—but by 27th century BC they were complaining that erosion had set in this process was no doubt later accelerated by Hebrew destruction of the forests in the hill country[20]. Ipuwer complained that cedar-oil for embalming mummies and cedarwood for coffins were hard to get after the fall of the Old Kingdom (2270 BC); vessels in the Giza tombs contain coniferous residues left by the evaporation of this cedar oil. These commodities were also exported to Crete which points to the existence of ships large enough to go out of sight of land.

Egyptian ships whether built of wood or bundles of papyrus—which Heyerdahl's experiments show to be quite feasible for long rough voyages —were capable of reaching the Hellespont whence they presumably set out for Crete[21]. At Dorak, south of the Sea of Marmora, in Anatolia a gold-covered chair bearing the title of King Sahura of the Vth Dynasty has been found, deposited with artefacts similar to those of Troy II (2500-2100 BC) and contemporary Mesopotamian material of the IIIrd Dynasty of Ur; in support of this, Sahura's funerary temple inscriptions show large Egyptian ships bound for Syria, where Byblos was now strongly under Egyptian influence. Another contemporary inscription found on the island of Kythera bore the name of a ruler of Eshnunna whilst a small cup with the name of the Sun Temple of Weserkaf, the first king of the Vth Dynasty was found with it, but these were probably

600 years old when they were deposited. More relevant is the representation of 'Asiatics' in Egyptians vessels alongside granite transports from Aswan; these appear in the funerary temple of Unas, also of the Vth Dynasty, and show that peoples from the Levant were working in Egypt over 1,000 years before the Exodus.

Slightly later the Minoans migrated from Asia Minor to Crete, and the Early Minoan period began. They lived in caves at first and no palaces were built, but the two ports of Mochlos and Komo (the point of departure for Egypt) were founded. Within a century all trade in the Eastern Mediterranean fell into their hands[22] and the Cretans established their first colonies in Cyrenaica. Egypt felt her power challenged, and in her attempts to strengthen her suzereignity over the land-bridge she caused great destruction at Ugarit, Byblos, Hama, Bethshan, Ai, Jericho, Gezer, Askalon, Tell Beit Misrim (Kiriath Sephor), Tell el-Hesy, Tell el-Ajjul and perhaps Taanach and Megiddo. The Abydos inscription of Weian gives the account of these campaigns which are confirmed by archaeological evidence. The Egyptians had good reason to be worried, for the Amorites, the ancestors of the modern Palestinian 'Arabs', were on the move and during the 24th century BC the Amorite Kingdom of Akkad, destined to become the first Semitic Empire, was founded. The traders of Akkad were quick to establish trade with India, for at Tell Asmar, close to their city, seals have been found, showing rhinoceros, elephants and crocodiles similar to the seals of Mohenjo-Daro. No doubt this trade was conducted through the clearing centres of Dilmun.

During this period Early Minoan II started, and Egyptian imports of Dynasties VII to X entered Crete, whilst ivory Cretan seals bore designs similar to contemporary seals of Egypt[23]; the ivory of which they were made was probably brought in from Syria and a dish found at Mochlos, decorated with thick red concentric circles is almost certainly of Syrian origin. An ivory signet found at Hagia Triada shows an Egyptian draughtsboard with three 'men' shaped like chess-pawns on top. The migrations from Anatolia which had founded Minoan power in Crete may have been prompted by the same sort of disturbances as those which now led to the beginning of the Early Bronze Age in Cyprus; certainly Anatolian pottery entered Cyprus during the 23rd century BC.

Egypt still maintained her influence in the land-bridge[24] for an inscription of Pepi I, found at Byblos, refers to Hathor of Dendera (the principal centre of Hathor-worship in Egypt). This may again point to early identification of Hathor with Baalat (the mistress of) Byblos. A hundred years later stone vessels of Pepi I, Mernera and Pepi II were deposited at Kerma in the Sudan.

Amorite strength was now growing. During 23rd century BC Sargon I of Akkad claimed to have conquered 'the land of the sunset and the mountains of cedar, all of it'; in the Gilgamesh legend the heroes kill Huwawa, the wild guardian of the cedar forests[25]. He mentioned ships from Magan (probably Buraimior Muscat) Dilmun and Molukha moored at Akkad. From the Amarna period and later the name Molukha denoted Nubia, but the nature of the merchandise imported therefrom in the records of Sargon almost certainly indicates the Indus Valley. About the same time Ea-Nasir of Ur was also trading with Dilmun for copper from Makan (Magan). A century later Sargon's grandson Naram-Sin built a palace at Brak, strategically sited between Cappadocia and Northern Iran whence he drew the metallic ores needed for making the equipment of his army[26]: this would indicate an efficient means of land transport for heavy loads. The earliest iron implements which still survive date from this period and were found at Alica Huyuk; meteoric iron, called 'the metal of heaven', had been known in Egypt and Mesopotamia before this, and was used in Egypt for tools and weapons, but of course the supply was minimal.

The Amorites were now well settled in Canaan, and Egyptian texts from the XIth Dynasty are full of execrations against them; Egyptian fears were well founded and an Amorite invasion of the Nile Valley began. The date was about 22nd century BC. These events were destined to be one of the most determinative ever to take place in world history; it was the watershed between the religious beliefs of remote antiquity and those of modern man, for this Amorite settlement of Canaan introduced into the future Holy Land the worship of Semitic El—the god whom the Old Testament patriarchs[27] and writers took over from the Canaanites and synthesized with YHWH of Sinai, the God whom Jesus called Father and whom Muhammed identified with the source of his own revelation. It was also a watershed in Mediterranean civilization for Greek speakers, worshippers of Olympian Zeus whom El closely resembled in many ways, were now invading Greece, imposing their language and culture as they spread out from Argos; about this time the olive, which had centuries before reached Crete from Canaan, now penetrated Egypt, but Egyptian olives are still inferior to those of the Mediterranean islands. Egypt also received the donkey from Syria and Palestine about this time. Assyrian influence was also starting to spread widely, and Ashurbanipal referred to Dilmun in the Lower Sea and Tyre in the Upper Sea; probably the Assyrians learnt the latter route from the Sumerians for about 2080 BC Gudea of Lagash was importing cedar from Lebanon, probably carried in the great waggons now in use in Mesopotamia to the nearest point on the Euphrates and then floated downstream. But the Hittite domination of the whole Euphrates area was beginning—to reach its climax a century later—and the Assyrians were being forced to develop an overland route to Kanesh due north of Ugarit.

Egyptian influence was now strong amongst the Phoenicians who were copying Pharonic building styles at home and were transmitting them to their North African colonies[28]. It must be stated here that the dating of Phoenician activity is not generally held to be as early as I assume, and that the foundation of Carthage is usually placed about IXth century BC on existing archaeological evidence[29]. But Tyrian tradition claimed that the city was much older and Herodotus (ii.44) says that the city was 2,300 years old when he visited it in the middle of the Vth century BC, which would place its foundation about XXVIIIth century BC; it was apparently not under Sidonian control at the time. Similarly Ugarit can trace its foundation to IIIrd Millennium BC. Even Homeric legend, which is probably to be dated to Mycenaean times, speaks of the Phoenicians, and it seems probable that their expansion to the Western Mediterranean should be dated no later than the IInd Millennium BC. I have seen at Motya in Western Sicily a Phoenician gateway very reminiscent of the main gate of Ugarit, and Phoenician historians themselves claimed that Utica, Gades, and other Western cities were founded earlier than Carthage. I am disposed to regard these as the Phoenician colonies which developed as the result of trade, and Carthage as a city founded—to meet an emergency—the forced emigration of people brought about by Assyrian and other pressures on their native homeland. In any case, Ugarit was known to Egypt at the beginning of IInd Millennium BC, for votive objects bearing the cartouche of Sesostris I (1980-35 BC) have been found near the Temple of Dagon, and the travels of Sinuhe who fled to Syria seeking sanctuary after the death of King Amenernhet whom he had served as an official not only indicates the general unrest of Egypt but also the extent of her contacts with the land-bridge.

'Some Grave Tyrian Trader from the Sea' (Matthew Arnold)

The overseas expansion of the inhabitants of Phoenicia is indicated by the beginning of settlement at Enkomi in Cyprus, whilst in Thessaly the neolithic period was now coming to an end. In Crete the old Palace period was beginning together with the appearance of a new type of pottery. Large sea-going ships, reminiscent of Egyptian and Phoenician vessels, now started to appear on Minoan seals. Possibly the dessication of the Sahara now began; it is usual to attribute this to the root-eating and bark-stripping propensities of the goat, combined with *excessive* cultivation but I would be more inclined to ascribe it to the *wrong type* of cultivation. Cross-ploughing was now starting in Europe[30], and whilst land so treated is more productive in the cold wet climate of the north it is not too apt to pulverize in a dry hot climate, especially when the soil is light. Contact between Europe and the Levant is undoubted at the start of IInd Millennium BC; in areas of modern South Germany and Austria ornaments and weapons appear which can be identified with types found at Ugarit and elsewhere in Syria. There were trade routes from the cities of Babylonia and Assyria to Anatolia or Ugarit; or else a traveller could follow up the Euphrates to a point where a route passed over the Taurus and Anti-Taurus Mountains to central Asia Minor. Trade routes also led from Central Asia—Samarkand, Bukhara and other immemorially old cities of Soviet Central Asia—to Hungary and thence to Denmark, but it is significant that Middle Eastern influences did not appear in Eastern Europe, further east than Vienna, which seems to rule out the Danube as a trade-route. The most likely journey from the Middle East would have been from Ugarit or Sidon by ship to the head of the Adriatic and then over the St Gothard Pass to Central Europe where Mediterranean seashells were used as ornaments or from the head of the Gulf of Lyons through the Carcassone Gap to the north of the Loire and thence to Western Europe and England. So a traveller from the Egyptian trading city at Kerma in the Sudan, or the Indian traveller from the Indus Valley, a couple of centuries before the time of Abraham, could have followed recognized trade routes to Aleppo and thence to England. Contact between Egypt and Mesopotamia was distinct at this time, for about 1934 BC a seal of the royal family of Larsa was deposited at the Lod Temple of Luxor; Egyptian figurines and other artefacts were widely distributed throughout the Land of Canaan. This wide Canaanite expansion was perhaps due to the presence of the Upper and Lower Sutu (Egy. Styw *Asiatics*), and it is highly probable that the first impetus to overseas colonization was caused by them. Shum-abum, who founded an Amorite dynasty at Babylon, is probably Shmwibw, chief of the Upper Sutu mentioned in the Execration Texts. The Amorites established Carchemish under an Amorite dynasty on the crossroads connecting Mesopotamia, Anatolia, Syria and Egypt. Amorite pressure was responsible for the rise of the Hyksos. Jerusalem was now sufficiently important, some centuries before the time of Abraham, to be mentioned in the Egyptian Execration Texts which cursed her Amorite (i.e., Jebusite) kings.

There is evidence that Byblos, which was now ruled by a Council of Elders—the zkenim of the Old Testament—had a vigorous trade with Ugarit and Egypt. Her temples had votives and gold-offerings of Egyptian origin, and Amenemhat II deposited silver vessels of Aegean and Syrian origin in two copper chests with gold ingots and lapis lazuli from Afghanistan and seals from Ist Dynasty of Larsa in the foundation of the Lod Temple at Luxor. His daughter, Princess Ita, when she was wife of Senusset II, was represented by a sphinx found at Qatna, eleven miles N.E. of Homs, and another wife of Senusset is represented by a figure found at Ugarit. Here, then is evidence of wide cultural contacts and diffusion at the beginning of XIXth century BC which was centrifugal from the Middle East and which extended to India (and beyond) in the east and to the North Atlantic in the west.

Population pressures in the land-bridge forced nomad Semites, depicted at Beni Hasan, into Egypt, and Senusret III led a military expedition to Skmn (Shechem?). The Canaanite chiefs of the period bore Amorite or poto-Aramaean theophoric names; similar names were borne by the Semites who invaded Mesopotamia from Arabia during IIIrd Millennium BC, and both groups resemble the theophoric names of Hebrews in the Old Testament. The period was one of great movements of peoples; in Greece this was the Middle Helladic period, and the migration of Greek-speaking peoples from the north was continuing, Mycenae becoming an important centre. Megaron-type houses and

Minyan-type pottery appeared. An influx of Indo-Iranians set up an Aryan ruling class over Northern Syria; and the Mitanni were settling between the Tigris and the Euphrates. The Hurrian states were now established by great hordes of people from an area between Lake Van and the Zagros Mountains, first appearing in the Upper Euphrates area about 1730 and gradually spreading south into Palestine until Palestinian chiefs of the time of the Amarna letters (*c.* 1350 BC) bore Hurrian names, the Hyksos were probably recruited from them and from Bedawin, or Habiru, whose personal names indicate a mixture of Semitic, Aryan and even Egyptian people. Seals from Kanesh show that horses had now been introduced into Anatolia by these Aryans who later took horses and war-chariots into Canaan via Assur. Their origin is indicated by the close resemblance of the horse-burials at Tell el-'Ajjul and Jericho to those in South Russia and the Caucasus during the preceding millennium. The horse now made its first important appearance in Egypt along with certain Aryan words such as wrjt, *chariot*. As early as the Middle Kingdom the horse had been peripherally known at such places as Buhen, well before the Hyksos period, but now its use became common, as early as 1775 Zimiri-lim of Mari was buying, white chariot-horses. The spread of the light Chariot in Mesopotamia, Egypt, Crete and Mainland Greece marked the direction or results of Amorite/Hyksos expansion. Horses and chariots need specially-trained staff to care for and handle them, and this led to the establishment of a feudal system which the Hebrews adopted and preserved under the monarchy. The narrative of Sinuhe referred to the inhabitants of Palestine during this period as the Retenu, a new term; at this time new pottery appeared, clearly modelled on a metal prototype—silver examples from XIIth and XIIIth Dynasties have also been found at Byblos. New burial customs and new weapons which have their only affinities in the Caucasus were introduced—e.g., a bronze belt with dagger attachments found at Tell el-Fara and Ugarit, dating from this period. Town life was resumed with a culture which was to survive for 700 years behind a new type of defensive wall strengthened by a glacis which prevented chariots being driven right up to the foot. These appeared not only at many cities in Palestine but also at Tell el-Yehudiah in Egypt. The evidence all seems to point to the Hyksos as the bearers of this new culture, involving a wider use of metals as well as better transport.

In Crete Middle Minoan III was about to begin and to make its influence felt abroad. The royal tomb at Byblos yielded Cretan metal vessels, and in Egypt Amenemhat II put silver vessels from an Aegean source into the foundation deposit of the Lod Temple at Luxor. Likewise, there was some contact between Crete and Mari, where paintings similar to, but earlier than, the Cretan frescoes were found, but this is not decisive evidence for Cretan cultural dependence, for a still-earlier piece of Middle Minoan II painted pottery also shows this style of painting. There is a probability also, that the paintings of Alalakh influenced the art of Middle Minoan III in Crete[31]. A possible route of diffusion is indicated ;it was the ancient trade-route later followed by Abraham through Haran whose Temple of Sin (the moon-god) is mentioned in a letter from Mari. Egyptian statuettes of the XIIth Dynasty have been found at Knossos, at Adana (perhaps the original home of the tribe of Dan) on the Cilician plain, and on the central plateau of Anatolia.

The pressure on the peoples of the land-bridge and the struggle of cultures naturally turned men to seek the sea-roads, and during XIXth century BC sea-trade developed rapidly in the eastern Mediterranean, as suggested above; the Hyksos reached Cyprus and Mycenaean objects appeared at Ugarit. The Amorites of Mesopotamia were expanding, and the mysterious 14th Chapter of Genesis is perhaps based on the experiences of Mesopotamian raiding-parties of this period who for their own protection or prestige associated themselves with the names of great rulers. These incidents were only a couple of centuries old by the time of Abraham and later became attached to his name. Mari on the Upper Euphrates had also become an important ship-building centre, making barges of a Sumerian type which not only indicates considerable waterborne trade but also may show how Sargon of Akkad, 600 years earlier, had carried heavy timber from the Cedar Mountains to his capital.

Mari was in communication with Ugarit and Byblos which, since they were the Levantine ports at the end of the sea-routes to Cyprus and the West, supplemented her eastwards sea-trade down the Euphrates and perhaps along the Persian Gulf to India. Ugarit was the vital port during this period for it received from Cyprus most of the exports of copper, the strategic metal of the Bronze Age. Mari was also in communication with Hazor (the ancient capital of the Canaanite kings), Qatna (which had access to the Mediterranean by the Eleutherus Valley to the coast north of Tripoli) and Yamkhad (i.e., Aleppo, whose port was Alalakh not far from the mouth of the Orontes). These contacts were clearly shown at Mari by the presence of Cypriot copper, Byblian textiles and goods from Crete; as already noted the decorations in the palace of Zimri-lim bore some relationship to Aegean art. Over the next few centuries painted-face jugs showing Philistine-type head-dress spread throughout the Levant and indicated their association with the sea-peoples by appearing also at Phaestos in Crete and at the Mycenaean sanctuary of Asine in Greece. The Assyrians were also expanding, and later in the century Shamshi-Adad I was destined to conquer Mari and to build a Temple of Dagon at Tirqa. He reached the Upper Sea (the Mediterranean) and set up a stele at Lab'an.

The People of the Book break into History

During this period there was great Sumerian literary activity, the most notable achievement being the redaction of the Gilgamesh legend; some scholars believe that this ancient epic was the pattern which the Mycenaeans and Greeks were to follow later in the Homeric literature[32]. This was roughly contemporary with the beginning of non-Greek Linear

A script. It does not seem to have been quite unrelated, so far as the symbols were concerned, to the earlier Canaanite script, and as it *is* alphabetic and *is* non-Greek it seems that the idea of an alphabet may have been brought from the mainland by those fleeing before Hyksos and Habiru pressure. Radio-carbon dating indicates that the first Stonehenge structures were being built about this time, but I do not propose to comment on the Mycenaean axe said to have been outlined on one of the stones there; it serves to indicate the length of contact possible during IInd Millennium BC.

In 1740 BC, Egypt still controlled Byblos as the name of the Byblian prince, Yantin, on the wall-relief of Neferhotep I shows, and Egyptian sculptors and scribes were living in the ancient Phoenician capital. Four years later Sebekhotep IV erected his stele at Baalbek on succeeding Neferhotep. The Ugaritic writings also indicate that trade with Egypt was a two-way traffic. Egyptian craftsmen of various skills coming to Canaan, and Egyptian merchants sending home pottery and timber from Lebanon and turquoise from the mines of Serabit el-Khadem in the Sinaitic Peninsula. In order to exploit these mines in peace it was necessary that the Egyptians should subdue the local Arabs, thus creating a hostile environment on her frontiers which may have been relevant in the later occupation of the Delta by Asiatics, who by 1730 had taken over the whole of Egypt. The Hyksos brought prosperity to Egypt by their strong rule, efficiency in war and forceful control of the country's wealth. By the time they were expelled in 1580 BC, they had established communications with Kush, through the Western Desert. There can be little doubt that Josephus was right when he identified the Hebrews with part of the Hyksos movement; in this case they would have penetrated Egypt whilst under Hyksos rule, the only period in Egyptian history when a foreign Semite such as Joseph could have risen to top executive rank[33]—and the expulsion of their patrons would have marked the rise of the king 'who knew not Joseph'[34]—a matter to which we shall return presently.

About 1724 BC Hammurabi began his victorious campaigns, capturing Larsa, Isin and Mari. His greatest contribution to culture was his codification of Babylonian law; he collated the laws of various cities and produced a code quite similar to the much later Hebrew code. It is now recognized that the resemblance is probably to be attributed to the dependence of both upon a common ancestral Amorite code. Whether Abraham was a refugee fleeing before Hammurabi's armies, or whether he was a trader following in their wake, is quite immaterial; the following timetable emerges in either case.

Convenient point in the very long life of Abraham	*c.* 1730[35]
Isaac's birth	*c.* 1670
Jacob's birth	*c.* 1640
Joseph's birth	*c.* 1610
Expulsion of Hyksos	1580
Three generations of servitude	*c.* 1460

This date ties in quite well with the first explosion of Thera, which took place about 1470-47 BC (see later) and judging by the effects of the explosion of Krakatoa last century, could together with succeeding explosions, have produced all the phenomena of the miracle at the Red Sea, the blocking of Jordan, the fall of the makeshift rebuilt wall of Jericho etc[36]. The entry into Canaan was a gradual affair, probably beginning with the conquest of Jerusalem about 1420 by Caleb and other Judamite and Benjamite groups, then delayed by the defeat of Simeon at Hormah, and culminating with the incident of Joshua and Jericho. The account of the settlement tells us that the Hebrews were unable to dispossess the Canaanites and were compelled to dwell in the mountains[37]. This statement is supported by Merneptah's stele (1135 BC) which refers to Israel as a people without a land of their own.

During the XVIIth century BC the New Palace Period began at Knossos, Phaestos and Mallia; Mycenaean objects began to reach Ugarit; it is hard to say to what extent this is to be linked with the spread of the use of the light chariot to the mainlands of Greece, Egypt and Crete. The Sea-peoples were extremely vigorous, and by 1658 BC had captured from Shamshu-iluna of Babylon, the successor of Hammurabi, all the country as far east as Nippur. Alalakh was destroyed eight years later by Hattusilis I, king of the Hittites who then circumvented the powerful fortress-city of Yamkhad (Aleppo) and crossed the Jordan further south on his way to attack Egypt. Later he decided to attack both Yamkhad and Babylon, and as a first step sent a force, which included 80 chariots, against the North Syrian town of Unshu. Babylon, threatened in the east by the Kassites and in the west by the Hittites, began to erect fortifications which stretched as far south as the mouth of the Euphrates; but their defence was in vain for in 1595 Mursilis I, the Hittite king, destroyed Mari, then captured Yamkhad and subdued Syria. The Hittites then prepared to attack Babylon, after which quick political decline set in; culturally, this weakening of Babylon was important for Syria, for local art now began to free itself from Mesopotamian forms. The pressure from the east exerted by the Kassites upon Babylon was possibly due in part to the southward invasions of the Aryans whose destruction of the Indus Valley civilization early in the XVIth century BC set up great population movements.

The Hurrians were now dominant in Assyria and began to form states in Northern Mesopotamia under Indo-European rulers of the Indic branch of that race. The Hittite Empire was at its peak and extended from the Black Sea to the Mediterranean; the Hittite Code probably belongs to this period. It reveals a patriarchal state of society and an agrarian economy not unlike that of the Hebrew patriarchs, but it is socially more advanced in that there is no lex talionis, since its object was not so much to punish the offender as to help the victim. In spite of the threat from the Hittites to the small Aramaean and Canaanite states, Ugarit, where Hurrian and Hittite influences were apparent, was also at the height of its power and showed evidences of trade with both Egypt and Mesopotamia.

Life in Canaan generally was rather precarious, few reaching the age of 50. This probably was the stimulus to the growth in a belief in a future life, evidence of which is to be seen at Jericho where tombs contained deposits of food and drink as well as contemporary furniture. Ugarit and its Cypriote colony Enkomi were now both very prosperous as a result of the demands of the Bronze Age for copper, and control of this supply may have been one of the motives which induced Ahmosis, as he pursued the Hyksos into Palestine and as far north as the Euphrates, to seek to re-establish Egyptian suzerainity over the land-bridge by destroying the strong strategic cities of Jericho and Megiddo. His successor Amenophis I (c. 1555-30 BC) also claimed to have reached the Euphrates; the Egyptians divided up the land-bridge as follows:—

Upper Retenu: the Palestinian highlands, the Phoenician hinterland and Lebanon;

Lower Retenu: Naharaim (the land between the Euphrates and the Orontes) and north to Asia Minor.

Thutmosis I consolidated these conquests, setting up his stele on the Euphrates about 1525. He was the first native-born Egyptian Pharoah whose use of chariots is attested, by an engraving on a scarab. About 1575 the horses and chariots appeared on Mycenaean vase-paintings in Cyprus, whilst in Crete, where the period was that called Late Minoan I, horses appeared together with figure-of-eight shields so heavy that they were probably used in chariots; a horse and chariot were depicted by a painter in the palace of Hagia Triada. Slightly later, Minoan artefacts appeared in Santorin, for Minoan influence was still dominant in many places, such as Melos, and even the Mycenaean art of Greece itself still showed a distinct debt to Minos. Crete was in its most brilliant period and Kekrops, according to the Parian Chronicle, founded Athens about this time; it shortly became tributary to Crete. Minoan hegemony is probably reflected in the story of Theseus which may well preserve a genuine fragment of history. Minoan influence also became apparent in Cyprus, the first Cypriote syllabic script perhaps being borrowed from Crete since it seems to show affinities with Cretan Linear A. This form of writing was roughly contemporary with but clearly inferior to the alphabetic script of the Sinaitic inscriptions.

But the Mycenaean period was shortly to become dominant in Greece and throughout the Aegean as the Mycenaean Greeks began to settle in the islands. The Mycenaeans ranged extremely widely, and a Mycenaean dagger was carved on the Sarsen stone at Stonehenge; these sarsen stones had been shaped by the Egyptian technique of batter with stone mauls; this contact is not impossible, for amber from the North Sea which was coming into use as an ornament in Greece, confirms that the overland route to Western Europe was still in use. A natural disaster broke the power of Crete; the explosion of Santorin, referred to above, took place about 1470 BC; Millia and Phaestos were damaged and abandoned; Knossos was damaged but repaired. This gave the Mycenaeans an apportunity to take over Minoan sovereignty; archaeology approximately confirms the date of these events in the Parian Chronicle, which dates Deucalion's Flood at 1447 BC; radio-carbon testing on Theran material fixes a date between 1510 BC and 1310 BC. The Greek-speaking Mycenaeans captured Knossos and non-Greek Linear A script was replaced about the same time by Greek Linear B script which came into use in Knossos but not elsewhere in Crete[38]. The 'palace style' pottery of Knossos was similar to that of the Mycenaeans at their other centres and on the Greek mainland. Enkomi in Cyprus became very prosperous, due to the expansion of Mycenaean trade, and Aegean peoples began to penetrate Anatolia and to settle on the coasts of the Levant.

Towards the end of the century the epoch Mycenaean III began in Greece and was characterized by the Cyclopaean walls which were built around the acropolis at Tiryns and Mycenae[39]. Palaces here had frescoes on their walls in the earlier tradition of Mari and Knossos. There was considerable trade with the Eastern Mediterranean, Egypt and Sicily; Mycenae established her own trading-ports in Rhodes, Cyprus and at Minet el-Baida which served Ugarit. In 1410 BC, according to the Parian Chronicle, Thebes was founded by Cadmus; the name Cadmus is derived from the Semitic root qdm *east*. His daughter Semele preserves a memory of the Semitic moon-goddess and her son Dionysius begotten by Zeus[40], is a parallel figure to Baal who proclaims himself as a son of El. It would thus seem that memory of some Semitic (Phoenician ?) settlement survives in this legend.

Ugaritic and Atchanan documents now confirm the establishment of a class of professional soldier around the swift horse-drawn war chariot, and the concept seems to have been given divine approval by one of the Ugaritic traditions which tells how the goddess Astarte rode on horseback; this legend is depicted in a seal (*c.* 1425 BC) of Thutmosis IV and should perhaps be understood in the light of the Astarte Papyrus, surviving in a XIIth century BC copy, which tells how the goddess, whilst walking along the shore, was taken by the sea-god Yam the forerunner of Poseidon[41].

Central Palestine—Hazor, Beth Shean, Jaffa, Megiddo, Askelon, Lachish—now became the focal points of local culture, and Egypt decided to reassert her lost suzerainty by force. Thutmosis III (*c.* 1473-36) sent sixteen expeditions into the land-bridge; he defeated a coalition of 330 Canaanite chiefs at Kadesh capturing booty and prisoners in great abundance. The lists of gold and silver vessels, ebony and ivory carvings, statues and other *objets d'art* illustrated the enormous wealth of Canaan at this time. Pushing ahead, he took Aleppo and Carchemish and received tribute from Assyria. He took with him two-wheeled carts, pulled by oxen, on which were loaded the boats he needed to cross the Euphrates for an intended attack on Mitanni whom he subdued. Egypt, after these victories, sought to retain the loyalties of her former enemies by contracting diplomatic marriages—thus Amenophis III married a daughter of the King of Mitanni, and Amenophis IV followed his example and maintained friendship with the kings of Babylon, Mitanni and the Hittites. Egypt's foreign trade was prospering and widespread; Thutmosis III stated that ships from Keftiu, Byblos and Sektu were loading in Syrian harbours with beams and large timbers for Egyptian ports whilst his own ships were at Memphis preparing to go to Keftiu. Domestic poultry, originally from India, now reached Egypt; they could have been brought either by the Persian Gulf route and then down the land-bridge, or else across the Indian Ocean from the Malabar Coast to Mukalla and then along the ancient trade-route through Teima to the Gulf of Akaba.

The art of writing in an alphabetic script, invented by the inhabitants of Phoenicia, was now widespread. There were a number of Canaanite groups of symbols, but they all represented the same basic alphabet; their very diversity is evidence both of the age of the original and of its Palestinian provenance. The older theories of Egyptian origin, to which Sir Grafton Elliot Smith subscribed, now appear unlikely. The obscurities in the old Accadian diplomatic language in the Tell el Amarna letters were glossed in Canaanite and documents in Ugaritic script were now used in other parts of the country such as Beth Shemesh. The earliest 'Hebrew' compositions may belong to this period, presumably written in the 'Phoenician' script; the writer believes that the square Hebrew script of later times is not derived from this but may be based on Ugaritic cuneiform[42].

By XIVth century the Egyptians were using iron extensively for tools and weapons having learnt the art from the Hittites who still controlled supplies of the raw metal. This control probably explains Hittite power to interfere in Egyptian controlled territory.

A great disaster befell Crete. The period is late Minoan III. An unidentified enemy destroyed Knossos by fire, the palace ruins were deserted and the Dark Age of Crete began. Colonies appeared in the island, either Phoenician[43] or Mycenaean[44]. It was certainly a period when Phoenician power and interest in expansion was rising but it was also a time when the Mycenaeans were replacing the Minoans in foreign trade. Although they formed no colonies in Cyprus a great amount of Mycenaean-style pottery is to be found there. The Lion Gate at Mycenae was built after the fall of Knossos. The Phoenician unrest was probably part of something more general for about this time the Canaanites, according to the Tell el-Amarna letters, were asking Babylon for an alliance so that they could revolt against Egyptian rule. The Aramaeans were constantly pressing into Canaan around the source of the Jordan. Damascus and Harran. The tales of Laban and Jacob give a true picture of Aramaean peasant life of the period[45]. Moreover, the Canaanites of this period possibly provided an element in the racial makeup of the modern 'Palestinian Arab'[46]. Hurrian influence was now strong in Ugarit, one eighth of the personal names being Hurrian. The Egyptians called all Palestine and Syria 'Huru'. Palestinian chiefs such as Arad-Khepa of Jerusalem had Hurrian names. Hurrian had official standing as the language of Mitanni and the Mitannian rulers bore Hurrian names. The Huru were the Biblical Horites. The Ugaritic texts were now written down in the existing recension, and as further evidence of their expansionism 'Phoenician' copper pendants began to sell as far away as Central and Eastern Europe. Canaanite and Egyptian influences were now reciprocal in art and religion, and it is possible that the long residence by the Hebrews in Egypt may have contributed to this. Hebrew cultic arrangements owed much to Egypt; Ikhnaton's Hymn to the Sun's Disc and the Hebrew Ps 104 are probably descended from a common Syrian ancestor, and portions of the Baal Epic from Ugarit were translated into Egyptian[47]. There was much Egyptian literary activity at this time.

Growing nationalism amongst the Amorites of the north encouraged the Hittites to interfere in the affairs of Syria and Palestine since they found them a useful tool against Egypt. Shubbiluliuma received tribute from Ugarit and raided as far south as Byblos. The Habiru are identified with the SA+GAZ by evidence from the Hittite capital Hattusas, Ugarit and Alalekh (Atchana); they were employed as mercenaries by chiefs seeking Amorite independence. About 1360 Aziru, son of Abda-shirta, king of the kingdom of Amurru in central Syria conquered a strip of country stretching from the Syrian Desert to the sea at Ugarit, forcing Rib-Addi, king of Byblos who had remained loyal to Egypt, to flee to Beirut. Zimridu king of Zidon joined with Aziru to attack Abi-Milki, the pro-Egyptian king of Tyre. The Egyptians were employing the Sutu as mercenaries according to Assyrian inscriptions. The Battles of Qadesh (1308, 1296) arose from these movements. This also covered the period of the reign of Ikhnaton (1375-58) when weakness in the central government of the empire left it wide open to attack by the Habiru. There is almost certainly some connection between these attacks and the entry of the Hebrews, and at no other time would entry and settlement have been easier[48]. During the following century Ugarit extended its control to cover 2,300 square miles, aided no doubt by the recession of Egyptian power and was, just a century before her violent death, at the height of her strength.

Mycenaean Miracle

During the thirteenth century the Minoan traders on Melos in the Cyclades were replaced by Mycenaeans who also gained control of Delos. Carved ivories found here may indicate Phoenician contacts, perhaps in Minoan times, for at Deiralla in the Central Jordan Valley clay tablets, written in a script resembling Minoan Linear A were deposited at this time beside a metal-working furnace[49]. The Phoenician sites of Enkomi, Sinda and Kition were re-established in Cyprus partly by Mycenaean influence. Kition stated a close contact with Egypt. Aegean settlements in Cyprus were destroyed by the sea-peoples who attacked the Nile Delta but did not get as far as Thebes. This expansion by the Sea-peoples may be connected in some way with the apparently steady migration of the Etruscans traditionally from Anatolia—into Italy over the next two centuries; swords found in the Papulonia Etruscan tombs resemble those used by Hittites and Sherdans at the Battle of Qadesh (1285) and certain elements in Etruscan inscriptions seem to be reminiscent of the Levant. There may well have been Mycenaean pressure behind the Etruscan migration for a dagger from Taranto shows Mycenaean influence and resembles a sword from Enkomi, and lugged axes, of the type cast in Troy VII have been found at Pozznoli, Rome and Civita Vecchia. This coincides with the fall of Troy VIIa at a time when the Greeks were trying to force a trade-route through the Hellespont against Trojan opposition. At the time of the Trojan War the rulers of Crete were Achaeans, with Agamemnon as Supreme king; Attarssiyas the Ahhiyian[50] was attacking Lydia which may be connected with the probability that the Hebrew tribe of Dan was non-Semitic in origin and was part of the Danuna movement from nearby Adana[51]. Further invasions of the Sea-peoples were defeated on the Egyptian coast by Merneptah who records the event, along with the destruction of part of the population of Palestine, in his stele (1220) which was found at Lachish; a sword bearing his name was found at Ugarit, which was then ruled by King Ammurabi. The King of the Hittites had written to the King of Ugarit warning him of this attack which he ascribed to famine, and this is confirmed by Etruscan records and Herodotus[52] mentions disastrous world-wide starvation. Merneptah sent grain by ship to 'keep alive the land of Kheta' (the Hittites) and found himself attacked by the starving Libyans. This famine was probably the instrument by which the Hittite monopoly of iron-production was broken. Their empire collapsed because the Aegean peoples had learnt from them how to produce iron and had turned it against them. The Philistines of Tell el-Fara in Palestine tried in turn to keep the monopoly for themselves and succeeded for some centuries[53]; when this attempt failed iron weapons became available to the peasants, and the cultured aristocracies and monarchies of the Bronze Age fell before them. A cultural recession took place which made Palestine less pleasant, as a place to live in, for a considerable period[54]. The Phoenicians, armed with superior weapons were now able to establish some of their earlier colonies in Africa[55]. The Aramaeans had mastered the use of the camel which made possible long desert journeys by short routes inaccessible to ass-nomads. Cities such as Shiloh, Bethel and Tell el-Fal (later to become Gibeah of Saul) were conquered and destroyed by them.

There was also great activity in the Aegean world; Troy VII had fallen and a great surge of displaced peoples were seeking new homes. The southward move of the Dorians overwhelmed all Mycenaean cities except Athens and the homeless Sea-peoples, having failed in their two-pronged attack on Egypt went further west, the Sekels to Sicily, the Sherdans to Sardinia. Perhaps the Teresh joined the Etruscans whose first saecula started at this time. Simultaneously the Chariot people invaded the Sahara: it is possible that these too bore some relationship to the Sea-peoples since the two-wheeled carts of the type which the Egyptians were to use for nearly a Millennium were first introduced to them by the Philistines during this period. The Philistines, foiled by Rameses III, then augmented their existing settlements along the south-west coast of Palestine. This is the period of Biblical Samson, the scenes of whose life are now being uncovered by Israeli archaeologists at Ascalon.

All these political disturbances on the mainlands of the Levant threatened the prosperity of trade which was the lifeblood of Phoenicia and compelled the Phoenicians to concentrate upon developing their colonies in the Western Mediterranean. There is considerable disagreement about the dates of the foundation of these colonies. Some French scholars maintain that Gades, Lexus, Utica and even Cathage may have been founded during the XIIth century BC, but archaeological evidence does not support such an early date. It is certain that the Phoenicians were eventually forced to set up these bases in order to safeguard their sea borne trade, for the collapse of Greek power had, whilst it removed one threat, left the oceans open to swarms of pirates. This was one of the results of the social revolution brought about by the coming of the Iron Age; the Greeks even lost the art of writing and the great literature of the Mycenaean age was only kept alive by the itinerant bards, one of whom was Homer[56].

Tyre, like the Hebrews a century later,[57] realized her need for a strong central government if she were to survive her external pressures. Sidonian power faded and the Tyrian monarchy arose; the need for monarchy was also felt in their colonies overseas, and the Egyptian Wenamon refers to the queen of a Cypriote city who was also probably Phoenician. The Hebrews made their first unsuccessful attempt to establish a monarchy[58] to meet the threats of the Midianites and Philistines, but their search for a cohesive centre for political unity came too late—the Philistines had won a great victory at Aphek, capturing the Ark, the focal point of the Hebrew cultus, and destroying the ancient temple at Shiloh. The Hebrews now realized that in a strong central government lay their only hope of political survival, and they accepted a monarchy under Saul[59]. It was their good fortune that their second king, David, was a master-politician as well as a poet and religious synthesizer who did not hesitate to borrow the ancient hymnbook from the Jebusite-Judahite temple at Jerusalem. Much of the greatest Hebrew poetry comes from this period.

Then destruction struck Cyprus, both natural cataclysm and political catastrophe. According to Homer Salamis was founded about this time by Teucer on his way back from the Trojan War; archaeological evidence supports the need for this foundation, for Enkomi had been abandoned because her harbour had become silted up.

The foregoing brief outlines of cultural diffusion in the A.N.E.

during the IInd Millennium BC is necessarily heavily coloured by the contacts of warfare since this is the subject matter of most of the surviving records. But the evidence is quite clear—about the time of Abraham people were travelling from the Indus Valley to the hub of the cultural wheel in the middle East and thence, by whichever spoke suited them, to North Africa, or Spain, or Northern Europe, or the Caucasus, or to Egypt or the land of Punt, taking with them trade-goods required in their destination. The standpoint of the cultural diffusionist is vindicated, for who will invent when a prototype is available from the salesman just arrived from abroad? But man's inborn spirit of adventure was a greater motive-force than trade—

> We travel not for trafficking alone
> By hotter winds than these our hearts are fanned
> For lust of knowing what should not be known
> We make the golden journey to Samarkand.
>
> —FLECKER

NOTES AND REFERENCES

Exigencies of space compel me to be content with general rather than detailed references.

1 A selection of his published works includes such titles as *The Migrations of Early Culture*, 1915; *The Influence of Ancient Egyptian Civilization in the East and in America*, 1916; *Ships as Evidence of the Migrations of Early Culture*, 1917; *The Evolution of the Dragon*, 1919; His *Ancient Egyptians* first appeared in 1911; 2nd edn, used in the preparation of this article appeared in 1923 and is referred to as *A.E.*; *The Evolution of Man*, 1924; *Elephants and Ethnologists*, 1924 and many medical and anatomical studies and articles in the Encyclopaedia Britannica and in many journals, Festschrifts, etc.

2 Sir Grafton took an opposite view, *A.E.*, Ch. 3.

3 *A.E.*, Ch. 2.

4 Plutarch, *Isis and Osiris*.

5 Sir James Frazer, *The Golden Bough* (vols on Adonis, Attis, Osiris, 1914, p. 7).

6 E.g., H. Wheeler Robinson, *Inspiration and Revelation in the Old Testament* (Oxford Paperbacks 1946, p. 100 ff.); W. Eichrodt, *Theology of the Old Testament*, SCM London 1964, Vol. II, p. 510 ff.

7 The portrait skulls of neolithic Jericho, and the presence of grave goods through a long period of Palestinian life, seem to me to indicate belief in a resurrection. On the Jericho excavations see K. M. Kenyon, *Archaeology in the Holy Land* (London 1960), and *Digging Up Jericho* (London 1957). For Egyptian belief that the earth was a male being see E. O. James, *The Cult of the Mother Goddess*, Thames & Hudson, London 1959, p. 58.

8 N. Walker and many others have contributed or commented on this view, but see my *YHWH* in Vetus Testamentum XII 1964.

9 This has long been recognized; cf. H. R. Hall, *The Ancient History of the Near East* (London 1913) p. 89; L. E. Street, *Peoples and Cultures of the Middle East*, National History Press, N.Y. 1970, Vol. 1, p. 44 ff.; Sonia Cole, *The Neolithic Revolution*, British Museum, London 1961, p. 8. Cf. *Palestine and Jordan*, Naval Intelligence Division, Geographical Handbook Series, 1943, p. 82.

10 G. Bibby, *Looking for Dilmun*, W. W. Hallo & W. K. Simpson, pp. 11, 15; *The Ancient Near East*, Harcourt, Brace, Javanovitch, N.Y., 1971 gives a useful summary of N. E. archaeology.

11 Beautiful illustrations on p. 18 of R. Tobley, *Ships Through the Ages* (Octopus Books, London 1972) enable one to compare the Ethiopian hobolo with the papyrus boat of Lakes Chad (Africa) and Titicaca (South America); see further Thor Heyerdahl, *The Ra Expeditions* (George Allen and Unwin Ltd, London 1971) and Bibby, *Looking for Dilmun*.

12 Judaism, Christianity and Islam, all of which show the influence of their great forerunner, have followed in her wake, cf. E. O. James, *The Cult of the Mother Goddess* (Thames & Hudson, London 1959); Erich Neumann, *The Great Mother* (Routledge & Kegan Paul, London 1955).

13 R. W. Hutchinson, *Prehistoric Crete* (Pelican, London 1962) to which most of the Cretan references are made.

14 All Ugaritic quotations are taken from Sir Godfrey Driver, *Canaanite Myths and Legends* (T. and T. Clark, London and Edinburgh 1971). The Ugaritic legends are briefly summarized by S. H. Hooke, *Middle Eastern Mythology* (Pelican, London 1963).

15 Bibby, *Looking for Dilmun*.

16 A useful summary of Egyptian scientific achievement can be found in R. Arnoldey, *et al, La Science antique at médiévale* (R. Taton (ed.), P.U.F., Paris 1957).

17 1 Sam. 13:19 f. shows that the Hebrews were dependent upon the Philistines for metal-working; 1 Sam. 17 gives a fascinating account of a Stone-Age warrior with a Bronze-Age opponent.

18 F. Gladstone Bratton, *A History of Egyptian Archaeology*, Robert Hale, London, 1967, p. 21 f.

19 Josh. 5:6.

20 Josh. 17:18; cf. Deut. 19:20.

21 The Egyptian material and the diffusion of its influence quoted in this essay has been collected from so wide a range of sources that it is convenient to indicate some of those most frequently used. W. Stevenson Smith, *Interconnections in the Ancient Near East* (Y.U.P., New Haven 1965). A. Mekhitarian, *Egyptian Painting* (Skira, Geneva 1954). M. Vilimkova, *Egyptian Art* (Peter Nevill, London 1962). Seton Lloyd, *The Art of the Ancient Near East* (Thames & Hudson, London 1961). Doubt has recently been cast on the reliability of dating based on the Dorak hoard, but I see no valid reason for this.

22 A. Galanopoulos & E. Bacon, *Atlantis; the Truth behind the Legend* (Nelson, London 1969).

23 Most references to Aegean Art can be traced to P. Demargne, *Aegean Art* (Thames & Hudson, London 1964) and to articles by Marinatos and others.

24 Most references to the archaeology of Canaan are to be found in J. Gray, *The Canaanites* (Thames & Hudson, London 1965). H. J. Franken & C. A. Franken-Battershill, *A Primer of Old Testament Archaeology*, Brill, Leiden 1963. K. Kenyon, *Archaeology in the Holy Land*. W. F. Albright, *The Archaeology of Palestine* (Penguin, London 1951).

25 References to early Mesopotamian archaeology are mostly to be found in M. E. L. Mallowan, *Twenty-five years of Mesopotamian Discovery* (The British School of Archaeology in Iraq, London 1959).

26 Albright, *The Archaeology of Palestine*.

27 Gen. 14:18, 19.

28 References to Phoenician influence and spread of culture are mostly derived from M. Cheban, *et al.*, *The Role of the Phoenicians in the Interaction of Mediterranean*

Civilizations (W. Ward (ed.), A.U., Beirut 1968); W. Culican, *The First Merchant Venturers* (Thames, London 1966); S. Moscati, *The World of the Phoenicians* (Weidenfeld & Nicholson, London 1968).

29 Cr. M. Yacoub, *et al.*, *Carthage* (J. de Moreuil (ed.), Archaeologia Viva 1, Paris 1969); B. H. Warmington, *Carthage* (R. Hale & Co., London 1969); G. Picard, *Carthage* (Elek Books, London 1964). Future references to Carthage are mostly based on the above.

30 References to M.E. and European cross-influences are mostly based on Stuart Piggott, *Ancient Europe* (E.U.P., Scotland 1965), p. 150 and various works already mentioned dealing with M.E. archaeology.

31 Sir Leonard Woolley, *A Forgotten Kingdom* (Pelican, London 1953), p. 76.

32 C. H. Gordon, *Before the Bible* (Collins, London 1962); *Homer and Bible* (H.U.C.A. 26, 1955).

33 Gen. 47:14 ff.

34 Exod. 1:8 ff.

35 Gen. 12:17, seeking to account for the expulsion of Abraham and Sarah from Egypt, says that the Egyptians blamed them for introducing 'grave diseases'. The nature of these is not stated but Sir Grafton, in association with Warren Dawson (*Egyptian Mummies*, p. 157) established that no syphilitic symptoms occur in any ancient Egyptian remains.

36 Cf. J. V. Luce, *The End of Atlantis* (Thames & Hudson, London 1969), p. 174.

37 Josh. 15:63; 17:15 ff.

38 Sir Godfrey Driver, *Semitic Writing* (Schweich Lectures, British Academy, London); Frank H. Stubbings, *The Rise of Mycenaean Civilization* in *Cambridge Ancient History*, rev. edn C.U.P. 1963, Vol. II, Ch. XIV.

39 Stubbings, *The Rise of Mycenaean Civilization* . . . VIII.

40 Sir Robert Graves, *The Greek Myths* (Penguin, London 1955), Vol. 1, p. 56.

41 Yam (Semitic *sea*) probably conceals a name long-lost and refers to a deity who was also called Potei-dan and identified by Minyans and Ionians with a land deity (cf. Charles Seltman: *The Twelve Olympians and their Guests*, Max Parrish, London 1952, Ch. XI).

42 This proposition may appear unlikely, but there seems to be some evidence that the three-fold vocalized aleph of Ugaritic is sometimes represented in Hebrew by the three different bearers aleph, yodh and waw.

43 Thucydides quoted by Hutchinson, *Prehistoric Crete*.

44 Hutchinson, *Prehistoric Crete*.

45 Gen. 25:20 etc.; Deut. 26:5.

46 Jos. 7:9f.; Gen. 36:2, 20; Jud. 3:3f., 2 Sam. 24:7 etc. 'Today, many peoples of western Asia are inaccurately called Arabs, among them . . . the Palestinian Arabs who now live mostly in Jordan'. C. S. Coon, with E. E. Hunt, *The Living Races of Man* (A. A. Knopf, New York 1965, p. 79).

47 The Astate Papyrus (extant copy XIIth century BC), formerly in the Amherst Collection, is almost certainly part of the Baal Epic.

48 An entry date for the first wave of attackers about 1360 BC would hardly satisfy the biblical statement that the Exodus took place 400 years after Jacob's descent into Egypt, but this is probably an idealized figure; the invasion and settlement was probably still in process at the time of Merneptah's stele, *c.* 1220 BC, cf. D. Winton-Thomas, *Documents from Old Testament Times* (Nelson, Edinburgh 1958).

49 This may be further evidence for the suggestion that the original idea of writing may have spread from Canaan to Crete.

50 Achaean?

51 Yigeal Yadin, *And Dan, why did he Abide in Ships?* in *Australian Journal of*

Biblical Archaeology, Vol. 1, No. 1, 1968, p. 9 ff.

52 *History*, I 94.

53 1 Sam. 12:19-22.

54 Jud. 5:6; 13 ff.

55 The Archaeological evidence is not conclusive being negative; no deposits of this period have been found on the sites. But the earliest havens were probably entirely transitory, and the traders probably lived on their ships for comfort and safety and threw their pot-sherds overboard.

56 The Homeric device of using old familiar 'jewels five words long' was earlier practised by the West Semites, and has caused much waste of time by textual critics seeking to remove 'dittographs'.

57 Jud. 8:23.

58 1 Sam. 4 ff.

59 1 Sam. 9:16.

14 CHINESE CIVILIZATION AND THE DIFFUSION OF CULTURE

Wang Gungwu

The place of China in world history has undergone many changes during the past centuries. China itself has been persuaded that it is not the centre of the world, and this has led to profound changes in China. What was more difficult for the Chinese has been the problem of fitting China into a wider but essentially Western scheme of world history. By this scheme, I do not mean that any other region is seen as the centre of the world. I refer to the scheme whereby the origins of Western civilization having been traced to Mesopotamia, Egypt and other centres in Western Asia, a great deal of effort has been expended on trying to fit the Far East, Africa and the Americas into the scheme as similar extensions from the same origins. Although the debates which arose have been acrimonious during the past two centuries in Europe and North America[1], the efforts have not been wasted. We know a great deal more about history today and much more about the nature of cultural and technological change than ever before. What happened in history is clearer to us; we are better equipped than before to know what was possible and what was probable. For this, we must acknowledge the contributions of many men—not only the patient collectors of facts but also the exponents of theories and stimulators of educated opinion. Of the latter group, one of the most notable protagonists some two generations back was Sir Grafton Elliot Smith.

Many of you knew the man personally. I was not so privileged. I came to know of him through his several books, most notably *Human History* and *The Diffusion of Culture* which he wrote during the last years of his life. I first read them some twenty years ago at a time when his views on the origins of civilization and the diffusion of culture were no longer widely accepted. All the same, the books made engrossing reading and contributed to my long interest in the history of culture-contact in Asia both in the dim past and in modern times. Two things I did not know at the time—that he had made lasting contributions to the field of anatomy and that he was born only a few hundred miles from here. This new knowledge has given me added interest in associating myself with this commemoration of the man.

As you know, Sir Grafton Elliot Smith started on something of a new career at the age of 40 when he published the first of his books on diffusion theory, *The Ancient Egyptians and their Influence upon the Civilisation of Europe*, in 1911. He had already won a reputation as a scholar of anatomy and physical anthropology and was regarded as an expert on Egyptian mummification. From then on, for twenty-five years, he wrote and lectured on the ramifications of his theory that civilization had begun with the discovery of cereal agriculture in the Nile Valley and that this had gradually stimulated the rise of civilizations in other centres in Asia, Europe and the Americas. Among the centres was the Yellow River Valley, the home of Chinese civilization, about which at that time little was really known.

Elliot Smith began modestly. In the first edition of *The Ancient Egyptians*, he makes no mention of China. He concentrates on establishing the case for diffusion from Egypt to the neighbouring Tigris-Euphrates valley, to Central Asia, to the Mediterranean and Western Europe and to East Africa. It was not until 1915 when he published *The Migrations of Early Cultures*, where he examines the geographical distribution of the practice of mummification, that he implies that China, Korea and Japan were all 'on the heliolithic track'. He says, 'The great stream of "heliolithic" culture exerted a profound influence and played a large part in shaping the peculiar civilisations of China, Korea and Japan', but also adds that, 'as the practice of embalming does not play an obtrusive part in this influence, I do not propose (in the present communication) to enter upon the discussion of these matters'.[2] This was followed by a number of other lectures which commented briefly on Chinese ships and Chinese writing having been stimulated by influences traceable to Egypt.[3]

Although Elliot Smith was already firmly convinced of the errors of the 'evolutionists' and had begun to attack fiercely the view that independent development of cultural traits and technology was possible because of the 'psychic unity' of all mankind, he had not paid much attention to China. But in 1916 and 1917, he began to include China in a series of lectures which explained what led men to move into Central Asia and Siberia: the search for gold and other magical stones. Quoting mainly from the monumental study of Chinese religion by the Dutch sinologist J. J. M. de Groot (in six volumes, 1892-1910), he became confident that 'the essential elements of Chinese civilisation were derived from the West'.[4] Three of these lectures were expanded and published in 1919 as *The Evolution of the Dragon*. The most striking where China was concerned was his second lecture on 'Dragons and Rain-Gods' where he links the Chinese dragon to the Indian Naga, the Babylonian Ea and the Egyptian Osiris and this link confirms him in his belief that the route to China was via Sumer and Elam, Turkestan and Baluchistan to the Tarim valley and then into Shensi and the Yellow River plains, and by the seventh century BC also to China by sea.[5]

It has long been clear that Elliot Smith had gone too far with the materials he used for China. He cannot, however, be held responsible for the widely accepted view before 1920 that the maturity of the bronze technology of Shang China in the middle of the second millennium BC could only be explained by cultural diffusion from Western Asia. Even a great scholar of Chinese exotics like Bertold Laufer rather assumed that this was the case because no example of neolithic cultures had been found in China. The picture was to change dramatically during the 1920s. It began with J. G. Andersson's discoveries of painted pottery ware at Yang-shao in North-Central China and culminated in Li Chi's discoveries of black pottery at Lung-shan in Shantung as well as P'ei Wen-chung's discovery of *Sinanthropus pekinensis* at Chou-k'ou-tien outside Peking. Our knowledge of the prehistory of China was completely transformed in the course of a decade.[6]

Elliot Smith kept abreast of the main outlines of these developments and even personally examined the Peking Man fossils in Peking. But he found nothing to shake his confidence in the Western origins of Chinese civilization. In 1928, he launched the series called *The Beginning of Things* with his own book *In the Beginning: the Origin of Civilisation*. Two years later, he produced his major full-length work, *Human History*. By this time, he had met with strong opposition from professional ethnologists and archaeologists concerning his claims for the centricity of Egypt as the source of all civilizations. Despite his fierce counter-attacks, he could not overcome the weak arguments he had used about diffusion to China and Central America. For example, in *In the Beginning*, he mentions paper from China and could only say

> the Chinese obtained the *idea* of making such a writing material *indirectly* from the Egyptians, who for more than twenty centuries before the peoples of Eastern Asia made rag-paper were making papyrus from the piths of the plants growing in the Nile, and writing upon it in ink with pens.[7]

Later, he suggests that gold-seekers went east about 2500 BC along the Tarim valley to Shensi (past the Kansu Ma-Chia-yao/Pan-shan sites excavated by J. G. Andersson in 1921-3) and the 'colony' settled there working on gold, copper and jade and 'planting the germs of Western culture, germs which provided the stimulus to the development of the distinctive type of civilisation which we characterise as Chinese'.[8]

His specific references to China remain weak in *Human History*. At one point, he warns us rightly not to confuse race and culture and not to think that the Chinese came from Mesopotamia even if their culture was similar to that in Sumer and Elam; then a few pages later he refers to his 'few Elamite prospectors' when arguing that Chinese civilization was 'inspired by certain alien influences'.[9] His uncertain grasp of Chinese history is further revealed when he emphasizes the benefits of agriculture and says, 'The Chinese are said to have doubled their numbers during the historic period at least once in each 250 years'.[10] This was totally wrong as all sources indicate how remarkably stable the population of China remained from the first to the fifteenth century AD, somewhere in the region of 40 to 50 million people over some 1,500 years.

I mention these examples not to quibble about minor points, but to say with regret how Elliot Smith had abandoned caution in his aggressive defence against contemporary criticisms. Indeed, his zeal had already established the validity of the idea of cultural diffusion. Even his strongest critics did not deny the significance of the concept, but merely questioned his insistence that *no* independent development was possible anywhere and that everything civilized began with Egypt. But he was unyielding, and even after his stroke in 1932, brought out vehement attacks on early New World scholars like William Robertson and W. H. Prescott and even turned against the great ethnologist he had long admired, E. B. Tylor himself; this was in his last book, *The Diffusion of Culture.* In this work, he says little of China except to mention the spread of Islam and Buddhism and the possibility of Buddhist travellers being the source of diffusion to America.

Let me not labour the point. The critics of Elliot Smith have not spared him. For thirty years after his death, the scathing attack on him by Robert Lowie in 1938[11] was read with awe and the names of Elliot Smith and W. J. Perry are still mentioned as negative examples for most professional anthropologists and archaeologists. But there is a positive side to this controversy where China is concerned. I refer to the influence of the debates on diffusion on the Chinese scholars themselves. They, too, went through controversies among themselves during the years Elliot Smith was active in the West. I believe this is a suitable time and place to outline the chief developments about diffusion and the origins of Chinese civilization among Elliot Smith's contemporaries in China.

Before I begin, I should emphasize that the Chinese underwent a traumatic intellectual experience during the first four decades of this century. A flood of contemporary Western ideas arrived in China almost all at once. Among the younger scholars, the experience was both exciting and exhilarating, but it was not always clear what ideas were more important and what more relevant; what priorities to give to the new ideas and how to distinguish between some of them. Among the first major sets of ideas to take root were those associated with the theory of evolution, with the works of Darwin, Huxley and Spencer. As Yen Fu, the great translator of Huxley and Spencer, says in 1895, in trying to sum up Darwinism in terms relevant to contemporary China,

> Living things struggle among themselves in order to survive. Nature selects among them and preserves the superior species. It is Darwin's view that humans and living things are born within a given space and together feed on the environment and on the benefits of nature. They come into conflict with each other. Peoples and living things struggle for survival. At first, species struggle with species, then as men gradually progress, there is a struggle between one social group and another. The weak invariably become the prey of the strong, the stupid invariably become subservient to the clever.[12]

Yen Fu was quite unequivocal about this and the elements of Social Darwinism spread very quickly. This was largely because the Social

Darwinism fed both the impending sense of doom which pervaded those who saw the fall of Chinese civilization as well as the exhilaration of those who wanted to re-gather forces to fight back, to adapt and change, to learn from the West to resist the West—as the Japanese had so successfully done by defeating China in 1894-5 and then by defeating Russia in 1904-5.

During the next two decades, evolution became the catch-word. There were a few Chinese scholars about the turn of the century who, through their readings of Japanese translations of Western writings, had begun to accept the view that Chinese civilization had come from Western Asia. But the theory of evolution was more attractive to the Chinese than any theory of diffusion at that time, and by the 1910s, the call was to change, to reform, to adapt, to evolve. But, of course, there was no sharp line between their use of the term evolution and what was in fact some form of diffusion. In order to adapt and evolve, there must be the will to learn and borrow from the West what was superior and beneficial, what could be used to achieve wealth and power for China.

In short, while the Western scientists could divide sharply on the subject of evolution and diffusion after 1911 and the controversy was fierce and long-drawn, the Chinese did not find it relevant to entangle themselves in this particular debate. It did not worry them to commit themselves to either one of two opposing views, and to imagine either that 'human nature is more or less the same everywhere' and therefore independent discoveries and developments are always possible, or that mankind is so uninventive that everything civilized must have originated in one place and then diffused over the rest of the world. Instead, they rather assumed that there was no contradiction between the biological need and will to survive which they took to be evolution and the conscious and unconscious borrowing and adaptation of ideas, institutions and techniques in order to survive.

For example, some of the nationalist traditional scholars at the turn of the century, men like Chang Ping-lin, Huang Chieh and Liu Shih-p'ei, were prepared to admit that Chinese civilization was the result of diffusion and migration from the West because this emphasized the difference between the Chinese and the Manchu 'northern barbarians' who conquered China in 1644 and had ruled over China since.[13] At the same time, the point had to be made that this civilization was facing destruction in the evolutionary sense of the struggle for existence and, therefore, action had to be taken to remedy that perilous position. The desire to survive makes human nature 'more or less the same', but salvation lies in the diffusion of new ideas, either directly from the West or indirectly from Japan.

Perhaps the most remarkable example of diffusion occurred within a few months of the publication of Elliot Smith's first book, *The Ancient Egyptians*, in 1911. This was the Wu-ch'ang rebellion in October 1911 which ended with the establishment of a republic in place of the two-thousand-year-old Empire. There was very little preparation for this new idea. The accepted models of the day were those of Japan, Germany and Britain, that is, of some kind of constitutional monarchy. Only a small group of rebels and young overseas students talked about a republic and they were never really in power during the 'revolution'. Yet a republic was declared, and thereafter, it was not possible for the clock to be turned back. Even though very few people in China understood what a republic was, the majority of the educated elite only three years later (in 1915) opposed vigorously President Yuan Shih-k'ai's attempt to make himself emperor. The important factor was the readiness of most people to try out something new—a vital ingredient in diffusion.

Yet I have not been able to find any deep interest in China concerning the theory of cultural diffusion during the next 25 years. Instead, with the intensification of nationalism, especially after 1919, the trend was towards arguing for the independent development of Chinese civilization. Their main criticisms were directed not so much against the British diffusionists as against Terrien de Lacouperie who had proposed a Mesopotamian origin for both the Chinese people and their civilization.[14] The reasons for this were that de Lacouperie had been very specific and that many Japanese scholars and some major Chinese scholars had accepted the main parts of his interpretation. Hence the concentration on demolishing his 'Babylon thesis'. And in doing this, it was rather assumed by most Chinese that all other views concerning Chinese origins in Egypt, India or Central Asia were similarly inappropriate and even ridiculous.

The main reaction against the idea of 'cultural diffusion' into China certainly owed something to nationalism, but a major factor was probably also the Chinese interest in Social Darwinism, in 'evolutionism', and their unwillingness to accept the fierce criticism against the 'evolutionists' set forth by Elliot Smith, W. J. Perry and W. H. R. Rivers. No less important were the scholarly links of the younger Chinese. By the time the republic was established in 1912, American missionary colleges had been strongly entrenched in most cities in Eastern China and many students had already been sent to America for higher education. During the next two decades, many more were to go and subjects like sociology and anthropology were introduced into Chinese colleges and universities, starting with the department in the Shanghai Baptist College in 1913. American influence remained strong and, when interest in China turned from social work to ethnology, Americans like L. H. Morgan, Franz Boas, and A. L. Kroeber received early attention. Before 1930, only a few like T'ao Lü-kung (L. K. Tao) were trained in England. Of the English scholars, the classics of ethnology and sociology translated into Chinese were, apart from Spencer, those of E. B. Tylor and Sir James Fraser; and later L. T. Hobhouse, Graham Wallas, B. Malinowski, A. R. Radcliffe-Brown and R. R. Marett. Significantly, other Europeans were, on the one hand, E. Durkheim, G. Simmel, F. Tönnies, Max Weber, V. Pareto, and F. C. Müller-Lyer and, on the other K. Marx, F. Engels, N. Bukharin and N. Lenin.[15] Bearing this list in mind, it is perhaps not surprising that little attention was paid to Elliot Smith and his friends, and the only substantial essay on diffusion theory by Wu Wen-hui in 1934 was very critical along the lines of the leading American anthropologists. In fact, Wu concludes as several Americans had done by saying,

> To be reasonable, we must admit that inventions in culture must have been very difficult and cultural diffusion very important. But to think that all cultures in the world originated among very few peoples or even one single people and only they can create culture, that is not something we would dare to agree with.[16]

In fact, diffusion theory never really had a chance to get off the ground in China. While it was developing in Europe in opposition to evolutionism, political developments took a sharp turn in China towards the left and a new generation of scholars shifted the debate to one between bourgeois Idealism and Empiricism on the one hand and Dialectical Materialism on the other. Neither evolution nor diffusion meant much when the intellectual world became divided more and more sharply between those who were pro-Western and followed Tylor, Kroeber and Malinowski and those who were 'anti-imperialist'; and therefore followed Marx, Engels, Morgan and Lenin, and, later, in the field of pre-history and archaeology, V. Gordon Childe. A good example of this was the controversy between Huang Wen-shan and Wang Yi-ch'ang in 1935, which exactly reflects the two schools of thought.[17] What was significant was that, in the field of ancient Chinese history, the archaeologists and sceptical traditionalists were providing data to the social historians who dominated the exciting and widely publicized debates about the nature of ancient history with their various versions of Marxist materialist arguments, notably those of Kuo Mo-jo and T'ao Hsi-sheng and the group centred on the journal *Tu-shu tsa-chih*.[18] Within a few years, several of the sociological and anthropological centres were closed down by the Nationalist government for being centres of radicalism. The political struggle had swallowed up the academics and the subject of the origins of Chinese civilization was no less political than any matter of political ideology and national survival.

Interpretations aside, the study of ancient Chinese history received a great stimulus from archaeological finds. First there were the oracle-bones of An-yang first discovered in 1898 and these became more and more significant with each new excavation in the area in the 1920s and 1930s. Then there were J. G. Andersson's discoveries of neolithic painted pottery sites in the early 1920s which revived the 'Babylon thesis' when it was realized that Mesopotamia and Russian Turkestan provided painted pottery of an even earlier type. More dramatic discoveries at the end of the decade curbed the 'Babylon thesis' somewhat. These were Li Chi's discoveries of black pottery sites (Lung-shan) in Eastern China which were clearly linked with the Shang sites at An-yang and suggested influences from Central-South China. Then there were P'ei Wen-chung's discoveries of *Sinanthropus pekinensis*. The latter, in particular, proving the antiquity of man in China Proper, was quickly seized by those scholars who had always doubted the idea of diffusion in the origins of Chinese civilization.

The more serious scholars realized that the situation was now very fluid and refrained from speculation and controversy. It was thought that this was only a beginning. If so much could be found within a few years of trying, then anything was possible and it would be wiser to stick close to what had been found and multiply efforts to find more, and possibly earlier, sites. Thus, up to 1937, the year Elliot Smith died, there were no serious discussions about his diffusionist theory. In Chinese eyes, his 'Egyptian thesis' was seen merely as another form of the as yet unaccepted 'Babylon thesis' of de Lacouperie.

But were the Chinese scholars averse to the idea of diffusion of culture? Clearly the major difficulty had arisen because of the confusion over race or people and culture or cultural traits. De Lacouperie had talked of a 'colony' from Babylon going to China rather as one of the lost Tribes of Israel was earlier supposed to have done. Elliot Smith had talked first of Egyptian and Phoenician sailors and traders diffusing culture and later referred to Elamite gold-prospectors wandering into Central Asia and then east into Shensi in Northwest China. W. H. R. Rivers was supposed to have been converted from 'evolutionism' and the 'psychic unity of Man' to the idea of 'racial mixtures and the blending of cultures'. Although Elliot Smith later insisted that *race* should not be confused with the *culture* of a race, and said, 'Any member of any race can adopt the culture of another people without undergoing any change in his physical characteristics', he did go on to say that, among the Mongol race, 'there was clearly no racial impulse to build up a distinctive type of customs and beliefs, nor in fact, an inevitable development of culture at all'. When he later said that 'the development of civilisation amongst the Chinese was inspired by certain alien influences', he added that 'the fact of the derivation of the foundation of Chinese civilisation from Elam and Sumer does not imply any close racial kinship between the peoples of Eastern and South-western Asia'. He concluded that it would be wrong to regard Mesopotamians in the third millennium as Mongolian and also wrong to regard the Chinese as Mesopotamian, 'even if it be admitted as conceivable that a few Elamite prospectors might have got as far as China at that time'.[19]

As the Chinese themselves often equated peoples and cultures, they would have found such comments about diffusion rather difficult to fit into their own preoccupations at the time.

What was the Chinese experience and perception of diffusion like? We have no clear record of conscious debate on this topic, but there is a great deal of historical and moral literature touching on this from earliest times. The orthodox Confucian fear of being 'barbarized' through contact with non-Chinese is well-known. Civilization had been hard-won through the genius of wise kings and leaders, the 'culture-heroes'. But, until the unification of the Ch'in Empire in the third century BC and the consolidation of the well-armed Chinese polity behind the Great Wall, there was no great confidence that this hard-won civilization could resist all threats to its survival. Strong 'barbarians' could destroy the civilized who were weak. Cultural influence and borrowings could not be separated from peoples who were in touch with one another. Trade, war, conquest, migration were brought to mind when the Chinese thought of such cultural imports and exports or cultural exchanges. The picture of cultural change and cultural diffusion was therefore a very concrete one associated with conscious dealings with non-Chinese peoples. It was only gradually and much later that the Chinese became certain that a culturally superior people 'absorbed' those who were inferior—and that this could happen even if the civilized ones were conquered by the 'barbarians'. Eventually the 'barbarians' would themselves become civilized. Cultural diffusion, therefore, took place by spreading from the superior to the inferior.

But here the Chinese were themselves mixing race or peoples with cultures and cultural traits. In fact, even when they were confident that other 'races' or peoples could be 'sinicized' or assimilated into Chinese civilization and that racial mixture through intermarriage would then quite naturally follow, they were aware that the Chinese had through the centuries taken many ideas and cultural traits from non-Chinese. These ranged from a fully-developed philosophy and religion like Buddhism to artefacts like some musical instruments, weapons and items of furniture to natural objects like some medical drugs, condiments, fruits and so on. At this level of cultural borrowing, no inferiority was assumed in the borrower who had adapted the borrowed item to his own use without necessarily losing anything of his own. The borrowing then had actually enriched the borrower. And this would apply to those people who borrowed from China, whether they borrowed the language as did the Koreans, the Japanese and the Vietnamese or whether they borrowed the Chinese use of silks, paper, gunpowder and so on. The crucial limits of such diffusion, as the Chinese saw it, was in not having to depend on a foreign supply. Hence the Chinese pride fully developed during the Ming and Ch'ing dynasties in their increasing self-sufficiency, a self-sufficiency that was almost a kind of perfection in itself, a perfection that needed no further cultural borrowing.

Thus it can be argued that, by the nineteenth century, the Chinese had an idea of diffusion, but the connotation of this diffusion from the examples in their history had become increasingly negative and unacceptable. Diffusion took place when unequal cultures met, and the inferior took from the superior, or diffusion was the cultural transfer of luxury unessentials, varying from harmless toys and trinkets to harmful habits, the most recent of which was the habit of opium-smoking leading to a dependence on large-scale opium imports. It was in this context that the Chinese viewed the West with deep suspicion at the turn of the twentieth century and had mixed feelings about the concept of diffusion.

It was not a question of denying that there was such a phenomenon, their own experience rather confirmed that there was. It was not even that the new concept of evolution, and the social Darwinism that they thought followed from it, was so overwhelming. It was simply that diffusionist theory applied to China at that time both denied the originality of China's ancient civilization and threatened to devalue existing Chinese values by having them replaced by superior Western ones. To accept both these negations would confirm that the Chinese were low down on the Social Darwinist ladder, and this the Chinese were determined to deny.

The quest for China's prehistoric origins, for China's original civilization, for diffusion not only to China but also from China, began in earnest in the 1920s and 1930s. It had begun with mere assertions about Chinese civilization being autochthonous and being as old as that of Egypt and Mesopotamia if not older, but soon this gave way to scientific opinion, the opinions of the archaeologists, geologists, palaeontologists, physical anthropologists and linguists. The debate in Europe and America over cultural diffusion had sharpened the wits of Westerners working in China, and Western scientists worked closely with their Chinese colleagues with the minimum of speculation and polemics. Men like J. G. Andersson, Teilhard de Chardin, Davidson Black, F. Weidenreich were followed by others like Owen Lattimore, L. Carrington Goodrich, and the incomparable Joseph Needham.[20] They worked in conjunction with, and with the help of, leading Chinese scholars like Li Chi, P'ei Wen-chung, Yang Chung-chien, Liang Ssu-yung, Cheng Te-k'un and Wang Ling. Since the war, there has been a new generation of scholars like Hsia Nai of the Chinese Academy of Sciences, Ho Ping-ti in Chicago and Chang Kwang-chih first trained in Taiwan and now at Yale. These are men who worked towards a wide horizon but with tighter discipline and well-controlled imaginations. They have rarely mentioned Elliot Smith and his friends and their writings suggest that they are not prepared to go along with the more extreme of Elliot Smith's claims. But what kind of picture have they, together and separately, created about the nature and development of Chinese civilization?

None of them deny the possibility of stimulus diffusion, but none of them would accept that this alone was responsible for the development of civilization in the Yellow River Valley. There are indications that the painted pottery sites within the 'nuclear area' in Central-North China were older than those to the northwest closer to the old silk route. There is evidence that the sequence of neolithic sites in North China can be related to that of similar sites in Central-South China although the precise relationship is still disputed. There are suggestions that the neolithic inhabitants in North China may have domesticated millet, the *Setaria italica*, not later than the domestication of barley in Western Asia. There are also suggestions that since rice may have become domesticated even earlier, with root-crops in mainland Southeast Asia or South China, this must make us reconsider the idea that cereal agriculture was entirely due to diffusion from the West.

But perhaps the most hopeful advances have been the recent laboratory reports of carbon 14 dates published in Peking related to key artefacts found in Upper Palaeolithic and Neolithic sites in China. The laboratory came into use for a short period in 1965-6 and then work began again in 1971, but these results have become available to scholars outside only in 1972. The latest issues of *K'ao-ku* (Archaeology) maintain high scientific standards for all periods of Chinese history and many valuable contributions should now follow. In the issues published so far, there is only one speculative article. This is the article by Kuo Mo-jo, the President of the Academy of Sciences, on the origins of Chinese ideographic writing found on painted pottery pieces at Pan-p'o (in the Wei River Valley in Shensi) dated about 4000 BC, more than 2,000 years before the oracle-bone writings of the Shang period at An-yang.[21] The remaining articles concentrate strictly on data; and the journal's editors have been quick to publish corrections to their own earlier speculations, for example, the carbon 14 results questioning the dating of the Tzu-yang man (found in Szechman, West China) as being Upper Palaeolithic.[22] As for the attitude taken on the subject of diffusion, there are no specific discussions about this, but we can perceive it in an article on the Inca civilization of Peru. This article ends with the possibility that the Inca civilization had received some outside influences, but insists that basically it was created by the indigenous people themselves. It then adds that it is nonsense to say that Peruvian civilization came from either Mexico or Polynesia, or that the Inca tribe had come from Asia via Alaska and Mexico and conquered the local tribes.[23] This clearly rejects the idea of diffusion of *total* cultures and the idea of migration and conquest as necessary factors in diffusion, but it does accept the possibility of stimulus diffusion and the influence of certain alien cultural traits. This is a sophisticated statement about diffusion which shows how far the Chinese have come from the crude views of diffusion current at the turn of the century and even when Elliot Smith was answering his critics some forty years ago.

Let me conclude with two quotations, one from a great Chinese historian and the other from a leading American anthropologist, neither of whom can be described as diffusionists. The Chinese historian, Ch'en Yin-k'o, doubts if many of the ideas borrowed from North America and Eastern Europe will survive long in China. But he concludes,

> For (new) ideas to be systematically developed and creative (in China), it is necessary on the one hand to assimilate the knowledge imported from outside and, on the other, not to forget the core-position of the (Chinese) people themselves . . . this is the lesson learnt from two thousand years of Chinese contact with non-Chinese.[24]

A grudging but significant acceptance of the central fact of cultural diffusion in recorded Chinese history!

The second quotation comes from George P. Murdoch of Yale University who said some 15 years ago, 'it is doubtful whether there is a single culture known to history or anthropology that has not owed at least ninety per cent of its constituent elements to cultural borrowing'.[25] While these are not exactly endorsements for Elliot Smith's theory of diffusion, I feel that those of us who remember him here might be content to see that the debate has come so far.

NOTES AND REFERENCES

1 The debate where China was concerned may be said to have begun with Joseph de Guignes, *Mémoire dan lequel on prouve, que les Chinois sont une Colonie Egyptienne*, Paris 1760, if we ignore the even earlier suggestions of Athanasius Kircher and John Webb, both of the seventeenth century. It continued desultorily throughout the nineteenth century until the full-scale efforts of Terrien de Lacouperie, *The Western Origin of Chinese Civilisation*, London 1894, followed by C. J. Ball, *Chinese and Sumerian*, Oxford 1913 and J. Ross, *The Origins of the Chinese people*, Edinburgh 1916. None of them, of course, offered anything like the all-embracing theory of diffusion developed by Grafton Elliot Smith between 1911 and 1915.

2 *The Migrations of Early Cultures*, Manchester 1915, p. 91.

3 Notably 'The influence of ancient Egyptian civilisation in the East and in America', *Bulletin of the John Rylands Library*, III, 1916-17, pp. 48-77 and *Ships as Evidence of the Migrations of Early Culture*, Manchester 1917.

4 *The Evolution of the Dragon*, Manchester 1919, p. 49.

5 Ibid., p. 76 ff.

6 The literature on these spectacular discoveries is vast. The early part of the story is well told in J. G. Andersson, *Children of the Yellow Earth*, London 1934 and H. G. Creel, *The Birth of China*, New York 1937. More recent synthesis of the subject are Li Chi, *The Beginnings of Chinese Civilisation*, Seattle 1957; Cheng Te-k'un, *Archaeology in China*, Cambridge, Vol. 1, 1959, and Supplement, 1966; and Chang Kuang-chih, *The Archaeology of Ancient China*, rev. edn, New Haven 1968.

7 *In the Beginning*, London 1928, p. 14.

8 Ibid., p. 84.

9 *Human History*, London 1930, p. 154.

10 Ibid., p. 288.

11 Robert H. Lowie, *The History of Ethnological Theory*, N.Y. 1938, pp. 160-9.

12 Yen Fu, 'Yuan-ch'iang', in Chien Po-tsan (ed.), *Wu-hsü pien-fa*, Vol. 3 of *Chung-kuo Chin-tai Shih tzu-liao ts'ung-k'an*, Shanghai 1953, p. 41 (Benjamin Schwartz's translation, *In Search of Wealth and Power*, Cambridge, Mass. 1964, pp. 45-6).

13 Chang Ping-lin, 'Hsü Chung-hsing', in *Ch'iu Shu* (first published in 1901), Shanghai 1958, pp. 41-53; Huang Chieh, 'Huang Shih', *Kuo-ts'ui hsueh-pao*, 1905, I/1, 47-60; Liu Shih-p'ei, 'Hua-hsia p'ien', in *Jang Shu*, and *Chung-kuo min-tsu chih*, both printed in his collected works, *Liu Shen-shu hsien-sheng i-shu*, 1936, Vols 17-18.

14 Some notable examples are articles by Miao Feng-lin, 'Chung-kuo min-tsu hsi-lai pien', *Hsueh-heng*, No. 37, 1925, 1-34; T'u Hsiao-shih, 'Han-tsu hsi-lai shuo k'ao-cheng', *Hsueh-yi*, 1920, Vol. 2, 1, 1-6 and 2, 1-6; Chang Ch'in, 'Chung-hua

min-tsu shuo-yuan lun'. *Ti-hsueh tsa-chih*, 1914-15, Vol. 5, No. 10 to Vol. 6, No. 1; and Chu Hsi-tsu, 'Wen-tzu hsueh shang chih Chung-kuo jen-chung kuan-ch'a', *She-hui k'o-hsueh chi-k'an*, Vol. 1, No. 3, 1923, 257-71. More recently, see Chien Po-tsan, *Chung-kuo shih-kang*, Vol. 1, Shanghai 1946 and Hsü Liang-chih, *Chung-kuo shih-ch'ien shih-hua*, Hongkong 1954.

15 A short summary of developments may be found in Leonard S. Hsü, 'The Teaching of sociology in China', *Chinese Social & Political Science Review*, Vol. 11, No. 3, July, 1927, and 'The sociological movement in China', *Pacific Affairs*, Vol. 4, No. 4, April 1931, pp. 283-307.

16 Wu Wen-hui, 'Wen-hua ch'uan-po lun chih yen-chiu', *Hsin shih-hui k'o-hsueh chi-k'an*, Nanking, Vol. 1, No. 2 (15 August 1934), pp. 57-75.

17 For example, Huang Wen-shan, 'Tui yü Chung-kuo ku-tai she-hui shih yen-chiu ti fang-fa lun chih chien-t'ao', *Hsin she-hui k'o-hsueh chi-k'an*, Vol. 1, No. 3 (15 November 1934), 1-26 and 'Chieh-chi lo-chi yü wen-hua min-tsu hsueh', *Ibid.*, Vol. 1, No. 4 (15 March 1935), 273-322; Wang Yi-ch'ang's reply 'Chung-kuo yuan-shih she-hui shih fang-fa lun', *Ibid.*, Vol. 1, No. 4 (15 March 1935), 251-72.

18 There is also a vast literature on these debates. The best-known and most influential are Kuo Mo-jo, *Chung-kuo ku-tai she-hui yen-chiu*, Shanghai 1930 and T'ao Hsi-sheng, *Chung-kuo she-hui chih shih ti fen-hsi*, Shanghai 1929. The major debates then followed, mainly in the pages of the journal, *Tu-shu tsa-chih*, edited by Wang Li-hsi, which published several special issues on this in 1931-3. Japanese scholars, too, took an interest in the British diffusionists, and the work of one of them, Nishimura Shinji, was translated into Chinese in 1936 as *wen-hua i-tung lun*, but this appeared too close to the Sino-Japanese War to generate interest and there seems to have been no scholarly response to this work.

19 *Human History*, pp. 145-55.

20 This list of Western scholars is highly selective. I have included only those who had actively worked with the first generation of archaeologists in China. A fuller list must include at least scholars like B. Karlgren, H. G. Creel, R. Heine-Geldern, C. W. Bishop, W. Eberhard, N. Barnard and W. Willetts.

21 *K'ao-ku*, No. 3, May 1972, pp. 2-13.

22 *K'ao-ku*, No. 1, January 1972, pp. 57-9.

23 *K'ao-ku*, No. 4, July 1972, pp. 58-63.

24 Ch'en Yin-k'o, Review of Fung Yu-lan, *Chung-kuo che-hsueh shih*, quoted in Chou Yu-t'ung, 'Wu-shih nien lai Chung-kuo chih hsin shih-hsueh', *Hsueh-lin*, Vol. 4, February 1941, p. 33.

25 Harry L. Shapiro (ed.), *Man, Culture & Society*, New York 1960, p. 254.

15 RELATIONSHIPS BETWEEN AUSTRALIAN ABORIGINAL MATERIAL CULTURE, AND SOUTHEAST ASIA AND MELANESIA

Frederick D. McCarthy

The Aborigines of Australia remained hunter-foodgatherers throughout their long occupation of a (relatively) isolated continent. There has been much speculation, however, on their origin and physical characteristics and on the migrations of various strains which contributed to their racial constitution. There has also been a continuing interest in their material culture, with which I am concerned in this paper, since Eden's discussion in 1787 of its composition based on Dampier's and Cook's primary accounts. This interest has led to some fantastic claims concerning Aboriginal rock art including the imaginative rock engravings of the Sydney-Hawkesbury region of New South Wales and the Wandjina cave paintings in the Northern Kimberley, Western Australia.

Theories of Cultural Dynamics

Before turning to the specific topic of this paper, I think reference to some of the 'classical' theories of cultural dynamics in relation to Australia would be helpful. Thus, the concept of evolution from savagery to civilization has little relevance to Australia where the so-called state of savagery survived until modern times, but it was a factor.* Examples of evolution in single traits exist in Aboriginal material culture, one of which is the development of the returning boomerang from the non-returning one; another is the extraordinary range of complex designs based on the concentric circle, parallel sinuous lines, animal tracks and dots incised on stone and wooden tjuringa by the Aranda tribe of Central Australia, which evolved from the simpler rock engraving motifs of this area in which compositions are rarely seen. Likewise environmental determinism has long been discarded as a decisive factor in shaping a people's cultural pattern (Lowie, 1937, p. 144), but it does set up limitations beyond which culture cannot advance. In Dixon's view (1928, p. 284) the development of culture depends on a people's genius, geographical position and history.

* See Lowie, 1937, p. 27, for a discussion of the concept.

In Australia there existed a basically uniform Aboriginal culture, modified locally in the differing habitats on the continent, from the desert to the tropics, the coast to the forest, the plains to the river banks; for this reason I believe the Aborigines imposed their culture on the Australian environment. This view is supported by Lawrence (1968, p. 58) in his detailed comparison of six different regional economies in Australia. He concluded that it is difficult to see the design of the material culture of any one group of Aborigines simply as a rational and distinctive response to life in a particular environment. As archaeological research has demonstrated that there were local changes only in Aboriginal stone implement industries, and no major cultural advance, except edge grinding until the Middle Stone Age began some 7,000 years ago, we have a situation of a relatively static culture stabilized with the environment for a long initial period after which many other factors came into force.

One school of thought insists that fixed laws of development or growth constantly impelled societies to duplicate one another's ideas. The Australian evidence does not support such an overall principle of independent development. Invention, in point of fact, is assigned minor importance by most culture historians who are prepared to accept parallel invention of simple devices, not of complex ones, by different societies. Davidson, as a result of his Australian distributional studies, concluded that a number of simple types of food and water containers— human skull, skin pouches and water bags, bark buckets, tree gnarl and wooden bowls, and bark containers—were invented by the Aborigines. Creative ability in the Aborigines is also evident in the primary or secondary invention of new kinds and shapes of spearthrowers, clubs and baskets, the stone and wooden *tjuringa*, returning boomerang, *kodja* hammer-axe, *leilira* blade, and in adapting basic nets, brush fences and pits in hunting and fishing techniques. Convergent evolution or parallelism was recently advocated by Golson (1971a, p. 135) as an explanation of

> similarities between the various kinds of hafted axe-like implements discussed by McCarthy in 1940 for a large area from Asia to Australia, which may, perhaps, be more realistically explained as parallels within the same technological tradition rather than successive migrations distributing individual items.

Finally, we come to cultural diffusion concerning which extreme and perhaps intriguing views have been advanced. Elliot Smith (1911, 1928, 1930, 1933) and Perry (1923) expounded the theory of the spread throughout the world of the advanced civilization of Egypt 3,000 to 4,000 years ago. Their views hold little relevance for Australian Aboriginal material culture as the central features of their heliolithic culture are megaliths, sun cults, mummification, dual organization and irrigation. The boomerang, however, is included in their claims (Elliot Smith, 1933, Figure 2). Whether the Egyptian and other ex-Australian occurrences of this weapon are related or not I cannot say. Pitt-Rivers (1916) believed that the boomerang, shield and club in Australia developed from a round stick, and Spencer (1922, p. 20) supported this claim for boomerangs and allied weapons. As the boomerang was not used by the Tasmanians it was either developed independently in Australia or came here after the arrival of the original ancestors of the Aborigines. Elliot Smith (1930, p. 129) stated that the Aborigines 'received practically every element of their culture from abroad in relatively recent times'. Available data, however, indicates that Australian Aboriginal stone technology, art and material culture received some stimulating injections from about 7,000 years ago to the present time, though not necessarily from an ultimate Egyptian source, even indirectly.

The problem with diffusion is that it leads the dedicated disciple on and on tracing like traits all over the world, and the difficulty is to know where to stop. This happened to Schuster with his studies of art motifs. In recent years Lommel (1957) claimed that the X-ray style of art featured in Arnhem Land in north Australia originated in the European Magdalenian as an element of older hunting cultures; Hallam (1971, p. 101) has compared the 1+3+1 spacing of wall grooves in the Orchestra Shell, Koonalda, Kintore and Cutta Cutta caves in Australia with similar markings in upper palaeolithic art in western Europe, and there is a close similarity between macaroni-type grooves at Koonalda and some western European art sites; the linear decorative art styles in Australia, based on both the concentric circle and the concentric diamond, have wide distributions in rock engravings, on pottery and other media elsewhere in the world; the Cleland Hills human face engravings, in a remote part of the Northern Territory, resemble faces painted on cave walls in Papua; the shapes of many kinds of stone implements, from geometric microliths to highly polished axes and adzes, are similar in many parts of the world. Undoubtedly, invention, convergent evolution and diffusion must all be invoked to explain these widespread occurrences of similar traits. In respect to Australia one can only say that Aboriginal culture forms part of the overall process of culture advance in Oceania generally, and its development cannot be separated as an entity in itself (McCarthy 1957a, p. 95). Australia is at the end of a chain.

Rivers, another British diffusionist, claimed that the numerous methods of disposing of the dead in Australia were each introduced by successive and very small groups of migrants whose racial strains left no mark on the Aborigines, and whose technology degenerated, so that the 'disappearance of useful arts should have taken place in Australia and on a scale unrivalled anywhere else in the world'. Australian Aboriginal culture, however, demonstrates steady advance, not decadence. Roheim (1925) thought that the human pointing bone was related to certain ways of disposing of the dead, and that it was introduced into Australia along with platform burial and anthropophagy.

The Vienna school of diffusionists, Graebner, Schmidt and Koppers, attempted to explain culture development in a system of strata which originated among small groups of primitive man, whose cultures spread outwards, and the earliest ones survived only in marginal, remote and inhospitable places. According to Lowie (pp. 180-2) Graebner defined six of these strata in Oceania as separate complexes from the most ancient, Tasmanian, through Old Australian (simple clubs, boomerang, windbreaks, etc.), Totemic (platform burial, circumcision, throwing sticks, circular domed huts, etc.), Moiety, Melanesian Bow and Polynesian levels. Certain of the traits in his strata, such as the penis sheath, headrests and circular domed huts in the Totemic complex, failed to reach Australia because the Aborigines were selective in adding to their range of possessions. Graebner further claimed (1905) that a West Papuan complex had penetrated Australia after a continent wide diffusion of East Papuan elements. Schmidt (Dixon, pp. 232, 238) applied his own version of the Kulturkreise theory to South America, as the Tasmanian and the Boomerang strata, which Rivet tried to prove by comparing the Tshon language of Patagonia with Australian languages in general.

The data available about Aboriginal culture at present proves that diffusion from Melanesia is an historical fact but not in the way proposed by the Vienna school. Nevertheless, Lowie (p. 193) believed the initial postulate of this school to be acceptable, that man at one time occupied a restricted territory and when he spread to other regions he carried part of his cultural inventory with him, some of which survived in remote places. Dixon (p. 266) referred to this as the spreading of man's Archaic culture. It is conceivable, therefore, that the ancestors of the Australian Aborigines, who came to Australia 40,000 or more years ago, were the carriers of a simple and widespread hunter-gathering culture, basically similar but varying locally.

The diffusion of culture has been approached in several significant ways by leading scholars of the subject, such as by the transmission of particular features or traits, whole cultures in adjacent or widely separated regions, and the geographical distribution or age and area approach, in addition to those discussed above. Few would deny the truth of diffusion but many would insist on a study of total cultures before relationships are claimed. It is essential to remember that neither evolution, environment, independent development nor diffusion in itself can explain the cultural inventory of any people—each of these factors played its own part in its formulation, and each people or group has its own unique history. I believe that Australian Aboriginal culture is a convincing example of multiple influences moulding a culture.

Students of Aboriginal cultural development have laboured under considerable handicaps in their efforts to ascertain the factors which have operated in this sphere until radio-carbon dates began to come through in the past two decades because there was no reliable data on the time factor and culture history had become an unpopular subject with the advent of functionalism. Davidson, an American follower of Wissler, rectified the situation considerably but his early death truncated his distributional study plan for the whole of Aboriginal culture.

FREDERICK D. MCCARTHY

An opposite view was held by Spencer (1921), that 'the Australian Aborigine has developed all the cultures necessary to his well-being, considering his wants and the material available, unaided from any other source', while Kenyon, Mahoney and Mann (1924), in supporting this claim, stated categorically that any attempt to compare the Australian Aboriginal culture with those of the Old World, with races subjected to periodic invasions of different cultures, or in contact with higher or lower cultures, will lead to error. Implicit in this local causation interpretation is an explanation of Aboriginal culture on the basis of invention and independent development, but it is only a partial explanation. Sollas (1924) concluded that though the Australian Aborigines had made a considerable advance on the Mousterian culture of Europe, possibly by their own efforts, there can be no doubt they borrowed from adjacent races.

Causes of Local Variation

It is necessary, also, to consider briefly factors generated within Aboriginal culture that I have termed causes of local variation (1940a). The influence of the material used—stone, bone, wood, bark, plant and other fibres—on the form of the objects made from them depends upon whether the shaping or processing technique employed enables the workman to control the material. There are examples of material influencing size and shape in the use of corkwood in Queensland which produced a short, thick and somewhat dumpy shield, and the huge flanged roots of giant fig trees in the Atherton area of Queensland which produced the largest shield in Australia. The nature of an ornament tends to depend upon material such as teeth, shells and twine, but the part played by material in the shape of knapped stone implements still needs intensive field research to determine. Material, however, is negatived to varying degrees by the deep knowledge of it possessed by the Aborigines, and tested by them over a long period of time; both the men and the women take great care in selecting materials and processing them to achieve their purpose, so that experience and selectivity have to be considered. Suitable materials, however, may be neglected in extensive areas because of another factor—the absolute necessity to have a shield, wooden container, spear or spearthrower made from the wood of trees growing at a sacred site where the article in question was first introduced by the ancestral spirits, as at Urachipma (Mt Sonder) for wooden bowls in Central Australia (Spencer & Gillen, 1914, pp. 536-7), Ngillipidji quartzite quarry in Arnhem Land for stone knives (Thomson, 1949), and ochres for paints from special deposits. This kind of preference leads to the standardization of a type of artefact, and to a greater distribution of it, in comparatively extensive regions.

The local elaboration of a universally distributed trait in Australia, or its evolution from a simple to a more complex form, is an important feature of Aboriginal material culture. I have cited above linear art designs in Central Australia, and in 1940(a) the development of widow's

214

caps from the widespread custom of mourners of the dead painting their bodies white, and there are many other examples. These secondary derivations of a trait lead into the problem of invention in Australia. Interpreted in its broadest sense, it is probably correct to say that invention can only be expressed in simple terms in a hunter-gatherer society, and applies mainly to new shapes or forms of weapons, utensils, ornaments, sacred objects and the like. One of the most important inventions of the Aborigines, in the Middle Stone Age, is the Central Australian hafted flake chisel, constantly re-sharpened during use and so worn down until the stub is discarded; it has not yet been found outside Australia. Likewise, the ground-edge axes of Oenpelli, the oldest in the world at 22,900 years (C. White, 1967) might also be regarded as an Aboriginal invention in the Old Stone Age unless older examples are reported outside Australia. Perhaps I could mention here the multiple uses of one artefact to eliminate several others, the factor of substitution, a classic example of which is the Central Australian spearthrower used also as a firesaw, haft for stone chisel, blood and fur container in ceremonies, and a digging implement. The Aborigines' need to fulfil a function in daily and ritual life led them to examine every possible resource in their own territory to find a suitable material or medium.

There are, finally, the modifications made to a basic pattern of Aboriginal life by adaptation to a local or regional habitat. It led to a lessening of possessions by the Western Desert dwellers in Western Australia, where the carrying of as few weapons and utensils as possible is essential to survival in a harsh environment requiring long distances to be covered daily on foot to obtain food and water. In central western New South Wales the spear was displaced by the cord hunting net and club in hunting kangaroos and emus.

Other aspects of the nature of the material culture to which attention should be drawn are areas of local variation, the absence of certain traits in extensive regions, and the progressive advancement in hunting and fishing techniques and apparatus, and of other appliances, from the south to the north of the continent. I have discussed these matters in detail in other papers (1940a, 1953a & b, 1957a & b) and would now like to look at the problem of culture relationships in the light of the new data revealed in recent years by archaeologists and allied workers.

Phases of Development of Aboriginal Culture

There appear to be three levels at which we should consider the development of Aboriginal culture, which I shall refer to as Phase I, the Basic or Early Stone Age, Phase II, the Middle Stone Age, and Phase III, the Proa-Canoe contacts. The first two of these phases have been called the Adaptive and Inventive, and the Hafted and Non-hafted, phases by Mulvaney (1970). I prefer Colonizing for Phase I and Progressive for II—III.

I. The Basic or Early Stone Age

Dixon (p. 266) suggested that the Aborigines carried an Archaic culture to Australia that was then widespread in the world, to which the use of fire, skins, stone, bone, wood and other artefacts belonged. To them in Australia might be added such traits as cremation (26,000 years old in Australia), the hand thrown spear, the club, rock art, painting on bark, twined basketry, red ochre on skeletons, a range of stone chopping, scraping and cutting implements of the Australian Core and Flake Tradition, and many other traits which formed the basic complex of possessions and customs brought to Australia at this time. It is equivalent in general terms to the culture of the Tasmanians who crossed the dry Bass Strait area prior to 11,000 years ago and preserved this complex in isolation across the later sea passage of the Strait, just as the mainlanders did for some 33,000 years until a quite noticeable enrichment of culture arrived in northwest Australia some 7,000 years ago in the Middle Stone Age. There is no data on the introduction of new traits into Australia during this Early Stone Age. Golson (1971b, pp. 208-9) stated that Malaysian man could readily have established and expanded his settlement anywhere in the northern regions of Australia because the vegetation complexes in the tropical regions were not unfamiliar to him in Arnhem Land and Cape York, and further, that the not insignificant degree of similarity in use between the Australian and Malaysian regions probably has an historical explanation. This raises an interesting problem as to the degree to which the Aborigines ascertained the food values of plants by trial and error elsewhere in Australia. We do not know what opportunities the Aborigines took to invent, discover or develop their basic culture, but it is apparent that their material culture remained comparatively static in this long period as part of a stabilized culture enforced by social rules, religious beliefs, magical and other legal punishments. Neither the environment nor the so-called genius of the people stimulated any real cultural advances, apart from ground-stone axes, in this initial period.

Unifacial pebble tools in Tasmania, Victoria, South and Central Australia, and Cape York were considered by Tindale (1937) and McCarthy (1940c, p. 33) to form a link with their occurrence as the Hoabinhien-Bacsonien assemblages in southeast Asia and Indonesia. Golson (1971b, p. 130) has recently argued for a late Pleistocene to early Recent age for them in this region on the basis of the Australian data. It is now problematical whether they were brought into Australia by a separate group of migrants carrying the Kartan culture, as Tindale claimed, or by diffusion as I believed, as they have not been reported in northwestern Australia and their greatest antiquity on the continent does not exceed 11,500 years. Parallelism appears to be a more logical explanation.

II. The Middle Stone Age

In the second phase of Australian prehistory, which both myself (1963) and Clark (1969) have called the Middle Stone Age, two important cultural changes took place in northwestern Australia. One was the introduction of the Australian Microlithic or Small Tool Tradition in the extreme northwest, the other that of the symmetrical point trait complex in the Kimberley region. With one of them, it is thought by some prehistorians, came the dingo, linear art based on the concentric circle, the spearthrower and compound disposal of the dead.

The Microlithic Tool Tradition has as its major tool types the geometric microliths, a range of well made tiny implements in triangular, trapezoidal, segmental and other shapes, and the backed blades or asymmetrical points; it is distributed from the Fortescue river in northwestern Australia down into and right across southern Australia. These implements occur in Sulawesi (Celebes) (Mulvaney & Soejono, 1970, pp. 27-8), and in south India, thus establishing a series of links between Australia and India. The radio-carbon dates for them form a satisfactory correlation, from 7,000 years ago at one site in India to 6,500 in Australia. Glover (1967, p. 425) believes this Microlithic Tradition was introduced into northwestern Australia from where it spread into its present known distribution on the continent. P. White (1971, p. 192) supported this view when he stated that the temporal correlation between the probable beginning of agriculture in Melanesia and Indonesia, and the start of Phase II or the Microlithic Tradition, is too marked to be simply coincidental, and the latter's introduction into Australia is related to the development and spread of agriculture into inland southeast Asia; the microliths, he said, did not penetrate New Guinea because they were of no use to agriculturalists. In his view, migration or diffusion based on sea travel to, but not from, Australia must have taken place to account for such an innovation of culture. Jones (1968, p. 190) also supported migration, and in his opinion 'the claims of W.A. as a potential bridgehead for Palaeolithic migrants, according to the distribution of the Microlithic Tradition, also strongly suggested diffusion from W.A., possibly derived from similar industries widespread in India, Ceylon and Sub-Saharan Africa'.

Similar reasoning could well be applied to the unifical and bifacial symmetrical points which have many links in southeast Asia and Indonesia, including Sulawesi (Mulvaney & Soejono, pp. 27-8). They belong to a different point-making tradition to the backed blades, were probably an addition from outside to the Sulawesi complex, and arrived in Australia at a different place to and diffused through the continent in a different area to the backed blades. They spread from the Kimberleys to South Australia, western New South Wales and western Queensland, into the desert region of Western Australia, and into Arnhem Land. They are dated at some 7,000 years ago near Oenpelli (White, 1967) and in my opinion were introduced by sea travellers from Indonesia.

Mulvaney (1970, p. 29), on the other hand, stated that evolutionary and diffusionist hypotheses are implicit in the origin of Phase II, marked by a significant change from standardization to variation; because of the dearth of Australian implement parallels in Timor and Australian New Guinea, and their noteworthy number in Sulawesi, it is premature, he thinks, to leap from morphological comparison to diffusionist inference. Subsequently (1971, p. 375), he favoured the view that the process of idea-migration-invention-diffusion of this Microlithic Tool Tradition occurred at more than one place, of which Australia was apparently one.

The linear concentric circle art has a similar distribution to the Microlithic Tool Tradition, from the northwest to the southeast of Australia, and it appears abruptly in rock engravings after the Outline phase (McCarthy, 1962, p. 45). In Central Australia it blossomed and survived till modern times as a ritual art. Previously I thought (1940c, p. 45) that this art was linked with the spread of Bronze age designs from southeast Asia; now it appears probable that it is connected with an earlier diffusion of curvilinear and circle motifs characteristic of the Kelanay ceramic tradition in Indonesia. This art style also occurs in New Guinea.

The third item mentioned, the spearthrower, has been the subject of much debate in the writings of culture historians. From his distributional studies of spears (1934) and spearthrowers (1936b), Davidson concluded that the spearthower was a relatively recent introduction into Australia, and that it came from New Guinea (where the female type unknown in Australia is employed) through the Torres Strait Islands, although he assigned it an Asiatic origin. Opinion, however, seems to have swung to an introduction on the northwest coast in recent years, although the spearthrower is not recorded in Indonesia.

There is thus considerable evidence to support the conclusion that two important cultural movements from Indonesia, representing a drastic change in stone tool types, entered northwestern Australia at different points between 7,000 and 5,000 years, and spread over a considerable portion of the continent. As several other traits are linked with them, and especially the introduction of the dingo, a detailed study of Aboriginal material culture as a whole, in the light of this Middle Stone Age enrichment, would probably add other items to these two trait complexes. There is collateral evidence of physical admixture in Cape York.

During this period, however, Australia missed or rejected cultural advances of much greater significance. Golson (1971a, p. 137) recently pointed out that the sequence of innovation in the heartland of southeast Asia was first the ground-stone technology, then horticulture based on tubers and fruits, and then pottery. New Guinea accepted all three, but the later version of agriculture based on cereals, known in Thailand 6,000 to 7,000 years ago, did not reach this island. In discussing the reasons why the Australian Aborigines remained hunter-gatherers in Cape York, and in fact why a Neolithic Revolution never took place in Australia, P. White (1971, pp. 185-7) suggested that the sea barrier, which existed prior to the spread of the early tuber-fruits type of agriculture into Oceania, may have prevented accretionary advances of agriculturalists entering Australia. The Torres Strait Islands are, as he said, a transitional zone of cultivators dependent upon fishing and collecting to a great degree in some of the western islands, and the islands do not represent a sharp break between the Papuan agriculturalists and the Australian hunter-gatherers. The fact should be stressed that although the Australian Aborigines had direct contact over centuries with agriculturalists they did not swing over to cultivation. One can only conclude that satisfaction with their own way of life, conservatism and selectivity based on their religion and mythology, were the real barriers to such a drastic change, and further, that agriculturalists did not settle in large enough groups to make a physical change in Australia where their contacts with the Aborigines were intermittent.

III The Proa-Canoe Contacts

We now come to the third and most prolific phase of cultural relationships between Australia and its neighbours, linked with the development of the proa and canoe trading voyages in the Indonesian and Melanesian regions respectively, involving both accidental and regular visits to Australia by peoples with more advanced material cultures than that of the Aborigines. Elliot Smith (1930, p. 126) pointed out that many customs on the northwest coast and Bathurst Island afforded clear evidence of influence from the Malay archipelago, especially, and in Queensland from Torres Strait and New Guinea; he believed, in fact, that the Aborigines received practically every element of their culture in relatively recent times. Three major points of contact have been revealed, two by Indonesians on the northwest coast and Arnhem Land, and one by Torres Straits islanders in Cape York. It is interesting to note that practically the whole of the northern coast of Australia was affected by these contacts from the Middle Stone Age onwards, but there is no evidence for cultural introductions on any other part of the coastline; moreover, the southern coast of the Gulf of Carpentaria missed both the Arnhem Land and Cape York contacts and their benefits.

The short distance and the island chain between Cape York and New Guinea naturally attracted attention as the most likely avenue of contact between Australia and contiguous cultural regions, and many writers since Eden in 1787 have discussed the traits introduced at a random level. They include Frobenius (1901), Hamlyn-Harris (1915), Haddon 1935, Thorpe (1924-31), Rivers (1926), Thomson (1933, 1952), White (1971), Lawrence (1968), Davidson (1933-57) and myself (1936-53). I cannot add to my earlier discussions of this subject because no reliable data is at yet available on the antiquity of this contact, and it was not affected by the Microlithic Tool Tradition, but archaeological research in progress in the area may unearth new evidence. Torres Straits islanders voyaged down both coasts of Cape York to visit communities of Aborigines, and Thomson's (1933) field study has documented the introduction of hero cult ceremonies with masked costumes, skin drums, wooden sculpture, and a series of camp dances with associated songs. It is apparent from Davidson's distributional studies that this contact has been long and intimate. It formed an extension of the canoe trading expeditions in the Fly River estuary and the Daudai coastal and island region of western Papua. It is conceivable, therefore, that the Cape York contact is as ancient as the introduction of the sea-going canoes into the region.

Davidson applied the geographical distribution method of culture analysis to Australia and wrote over forty papers on this subject. He concluded that the following traits were introduced through Cape York: three kinds of knotless netting and two techniques of coiled basketry (1933); spear barbs cut in the solid, detachable barbs with variation of wood and bone materials, and possibly the multi-pronged and stingray-spine heads (1934); throwing clubs as a class, and the pineapple-headed club (1936a); spearthrowers (1936b); gourd, coconut-shell, bamboo-stem, palm-leaf, and possibly improved marine shell containers and coiled basketry (1937); single and double outrigger dugout canoes (1937); and string figures (1941). They comprise a small proportion of the material culture traits analysed by him as he was just as intent upon distinguishing items that belonged to the basic mainland complex, and Tasmania, and those that were developed or invented by the Aborigines. He accepted continuous distribution from Australia to New Guinea as proof of diffusion, and in some instances non-continuous distribution by the absence of a trait in Cape York or Torres Strait Islands. In the latter instances, he believed the minimum antiquity of such traits in Australia to be the maximum length of time of the Melanesian occupation of the Oceanic region. In principle he accepted all Australian and New Guinea parallels as due to historical relationships, and where he had no evidence of the occurrence of a trait outside Australia he concluded that it had had an indigenous origin, and this reasoning led to some errors in his conclusions. An invaluable feature of his work lies in the continent-wide distribution maps upon which he based his analyses. Golson (1971b, p. 126) regards New Guinea as a locus of ancient settlement, exposed to influences from seminal areas in Asia and its archipelagoes, which it had the opportunity to absorb, to transmute and perchance to transmit, and as a recipient of influences from Asia, and the Pacific as a filter for their Oceanic dispersal. Australia participated in this dispersal.

Diffusion took place from Australia in a limited way. A culture hero named Kwoiam, equipped with Australian weapons, was of considerable importance in the western islands of Torres Strait (P. White, 1971, p. 188), and Australian weapons, examples of which are in the Australian Museum's collection, filtered their way into western Papua.

A clearer picture has now emerged of the contact between Indonesians and Aborigines in Arnhem Land and the Kimberley area since considerable research work has been done in both regions by archaeologists and social anthropologists. Radio-carbon samples obtained by Macknight from Macassan trepang sites in Arnhem Land date back some 300 and 800 years, but the concensus of opinion seems to favour the sixteenth century as the beginning of the voyages from Sulawesi, despite the proa captain Pobassoo's statement to Flinders that it began only twenty years prior to 1803, as a result of proas being blown to Australia from the Rottee trepang field (Mulvaney, 1966, p. 453). Attention has been drawn by Mulvaney in the same paper, and by Megaw (1967, p. 2) to the discovery of a piece of Ming porcelain of the fifteenth or sixteenth century on Groote Eylandt in 1948 (McCarthy & Setzler, 1960, p. 294, pl. 19), and the well known Shou Lao soapstone figure found in Darwin in 1879, as possible evidence of antiquity for these Macassan visits. One wonders in fact whether any of the Chinese merchants in Macassar who controlled the trepang industry (Mulvaney, 1966, p. 456) ever visited Arnhem Land on the proas and brought Chinese ceramic ware with them, but one must reject Megaw's view (1966, p. 2, pl. viiia) that a coin of Ptolemy IV found near Cairns, Queensland, in 1909, is possible evidence for the most southerly trade from southeast Asia; these coins, together with Roman and Greek billons, were always favoured as souvenirs by Australian tourists, and some of them have been found in equally strange localities in other parts of Australia, a matter in which I had direct proof during my curatorship at the Australian Museum.

The Macassans left huge quantities of potsherds at their trepang camps, also broken gin bottles on which dates of 1790 and 1838 are known. These bottles were reproduced in wood, with paintings of trepang on them, as totems by Glyde River Aborigines (Thomson, 1949), perhaps because they liked the gin so much.

The earliest reference to this contact by the Aborigines was recorded by the Berndt's (1954, p. 15), who stated that the Aborigines still sing of the ships in which the Baijini people arrived, of the women who came with them, the stone dwellings they built, the cloth they wove and the clothes they wore, and the way in which they speared fish and cultivated small gardens. The Baijini era is looked upon as belonging to the far distant past when the great spirit beings walked the earth, and the Baijini remain a mythical people.

The Macassans from Sulawesi, on the other hand, form a very important feature in the history of northern Australia. All writers agree that a comparatively long period of contact was necessary to explain the strong permeation of Macassan linguistic, artistic, technological, musical and ceremonial traits in Aboriginal life. It was a typical trading situation by strangers. The temporary Macassan camps were sited for defence, and protection, and a hostile or suspicious attitude existed between the foreigners and the indigenes (Mulvaney, 1966, p. 53). The Aborigines were employed in the trepang industry for a century or more, many of them were taken to Macassar to remain as menial workers or to return to Arnhem Land. Aboriginal women were made available to the proa crews. As there were 1,000 or more Macassans engaged in the industry, the Aboriginal life of coastal Arnhem Land must have been almost entirely disrupted during their visits.

As a result of his field research Warner (1937) considered the dugout canoe and its sails, smoking pipes, the mourning mast ceremony for the dead, a knowledge of metals and the Van Dyke style of beard to be the main items adopted from the Macassans by the Aborigines. According to the Berndts' (1948, 1949, 1954) the Macassan camps of stilt houses, and trepang processing boilers and racks, were bartering depots at which the Aborigines exchanged pearls, turtleshells and other natural products for East Indies currency, rice and sweetmeats, cloth, knives and tobacco, and the Aborigines learnt to use steel in making knives, spearheads and tomahawks. The Berndts' claim that the Macassans manufactured pottery in Arnhem Land is now disputed. In their view, it is in the realm of the great Aboriginal song cycles and stories that a colourful picture of Malaysian and Macassan life is unfolded, and the latter exerted a great influence in the diversions, entertainments and ceremonies of the Aborigines. They cited card playing, song rhythms and sounds of foreign instruments, and the Crook Man ceremony in addition to the traits mentioned by Warner. To these should be added floral and other decorative art motifs, sculpture in wood, stilt houses, folk tales, words and names, and the eating of tamarind seeds from the introduced trees. Thomson (1949) considered that the influx of Indonesian trade goods, particularly iron and glass, either created or extended the ceremonial gift exchange systems in Arnhem Land.

There was a further point of contact between Indonesia and Australia on the Kimberley and adjacent coast of northwest Australia visited by Timorese, Aru islanders and Macassans in recent times (Crawford, 1968, p. 61), and here it is thought the angular meander design incised on sacred boards and pearlshells, and the thread cross (Davidson, 1951) came in by random diffusion. Three Indonesian polished adzes found in Western Australia (Davidson, 1938, Figure 3) illustrate the latter point perfectly.

Summary

In my own evaluation of Aboriginal cultural relationships (1940, 1953, 1957) I have sought to define lists of the following: (1) Ancient traits whose distributions extend into Indonesia and Melanesia; (2) Traits which have a continuous distribution between Australia and New Guinea of which there are over sixty; (3) New Guinea traits in Arnhem Land and adjacent islands; (4) Australian traits in (a) Torres Strait Islands, (b) New Hebrides and New Caledonia, and (c) traits in Australia and New Guinea but not in Torres Strait Islands, of which there are only short lists. Many of these suggested relationships can, I think, be accepted but others remain to be proven.

To summarize the above discussion it is apparent that there was a very long static period of Aboriginal culture in the Old Stone Age, of which the ancient ground stone axes from Oenpelli are a notable feature. It was followed by a sudden phase of enrichment in the Middle Stone Age about 7,000 years ago at two points on the northwest coast of the continent, the origin and mechanics of which are still somewhat controversial between those who support migration, diffusion, independent evolution or secondary derivation within the one cultural tradition. Subsequently and associated with proa and sea going canoe traders to Australia, there has been a constant enrichment of Aboriginal material culture centred on three main areas—Cape York, Arnhem Land and the Kimberley coasts. They were contacts between cultures of highly varied levels from which the Aborigines selected traits useful and acceptable in their hunter-gatherer mode of life. Some of these additions are trait complexes, such as the dugout canoe with sail, paddles, stone anchor, harpoon with detachable head, and fish-hooks; smoking pipe with tobacco and sacred art designs; hero cult with music, dances, beliefs and elaborate paraphernalia; stilt houses with fire and sleeping pattern. The total abandonment by the Aborigines of their own culture for the adoption of a new sedentary one was still a long way off. Conservatism on the part of the Aborigines is notable in their adherence to hunter-gathering, and in maintaining their ancient religious beliefs and rites, though even to the latter they were prepared to add major beliefs and ceremonies in Cape York and Arnhem Land. Aboriginal economy survived in this situation of change because of the paramount importance of the sanctions imposed upon the people by their ancestral spirits. It could be argued that a much greater period of time was needed for the Aborigines in tropical Cape York to adopt the tuber-fruits agriculture, and for those in Arnhem Land the cultivation of cereals practised by their visitors. On the other hand, no group of Aborigines has voluntarily taken up cultivation since white settlement two centuries ago.

The local and trunk trade route network of gift exchange and barter that existed all over Australia (McCarthy, 1939) was an effective mechanism for the spreading of new ideas among widespread Aboriginal communities, as in New Guinea and all of the islands in the southeast Asia and Oceanic region. In addition, the network of canoe voyages in Oceania described by Lewis (1972) and others performed a similar function. As many of these networks linked up at hundreds, possibly thousands, of places in a vaster network which extended from southeast Asia to Australia and Oceania, the tremendous importance of borrowing, by diffusion, during these direct contacts of people cannot be over-emphasized. Differential diffusion or the spread of single traits and trait complexes at different times, instead of whole cultures as organic entities, has thus played a key role in the transmission of culture throughout Australia and Oceania.

REFERENCES

BERNDT, R. M. & BERNDT, C. H., (1948a) 'Sacred figures of ancestral beings of Arnhem Land, *Oceania*, 18, 309-26.
——, (1948b) 'Badu, islands of the spirits', *Oceania*, 19, 93-103.

——, (1949) 'Secular figures of northeast Arnhem Land', *Amer. Anthrop.*, 51, 213-22.

——, (1954) *Arnhem Land: its History and its People*. Melbourne.

CLARK, G., (1969) Australian stone age. In *Liber Isoepho Kostrzewski Octogenario a Veneratoribus Dicatus*, quem Konrad Jazdzewski, 17-23.

CRAWFORD, I. M., (1968) *The Art of the Wandjina*. Melbourne.

DAVIDSON, D. S., (1933) 'Australian netting and basketry techniques', *J. Polyn. Soc.*, 42, 257-99.

——, (1934) 'Australian spear traits and their derivations', *J. Polyn. Soc.*, 43, 41-72, 143-62.

——, (1935a) 'Archaeological problems of northern Australia', *J. roy. Anthrop. Inst. Gt Brit. Irel.*, 65, 145-84.

——, (1935b) 'The chronology of Australian watercraft', *J. Polyn. Soc.*, 44, 1-16, 69-84, 137-52, 193-207.

——, (1935c) 'Is the boomerang oriental', *J. Amer. Oriental Soc.*, 55, 163-81.

——, (1936a) 'Australian throwing-sticks, throwing-clubs and boomerangs', *Amer. Anthrop.*, 38, 76-98.

——, (1936b) 'The spearthrower in Australia', *Pr. Amer. Phil. Soc.*, 76, 445-83.

——, (1937) 'Transport and receptacles in Aboriginal Australia', *J. Polyn. Soc.*, 46, 175-205.

——, (1938a) 'Stone axes of Western Australia', *Amer. Anthrop.*, 40, 38-48.

——, (1938b) 'Northwestern Australia and the question of influences from the East Indies', *J. Amer. Oriental Soc.*, 58, 61-80.

——, (1941) 'Aboriginal Australian String Figures', *Pr. Amer. Phil. Soc.*, 84, 763-904.

——, (1951) 'The thread cross in Australia', *Mankind*, 4, 263-73.

DIXON, R. B., (1928) *The Building of Cultures*. New York & London.

EDEN, W., (1787) *The History of New Holland*. London.

ELKIN, A. P., (1930) Rock paintings of north-west Australia. *Oceania*, 1, 257-79.

FROBENIUS, L., (1898) *Der ursprung der africanischen kulturen*. Berlin.

——, (1901) Die kulturformen Oceaniens. *Petermann's Mitt.*, 46, 204-15, 234-8, 262-71.

GLOVER, I. C., (1967) 'Stone implements from Millstream Station, W.A.: Newall's collection re-analysed', *Mankind*, 6, 415-25.

GOLSON, J., (1971a) 'Both sides of the Wallacea line: Australian, New Guinea and Asian prehistory', *Arch. Phys. Anthrop. Oceania*, 6, 124-44.

——, (1971b) 'The remarkable history of Indo-Pacific man'. Fifth David Rivett Memorial Lecture. CSIRO, Canberra.

GRAEBNER, F., (1905) Kulturkreise in Ozeanien. *Zeitschr. f. Eth.*, 37, 28-53.

——, (1913) 'Melanische kulturen in nord-Australien. *Ethnologica*, 2, 15-24.

HADDON, A. C. (1920) 'The migrations of culture in British New Guinea', *J. roy. Anthrop. Inst. Gt Brit. Irel.*, 50, 237-80.

——, (1935) *Reports of the Cambridge Anthropological Expedition to Torres Strait*. Vol. I, General ethnography. Cambridge.

HALLAM, Sylvia, (1971) 'Roof markings in the Orchestra Shell cave, Wanneroo near Perth, W.A.', *Mankind*, 8, 90-103.

HAMLYN-HARRIS, R., (1915) 'Some evidence of Papuan culture in Cape York peninsula', *Mem. Qld. Mus.*, 3, 10-13.

JONES, R., (1968) 'The geographical background to the arrival of man in Australia and Tasmania', *Arch. Phys. Anthrop. Oceania*, 3, 187-215.

KOPPERS, W., (1955) Diffusion, transmission and acceptance. In *Yearbook of Anthropology*, Thomas, W. L., (ed.), 169-81, New York.

KENYON, A. S. & MAHONY, D. J., (1914) *Guide to the stone implements of the Australian Aborigines*. National Museum of Victoria.

KENYON, A. S., MAHONY, D. J. & MANN, S. F., (1924) 'Evidence of outside culture inoculations', *Rept. Aust. Assoc. Adv. Sci.*, xvii, 464-6

LAWRENCE, R., (1968) 'Aboriginal habitat and economy', *Occas. Pap., Dept Geogr., S.G.S., A.N.U.*, 6.

LEWIS, D., (1972) *We, the Navigators.* Canberra.

LOMMEL, A., (1957) Australische felsbilder und ihre ausser-Australische parallelen. *Baessler-Archiv*, N.F., 5, 267-83.

LOVE, J. R. B., (1930) 'Rock paintings of the Worora and their mythological interpretation', *J. roy. Soc. W. Aust.*, 16, 1-24.

LOWIE, R. H., (1937) *The History of Ethnological Theory.* New York.

MCCARTHY, F. D., (1936) 'The geographical distribution theory and Australian material culture', *Mankind*, 2, 12-16.

——, (1939) ' "Trade" in Aboriginal Australia, and "trade" relationships with Torres Strait, New Guinea and Malaysia', *Oceania*, 9, 405-38; 10, 80-104, 171-95.

——, (1940a) 'Australian Aboriginal material culture; factors in its composition', *Mankind*, 2, 241-69, 294-320.

——, (1940b) 'The bone point known as *muduk* in eastern Australia'. *Rec. Aust. Mus.*, 20, 313-19.

——, (1940c) A comparison of the prehistory of Australia with that of Indo-China, the Malay Peninsula and Archipelago. *Pr. 3rd Congr. Preh. Far East., Singapore, 1938*, 30-50.

——, (1944a) 'Some unusual cylindro-conical stones from N.S.W. and Java', *Rec. Aust. Mus.*, 21, 257-60.

——, (1944b) 'The Windang, or edge-ground uniface pebble axe in eastern Australia', *Rec. Aust. Mus.*, 21, 261-3.

——, (1944c) 'Some unusual stone artefacts from Australia and New Guinea', *Rec. Aust. Mus.*, 21, 264-6.

——, (1944d) Adzes and adze-like implements from eastern Australia, *Rec. Aust. Mus.*, 21, 267-71.

——, (1949) 'The prehistoric cultures of Australia', *Oceania*, 19, 305-19.

——, (1952) 'New records of tanged implements and pounders in eastern Australia', *Rec. Aust. Mus.*, 4, 361-4.

——, (1953a) 'The Oceanic and Indonesian affiliations of Australian Aboriginal culture', *J. Polyn. Soc.*, 62, 243-61.

——, (1953b) 'Ecology, Equipment, Economy and Trade', Sheils, H. (ed.) , *Australian Aboriginal Studies*, Melbourne.

——, (1957a) 'Habitat, economy and equipment of the Australian Aborigines', *Aust. J. Sci.*, 19, 88-97.

——, (1957b) 'Theoretical considerations of Australian Aboriginal art', *J. Pr. roy. Soc. N.S.W.*, 91, 3-22.

——, (1962) 'The rock engravings of Port Hedland, northwest Australia', *Pap. Kroeber Anthrop. Soc.*, 26.

——, (1963) 'The prehistory of the Australian Aborigines', *Aust. Nat. Hist.*, 14, 233-47.

——, (1967) *Australian Aboriginal stone implements.* Australian Museum handbook, Sydney.

—— & SETZLER, F. M., (1960) 'The archaeology of Arnhem Land', *Rec. Amer. Aust. Sci. Exp. Arnhem Land, 1948*, 2, 215-95.

MEGAW, J. V. S., (1967) 'Archaeology, art and Aborigines', *J. roy. Aust. Hist. Soc.*, 53, 1-28.

MULVANEY, D. J., (1958) 'The Australian Aborigines, 1606-1629: opinion and field-work', *Hist. Stud.*, 8, 131-52, 297-314.

——, (1966) 'Beche-de-mer, Aborigines and Australian history', *Pr. roy. Soc. Vic.*, 79, 449-57.

——, (1969) *The Prehistory of Australia.* London.

——, (1970) *Discovering Man's Place in Nature.* Sydney University Press.

—— & Soejono, R. P., (1970) 'Archaeology in Sulawesi', *Antiquity*, 45, 26-33.

Mulvaney, D. J., (1971) Aboriginal social evolution; a retrospective view. In Mulvaney, D. J. & Golson, J. eds. *Aboriginal Man and Environment in Australia*, Canberra, 368-80.

Perry, W. J., (1923) *The Children of the Sun.* London.

Pitt-Rivers, A. L-F., (1916) *The Evolution of Culture and Other Essays.* London.

Rivers, W. H. R., (1915) 'The boomerang in the New Hebrides', *Man*, 15, 59.

——, 1914) *The History of Melanesian Society.* 2 vols. Cambridge.

Rivers, W. H. R., (1926) *Psychology and Ethnology.* London.

Roheim, G., (1925) 'The pointing bone', *J. Roy. Anthrop. Soc. Gt Brit. Irel.*, 55, 90-114.

Smith, Sir G. E., (1911) *Migrations of Early Cultures.* Manchester.

——, (1928) *In the Beginning: the Origins of Civilization.* New York.

——, (1930) *Human History.* London.

——, (1933) *The Diffusion of Culture.* London.

Sollas, W. J., (1924) *Ancient Hunters and their Modern Representatives.* London.

Spencer, Sir W. B., (1921) 'The Aborigines of Australia', *Rept Aust. Assoc. Adv. Sci.*, 15, lvii-lxxix.

——, (1922) Guide to the Australian ethnographical collection exhibited in the National Museum of Victoria. 3rd edn.

—— & Gillen, F. J., (1914) *The Native Tribes of the Northern Territory of Australia.* London.

Thomson, D., (1933) 'The hero cult, initiation and totemism in Cape York', *J. roy. Anthrop. Inst. Gt Brit. Irel.*, 63, 453-538.

——, (1949) *Economic Structure and the Ceremonial Exchange Cycle in Arnhem Land.* Melbourne.

——, (1952) 'Notes on some primitive watercraft', *Man*, 52.

Thorpe, W. W., (1924) 'Some New Guinea cultural influences found amongst the Aborigines of Australia', *Rept Aust. Assoc. Adv. Sci.*, 17, 484-90.

Tindale, N. B., (1937) 'Relationships of the extinct Kangaroo island culture with cultures of Australia, Tasmania and Malaya', *Rec. S. Aust. Mus.*, 9, 257-73.

Tylor, C. B., (1861) *Researches into the Early History of Mankind and the Development of Civilization.* Chicago.

——, (1871) *Primitive Culture.* London.

White, P., (1971) 'New Guinea and Australian prehistory; the neolithic problem', in Mulvaney, D. J., & Golson, J. eds, *Aboriginal Man and Environment in Australia*, Canberra, 141-57.

White, Carmel, (1967) 'Early stone axes in Arnhem Land', *Antiquity*, 41, 149-52.

Waitz, T., (1858) *Anthropologie der naturvolker.* I. Leipzig.

Warner, W. L., (1937) *A Black Civilization.* New York.

Wissler, C., (1923) *Man and Culture.* New York & London.

INDEX